3/90

SAYING NO
IS NOT ENOUGH

Also by Robert Schwebel

A GUIDE TO A HAPPIER FAMILY
(coauthor with Andrew, Bernice,
Carol, and Milton Schwebel)

SAYING NO IS NOT ENOUGH

RAISING CHILDREN WHO MAKE WISE
DECISIONS ABOUT DRUGS AND ALCOHOL

Robert Schwebel, Ph.D.

Newmarket Press, New York

89   90   91   92 — 10   9   8   7   6   5   4   3   2   1   HC

Library of Congress Cataloging-in-Publication Data
Schwebel, Robert.
Saying no is not enough : raising children who make wise decisions
about drugs and alcohol / Robert Schwebel. —1st ed.
p.   cm.
Bibliography: p.
Includes index.
1. Teenagers—United States—Drug use.   2. Drug abuse—
United States—Prevention.   3. Teenagers—United States—
Alcohol use.   4. Alcoholism—United States—Prevention.
I. Title.
HV5824.Y68S35   1989   89-33775 CIP
649'.4—dc20
ISBN 1-55704-041-9

Quantity Purchases
Professional groups, firms, and other organizations may qualify
for special terms when ordering quantities of this title. For information call or write the Special Sales Department, Newmarket
Press, 18 East 48th Street, New York, N.Y. 10017 (212) 832-3575.

Book design by Rhea Braunstein

Manufactured in the United States

First Edition

To my wonderful parents,
who empowered my brother and me
with love and understanding,
and to all parents
who want to empower their children.

CONTENTS

Acknowledgments   ix
Introduction by Benjamin Spock, M.D.   xi

PART I   EMPOWERMENT

1 Why Saying No Is Not Enough   3
2 Drugs and Their Use, Misuse, and Abuse   22
3 The Empowering Family   53
4 Workbook for Early Drug Prevention   85

PART II   THE EXCHANGE OF INFORMATION

5 Opening the Dialogue   121
6 Listening to Each Other   145
7 Making Agreements   179

PART III   INTERVENTION

8 Drastic Measures   209
9 Families Working Together: Community Strategies for
   Reducing Drug Abuse   221

References   231
Index   233

ACKNOWLEDGMENTS

Many of the ideas in this book grew from my work with Berkeley colleagues Hogie Wyckoff, Becky Jenkins, Beth Roy, Michael Singer, Joy Marcus, Darca Nicholson, and especially Claude Steiner.

I had an opportunity to put the ideas into practice in Tucson with another set of colleagues who contributed more ideas: Craig Wunderlich, Rebecca Van Marter, Joan Meggitt, Joy Misenhelter, Linda Moreno, Chris Miller, Ginger Marcus, Anna Rascón, and Marilyn Civer. And I want to acknowledge colleagues in Phoenix: Nancy Hanson, Kris Bell, Steve Merrill, and Juanita Dressler.

Then there are my journalist friends in Tucson who taught me much about writing: Leo Banks, Nadine Epstein, and Mark Turner.

A first book is an opportunity to thank special teachers from the past such as Mrs. Stuart, Mrs. Helmcke, and Mrs. Skolnick in elementary school, Sam Baskin and the late Don Myatt in college, and Philip Cowan in graduate school.

Then there are family members who contributed in special ways: Andrew, Carol, Davy, Sara, and my parents, Milton and Bernice.

Best friends Brian McCaffrey and Sylvia Yee were important in many ways. Also falling into this category are Bob Calhoun, Martha McEwen, Don Oberthur, Jeri and Richard Briskin, Mike and Susie Cohen, Betty Anne Krause, Alex Zautra, Ann Gaddis, Mary Morgan, Carol Schaedler, Chris and Hope Nealson.

From over the fence came support from my neighbors David Boomhower and Barbara Brown.

And down the stretch, loving support came from south of the border, from Claudia Genda.

Acknowledgments

The National Institute on Drug Abuse funded much of the research that I found so helpful in understanding how to prevent drug abuse. The "parents' movement" helped stimulate action to bring the problem of drug abuse into the public eye.

I thank Al Zuckerman from Writers House and Esther Margolis from Newmarket Press for their confidence and commitment in making this book possible.

And I have special thanks to give to Theresa Burns, who is a gentle but strong and talented editor whose voice I know and handwriting I can recognize. I've not met her, but she made a very important contribution to the book.

Being a Spock baby, my gratitude to Dr. Benjamin Spock extends back a lifetime. I thank him for writing his classic child-rearing book and for all he has done to help make this a better world for everyone. I know how he responds when people tell him that they are Spock babies: "Your parents should be very proud." So now I thank Dr. Spock for writing an introduction to this book and for his kind offer to review a previous draft. I hope that *he* is proud of the product.

R.S.
April 19, 1989

INTRODUCTION

by Dr. Benjamin Spock

Drug abuse, including abuse of alcohol, is a frightening threat to all parents these days, whether their children are teenagers or are still just babies, whether they suspect their adolescents are already involved or are quite sure they aren't.

One serious aspect of the problem is that adolescents (and particularly preadolescents) are more apt than adults to slip into abuse easily and rapidly. Another is that they consider themselves miraculously immune to addiction just as they consider themselves immune to pregnancy and serious diseases. (I still remember how amazed and indignant I was in my youth when I came down with a serious disease.)

But the greatest problem of all is teenagers' need to be independent, which makes them pooh-pooh the opinions of their parents and believe that it's their pals who know and speak the absolute truth. They fear that their parents will continue to try to dominate them. Therefore parents have to avoid condescension, avoid acting as though their greater age automatically confers greater wisdom. They should speak in an adult-to-adult manner, show respect for their children's opinions, and listen as much as they talk—listen not impatiently, with frequent interruptions, but with nodding head and remarks such as "I see what you mean." Parents don't have to surrender or hide their own points of view. In fact they must give their own conclusions in the end, and if these are not agreed to, they may have to impose them, out of love and the desire to protect, with no ranting and raving. Adolescents are often influenced by friendly, respectful discussion even though they can't admit it at the time and appear unmoved. It is the most important reason for starting your prevention work before your children reach their teens.

Robert Schwebel, an old friend and colleague of mine, has written this book to cover all aspects of the child drug abuse problem for parents. To me the most impressive aspect of the book is that he has worked in the field of child drug abuse for twenty years, worked with many hundreds of children individually and in groups, counseled many hundreds of parents. He is not offering theories. He is making detailed, practical suggestions that he himself has worked out and tested many times over. They have proved their effectiveness.

Dr. Schwebel is sure—as I am—that the best protection against drug use is for children to grow up in a close-knit, loving family in which certain strengths are naturally fostered: open, easy communication between them and their parents; self-esteem, which comes not only from love and regular opportunities to succeed but from receiving more approval than criticism; the ability to think clearly and reasonably, which comes from discussions with parents, meeting rules, and learning the consequences of poor performance; problem solving, which is developed out of opportunities to analyze difficulties and to work out remedies.

Parental love should be unconditional in the sense that children should know that they can count on their parents' devotion no matter what problems they may get into. This does not mean submissiveness to children's rudeness, deceit, or abuse, but a belief in their ability to measure up, a willingness to give them another chance.

Dr. Schwebel explains that children take to drugs not for mysterious reasons but, like adults, to relieve tensions, to gain pleasure, and to achieve social acceptance. This knowledge guides us in our search for cause and cure.

One of the author's basic convictions is that you, the parent, must not evade the issue of drug abuse, or pull the wool over your own eyes. And you should stick to the belief that drugs, including pot, are not for children—whether or not you can get agreement from your child. There should be no compromise on this.

I find most illuminating and valuable Dr. Schwebel's recordings of actual conversations, or suggested conversations, between teenagers and their parents. For much of the book deals with the tricky problem of how to talk with an adolescent who has been found to be using alcohol or other drugs and who, after lengthy discussions, is still unwilling to come to a sincere agreement to quit. He insists that his use of pot could not possibly be a problem for him, so there is no need to discontinue. How do you reach a meeting of the minds and a valid agreement? And if you can't, which happens more often with the older adolescent, how do you express your recourse to parental authority so that it will be acceptable and followed?

Dr. Schwebel suggests the exact words that the parent might use, to steer between authoritarianism on the one hand and ineffectual blind alleys on the other. He shows how you can be persistent, even penetrating, while remaining friendly and supportive. These suggested questions and comments cover the age range from preteen, through early teen, to late teen. They cover the child who has not even experimented with drugs, the one who has used them occasionally, the one who uses them regularly, the one who is showing harmful effects (in grades, moods, neglect of chores, withdrawal from family and friends), and the one who is definitely dependent, addicted.

For example, if the reasonable approach fails, you might say, "You think pot is harmless but I think it's risky and it is illegal. I'm unwilling to allow it. I wish you would think it over and we'll discuss it again in a day or two." If this is not successful—and only then—you can take a harder line, such as stopping the allowance, or restricting social life and after-school activities.

Dr. Schwebel discusses steps that might be followed when a child has made an agreement and broken it, from a serious talk and another chance, to withdrawal of various privileges and perhaps to a confrontation with a group of well-wishing friends and neighbors, to a refusal to let a defiant youth stay in the home.

This is not all by any means, but it should be enough to show you the wide scope and the positive spirit of this book.

PART I

EMPOWERMENT

1

WHY SAYING NO IS NOT ENOUGH

Thirteen-year-old Daniel has a choice to make. It's Saturday night. He's sitting in his kitchen at home with his two best friends, Kevin and Michael. Kevin wants to smoke some marijuana that he got from his older brother. Michael suggests they wash it down with a cool beer from the refrigerator, Spuds McKenzie style. No adults are home. No one will notice.

This comes as a shock to Daniel, who never seriously thought about using drugs. He is scared and confused. Although he never discussed drugs with his parents, he knows from some of their comments that they would tell him to "just say no." He has seen scary television commercials suggesting that drugs "fry" your brain, but that message seems to be contradicted by Kevin's brother, who smokes pot, apparently without harm.

Beer doesn't scare Daniel. Marijuana does. But what worries him more is being called a "chicken" by his friends. So he smokes the joint and drinks the beer.

Did Daniel turn into a druggie that night? No, certainly not. In fact he gagged on the smoke and disliked the taste of the beer. But the episode was significant because Daniel, at age thirteen, had broken the barrier of using illegal drugs. He also committed an act that he kept secret from his parents.

Whether Daniel ever becomes harmfully involved with chemical substances in the future will depend to a great extent on his own personal development. The determining questions include: Will he become informed about drugs? Will he discuss drugs with mature and loving adults? Will he learn to meet his needs without drugs? Will he learn to resist peer pressure? Will he learn to make wise decisions?

Daniel's situation is similar to those faced by many of his peers. Like apples in the Garden of Eden, drugs are readily available to even the youngest and most vulnerable among us. Twelve-, thirteen-, and fourteen-year-olds, and often younger children, have important decisions to make. Even if they don't seek substances, it's likely that something—marijuana, a can of beer, or a stronger drug—will be placed in their hands. Regardless of their parents' wishes, they will have to decide for themselves.

Most children, like Daniel, were not prepared in their early years for decisions of this magnitude. Many decide about drug use without ever talking with an adult.

If you are frightened by this reality, you have plenty of company. Millions of other parents are also scared of what might happen or has already happened to their children. Although there is cause for concern, it's important not to panic and overreact as some have done, assuming that *all* teenagers are using drugs, and therefore *my* children must be using them. Many teenagers do not use drugs at all. Most important, parents should realize that they can take action to prevent and minimize drug and alcohol problems.

This book is written for those parents who recognize the dangers of drug abuse and want to respond in a positive way. It is not part of a "war on drugs," however, because drugs do not wage war. Many drugs are natural products that grow in the soil. Others are synthetically created by human genius and technology. Some drugs are used in religious practices, some for medicinal purposes, some in safe and socially accepted ways for fun and relaxation.

The goal of this book is not to fight against these substances. This is not an "anti" book. It is a "pro" book written to support parents in strengthening their children—to help their children learn to live healthy lives, to help them learn to make wise decisions that enable them to remain free from chemical dependence. The prevention of drug problems is nothing less than the promotion of healthy, competent, and informed children with positive attitudes and well-developed life skills. The challenge is to *empower* children.

Empowering young children means promoting positive attitudes such as high self-esteem. It also means teaching life skills such as problem solving and assertiveness. The development of these attitudes and life skills begins during early childhood, long before chemical substances are available. These attitudes and skills prepare children for the important decisions that lie ahead, including decisions about drugs.

Empowering teenage children means giving them a certain amount of freedom and responsibility, along with solid information, guidance, and supervision to help them learn to make good decisions on their own. Dialogue between parents and children is especially important during this period.

Too often the drug issue tears families apart. It doesn't have to be that way. Discussions about drugs can become an opportunity to help your children learn to think clearly and to develop a sense of true identity. Good discussions promote this type of personal growth and family closeness.

Drugs are not just a family problem. The availability and acceptance of drugs in our communities is also a major social problem, one that will not soon be solved. Long-term solutions include community action and changes in community standards. Until communities change, and while they do, you have to help your own children cope successfully with the existing dangers.

The starting point is to be informed yourself. Therefore, Chapter 2 presents basic information about types of drugs and their effects and also about how to evaluate the use, misuse, and abuse of drugs.

Chapter 3 is about good beginnings in a family. It describes how to establish an empowering atmosphere in which young children learn the basic life skills and positive attitudes that inoculate them against drug abuse. Chapter 4 is a workbook of techniques and practical exercises that you can use to strengthen your children during the elementary school years. It also offers guidance on how to talk with young children about drugs and other health issues.

The subsequent chapters are about empowering adolescents and teenagers to make wise decisions about drugs by engaging them in what is called the "exchange of information" process. This process gives parents a forum for their input and encourages children to think for themselves. Chapter 5 is about opening the dialogue. Chapter 6 is about listening to one another. Chapter 7 is about making valid agreements and handling broken ones.

When children are harmfully involved with drugs, it's too late for prevention. The task remains the same with remediation—to empower children to make wise decisions. But the strategies are different. They are discussed in Chapter 8.

Chapter 9 is about how families can work together in a community to create a positive social climate that encourages wellness, one in which drug use by teenagers is less accepted and less common. It is about families uniting to support one another and to improve their communities.

Throughout the book, true-to-life case histories are presented along with dialogue between parents and children. The dialogue not only gives you a sense of what is effective in drug prevention, but also reveals the concerns of children. Generations that wish to move forward together must listen to each other.

The case histories and quotes are drawn from my own professional experiences in the field of substance abuse that began twenty years ago. I was a graduate student at the University of California at Berkeley and worked in the community with Claude Steiner, who was just then writing his book *Games Alcoholics Play.* It was coincidence rather than special interest that brought me into the field. But I was startled and concerned by the prevalence of drug problems and the havoc they created in families. Since that time I have continued providing psychotherapy to people of all ages with alcohol and drug problems, sometimes with their families and sometimes separately.

In the course of therapy, drug-abusing adults often reflect on their childhood experiences and link initial problems with substances to earlier events in their lives, such as school failure or an inability to meet parental expectations. I watch these adults struggle—mustering power they didn't even know they had—to overcome their addictions. It's an uphill battle.

In contrast, I also work with teenagers who are having problems in school or in meeting parental expectations, but *not* yet using drugs. Often all they need is encouragement and a few study tips to turn things around. For them, a little advice on how to solve a personal problem sometimes makes a big difference. Their parents usually need a gentle reminder—although occasionally a strong one—to be less demanding and more supportive. Even when children have more serious problems, it's so much easier to prevent drug abuse during childhood than to face it years later, after so much suffering and so much damage has been done.

In addition to private practice, I served as the director of a publicly funded outpatient counseling center on substance abuse in Tucson, Arizona. Supervising a staff of counselors, I could see their exhaustion in trying to keep up with the demand for services. With limited funds available for treatment—a very expensive process—it became increasingly clear to me that the future in this field was in prevention and in early intervention. I then became the director of a large substance abuse prevention program that provided lectures, programs, workshops, and training for schools, families, and communities. Since leaving that job, I have remained active in public policy formation in the prevention field.

ALCOHOL, TOBACCO, AND OTHER DRUGS

With all this talk about drugs, some readers might be wondering where alcohol fits into the scheme of things. During my time as the director of a drug prevention program, one of the most disturbing statements I heard, and I heard it often, was made by parents who breathed a sigh of relief: "Glad to hear my child isn't involved with marijuana. He [or she] is only drinking alcohol."

Understandably these parents are pleased to think that their child is not using an illegal substance. (They forget that minors cannot legally purchase or consume alcohol.) However, alcohol is a drug—a powerful one with millions of addicts. Parents should find little comfort in discovering that their young children are "only" drinking alcohol.

When I talk about drugs in this book, I am referring to alcohol as well. Sometimes I use the expression "alcohol and other drugs" to remind you that, although it has gained widespread social acceptance and is easily obtained, alcohol is a drug, in fact a powerful one.

Another substance included in the discussion of drugs is tobacco, a dangerous and addictive drug, and one of the first ones that children use. It, too, is legal for adults to consume and therefore has gained considerable social acceptance. Preventing addiction to nicotine is a very important part of promoting the healthy development of children.

DRUG STATISTICS

Most books on the topic of children using drugs start with a drum roll and frightening statistics, the most alarming ones that can be found to prove that our country is experiencing a crisis. The most frequently cited statistics are from an annual survey of high school

seniors that asks them to indicate when they first used certain drugs.[1]
These statistics are interesting, but can be misinterpreted. The fact
that individuals use a drug once, the first time, does not mean that
they will necessarily continue to do so, or become addicted. Most
people who use drugs eventually stop, or use them without substantial
harm.

We don't need more hype about the drug problem. Most people
are well aware that children have access to drugs and that this is a
serious matter. Statistics will change from year to year. But the issue
of preparing children to face a drug-filled world remains constant.
What we need is not hysteria, but a strong, calm, and reasonable
response to the problem of drug abuse.

I'm not minimizing the importance of drug surveys. They are a
valuable resource for schools and communities in gearing their programs to the appropriate age level. Statistics also guide community
leaders in establishing and evaluating public policy.

But for your own family, statistics are less important. Drugs are a
health issue that *all* families must address. Regardless of the average
age at which a child is exposed to drugs or at which a particular drug
is first used, it is important that *your* children be prepared. It is important that they be informed about drugs and have positive attitudes
and the necessary life skills to make good decisions. In your own
family, you will want to maintain an ongoing, open dialogue about
drugs so that your children receive appropriate education *when they
need it.*

YOUNG CHILDREN AND DRUGS:
A SPECIAL PROBLEM

I believe that adults should give a clear message: *The use of alcohol
and other drugs is not for children.*

Drugs affect mood, concentration, and cognitive functioning, including memory. They can interfere with learning and impair school
performance.[2] They can disrupt healthy development. Furthermore,
children have not yet attained the maturity needed to manage powerful chemical substances, and therefore are more vulnerable to drug
problems than adults.

Young adolescents and teenagers have access to drugs at a time in their lives when they are struggling with their sense of personal identity, separating from their parents, and moving toward adulthood. They are beginning to find their own answers to these basic questions: Who am I? What is important to me? Where do I fit in the world? Without a fully established, firm sense of identity, adolescents are susceptible to peer pressure and likely to "do what everyone else does," instead of what might be best for them. When friends are using drugs, they will be tempted to do likewise.

Besides forming their own identity, adolescents are also involved in mastering the mental ability to think through *all* the implications of *all* possible actions. Until they have mastered this logical ability, they are not fully equipped to think through *all* the implications of their own actions, including the use of drugs.

Another concern about young people experimenting with drugs is that teens and preteens have trouble setting limits for themselves. Some adults can limit their consumption of chemical substances to weekends or other carefully selected times when alcohol or other drugs will not disrupt their lives. They may, for example, only drink an occasional cocktail or glass of wine with dinner or at a social gathering. Other adults cannot control themselves. Since children have less self-control than most adults, they are even more vulnerable to problems. Once children decide to experiment with drugs, they might find that it is difficult to stop.

An added problem with drug use, one which affects both teenagers and adults, is the psychological defense mechanism of denial. Drug abusers of all ages typically deny that they have a problem, saying, "It can't happen to me. I'm fine. There's nothing wrong."

The risk of such an attitude is greater among teenagers because, during this stage of development, young people have an exaggerated sense of invincibility. They believe that nothing bad could possibly happen to them.

One boy I counseled, Kenny E., age fourteen, denied his drug problem. "It hasn't affected my life," he stated without equivocation.

"How about school? How are your grades?" I asked.

"D's and F's" he replied. "School is boring."

"When did you start using drugs?"

"Last year."

"What were your grades back then?"

"B's and C's."

"Oh, but you say drugs haven't affected your performance in school?"

"No."

Denial also covered his difficulty in breaking his drug habit.

"I could stop whenever I want."

"Have you tried?"

"Yeah."

"Were you successful?"

"Well, it was a bad time. My parents were hassling me a lot, you know. So I started doing drugs again. They were being impossible."

With denial there is always an excuse for not stopping. Usually it is blamed on someone else, be it teachers, peers, or parents.

Kenny supported the denial by minimizing his drug use: "I don't smoke *that* much pot . . . it's not a problem." He exaggerated the drug use of his peers: "Everyone smokes," he said. "Nothing's wrong with me. It's normal."

His denial is further supported by a mistaken notion of what drug abuse actually looks like. He thinks that needle-popping addicts and skid row bums are the ones who abuse drugs. He is only aware of these extremes and doesn't understand that problems can be much more subtle.

Considering the level of maturity of young adolescents, the availability of drugs, and the age at which drugs are first used, it is not surprising that a substantial number of them develop serious drug problems.

Once this happens, the effects are devastating. Drugs shield children from dealing with reality and mastering developmental tasks crucial to their future. The skills they lacked that left them vulnerable to drug abuse in the first place are the very ones that are stunted by drugs. They will have difficulty establishing a clear sense of identity, mastering intellectual skills, and learning self-control.

The adolescent period is when individuals are supposed to make the transition from childhood to adulthood. Teenagers with drug problems will not be prepared for adult roles. They will lose the benefits of important years of schooling, leaving them ill-prepared for the job market. They will not deal directly—that is, with a clear head—with the emotional and social issues of dating. This means they will be ill-prepared to establish a committed, loving relationship. In short, they will chronologically mature while remaining emotional adolescents.

However, all of this can be prevented.

PREVENTING PROBLEMS

Much has said about the "Just Say No" campaign made famous by Nancy Reagan. Even before this particular campaign was launched, studies had shown that learning to say no was part of an effective way that children could resist negative peer pressure.[3] The former first lady used the slogan to rally public support against children using drugs and has no doubt made a valuable contribution to public awareness of this enormous problem.

It is important that young children hear the "Say No" message, as in: "Do what we tell you to do. We know what is best. Say no to drugs." But young children need more than a slogan. They need positive role models. They need to feel good about themselves. They need to know how to have fun and how to cope with stress, without drugs. In short: Saying no is not enough. Young children need a broad range of experiences to help them learn positive attitudes and basic life skills. They need support in succeeding at home, in school, and in their social life. By providing these experiences, parents go a long way toward assuring that their children are part of the vast majority of children—those who do not develop drug problems.

With adolescents, the "Just Say No" approach is entirely misdirected. Adolescents who are developing their own identity and learning to make their own decisions do not necessarily benefit from the campaign nor take it seriously.

Teenagers need clear standards of behavior and an objective presentation of the facts. They need an opportunity to think for themselves and to discuss their thoughts. They need to learn to make good decisions on their own about drugs and, for that matter, all health issues. Instead, they are being served one-sided information—all the negatives about drugs—and therefore are not prepared when they start hearing the positives. And they are told what to do—"Just Say No." This is not very helpful advice considering that rebelliousness is a major correlate of drug use by teenagers.

Simply saying no is not enough. Children need to be empowered. Young children need an opportunity to learn positive attitudes and basic life skills. Teenagers need dialogue and discussion with their parents. Given an opportunity, all children can learn to make wise decisions about their health.

IGNORING AND DENIAL

Many parents have failed to notice or have chosen to ignore the problem of teenagers using drugs. Some of them grew up in an era when drugs were definitely not an option and can't imagine that chemical substances are available to their children. They are too far removed from today's youth, including their own, to recognize what is happening.

Some parents hesitate to bring up the topic of drugs because of the issue of trust. They say: "My kid is a good kid. I don't want him to think I'm suspicious of him."

The implication of this statement is that talking about drugs with children means accusing them of something and that parents of "well-adjusted" children should steer clear of the topic. But this is a false assumption. Discussion does not mean accusing or condemning a child. The purpose of a discussion is to inform, to educate, and to empower. "Good kids" as much as any others need to be prepared for the tough decisions that lie ahead. They deserve support.

The "wait and see" approach is another way that parents avoid the drug issue. They hope that everything will be fine of its own accord. "I haven't yet heard about my kids getting in trouble with drugs, so I don't need to do anything." This is a dangerous outlook because the parents are waiting for a crisis instead of taking preventive action.

Then there is denial, the same defense mechanism applied by drug users themselves and one of the most common ways that parents overlook the drug scene. Parents deny the existence of the problem by making believe that nothing is, or could be, wrong. Some denying parents know that children elsewhere are using drugs but say it won't happen in their community. Or they see it in their community but say it won't happen to their children. Or they see their children using drugs but reassure themselves that there is nothing to worry about: "If I ignore it or don't think or talk about it, it'll go away."

An unsuspecting mother found a plastic baggie filled with marijuana hidden under her fourteen-year-old daughter's bed. She asked Heather to explain.

Heather: "It's not mine. I'm just holding it for a friend."

Mom: "Oh, I'm glad to hear that you're not involved with drugs, because they're dangerous."

These are the words of a parent eager to be reassured. Although there's always the possiblity that her daughter's explanation was true, there's also a possibility it was not. It so happens that Heather had been having serious problems in school. She had become moody and irritable in recent months. Something was wrong. But Heather's mother dropped the subject of drugs like a hot potato. This is the psychological defense mechanism of denial at work.

Still another way that parents deny drug problems is on the basis of an ungrounded and false sense of optimism. A composite of their wishful thinking goes like this:

"Kids will be kids. Teens will be teens. It's just a stage of life. Teenage behavior is always strange. My kids will grow out of it. They'll get over it."

Although some children who experiment with drugs manage to escape injury, others do not. There is no reason to panic, but, by the same token, there is no reason to presume that everything will be fine of its own accord. Children need help from their parents in dealing with drugs. Parents who ignore the issue cannot become an effective force in preventing problems.

THE ENABLING PARENT

Wishful thinking carried to its most destructive extreme is called enabling, which means doing what is needed to allow drug use to continue. On the surface, enabling does not appear to have much in common with ignoring, although they are indeed related.

Parents enable drug use by protecting their children from the consequences of their behavior. Instead of confronting the problem and trying to deal with the causes, they allow it to continue.

I worked with a wealthy family in counseling in which enabling had reached an unbelievable level before they sought help. When the son, Mark, started smoking pot, he began "ditching" school. His parents covered for him by writing notes to the teacher saying that he was ill. When Mark was caught burglarizing a home for drug money, the parents hired an expensive attorney to fight in juvenile court. The most amazing event occurred after Mark wrecked the family car while intoxicated—the parents bought him his own new car. By protecting Mark from the natural consquences of his behavior, they had allowed him to keep on doing what he was doing. The drug problem got worse.

Enabling is similar to ignoring in its basic premise: "Just leave the child alone. He will do fine." But, in addition, enabling parents clean up the messes of their children. They make excuses for them, sparing them the pain of their consequences but not helping them become more responsible.

In this day and age when drugs are readily available, parents cannot look away from reality. They cannot afford to ignore or minimize the dangers. Children need help and leadership. Parents who ignore or deny problems cannot possibly provide either.

THE AUTHORITARIAN APPROACH

Because solving the problem of drug abuse requires strong action, some parents attempt to dictate the behavior of their children. They rely on parental authority: "I'm the parent and I'll tell you what to do. I'm going to lay down the law under my roof." They impose strict rules. Children are expected to do as they are told, to behave as directed or else face serious consequences. Punishment or fear of punishment is supposed to keep children in line, to control their behavior. With the authoritarian approach, the emphasis is on obedience. It's not necessary that children understand the reasons for rules or that they participate in establishing them. All that matters is that they comply.

"Be home by ten," an authoritarian parent says to his daughter as she leaves for a friend's house on Saturday night.

"Why?" the fifteen-year-old girl asks.

"Because I said so," her father replies.

"But could you explain why it's important?"

"I don't have to explain anything to you," he says. "I'm the parent, and if you keep hounding me with questions I won't let you go at all."

Authoritarian parents consider requests for an explanation to be an affront to their authority and feel no obligation to justify or even explain their position.

Authoritarianism is a powerful response to a serious problem. It has special appeal to panicked parents who recognize the dangers of drug abuse and want to take immediate and strong action.

Unfortunately, it is ineffective. Worse still, it often leads to the opposite of the desired effect—to a decline in parental influence. Authoritarian parents lose their ability to influence their children through reasoned discussion. This is a great loss because teenagers are consumed with the task of forming their own independent identity, and they need the support of people they trust. If the family climate is one in which dialogue is seen as a threat to authority, they will be too scared to discuss what they think.

Because they are scared of their parents, teenagers will have to make difficult decisions, such as whether to use drugs, without the benefit of an open family discussion. They know that their parents would not support them in thinking through their *own* decisions, but would lay down the law.

It could be argued that the loss of independent thinking by teenagers is compensated for by clear directives about appropriate behavior. In other words, teenagers will do as they are told without explanation and eventually understand the reasoning behind the directives.

This sounds good on paper. But in real life, when teenagers are struggling—as they should—to form an independent identity, the typical response to authoritarian parents is rebellion. Younger children may jump into line when commanded to do something by their parents, but not teenagers.

I was counseling a family with a fifteen-year-old son, Steve. When the mother mentioned that she had heard that some of Steve's friends were using drugs, the father turned red in the face, jabbed a finger toward his son, and issued an ultimatum: "If I ever find out that you've smoked pot, you'll be kicked out of the house for good. Mark my words."

Unfazed, Steve replied with a smirk on his face, "Don't worry Dad, *you'll* never find out."

These are moves in the Scare, Catch, and Punish game played by authoritarian parents and their rebellious teenagers. It's an escalating power struggle involving strict rules, defiance, and harsh consequences. Parents impose strict rules that teenagers defy. Parents punish their children and see defiance as an indication of the need for stricter rules. Stricter rules lead to even more defiance and ultimately even more punishment. The result is angry and fearful parents pitted against their angry and fearful teenagers.

An unfortunate outcome of this power struggle is that, at a certain point when the stakes are high and the punishment is severe, the enraged teenagers finally pull the ultimate power play:

"I don't care how you punish me. You can't control me. Take away whatever you want. Lock me up. Kick me out of the house. It doesn't

15

matter. I'm still gonna do drugs and whatever else I want to do. I'll steal money and run away from home if I need to."

At this point the teenagers are out of control and the parents have lost all influence. On the surface, the teenagers look like rotten kids. But if you examine the interaction, their defiance can be seen as the predictable climax after a series of moves in the game of Scare, Catch, and Punish.

The authoritarian approach doesn't always lead to open rebellion. At a workshop I conducted for professionals, a juvenile court counselor talked about his work with a troubled youngster, Tom, and his authoritarian dad. With remorse and uncharacteristic tears in his eyes, Frank, the father, described his son's secretive rebellion. It was a story about deception. Frank laid down the rules—very strict ones. Tom said he would obey. For several years, Frank boasted about how well his son behaved and advised all his friends to get tough with their kids. "You gotta play hardball," were his exact words. He pointed to his son's behavior to demonstrate the truth of his pronouncement. Secretly, however, his son broke all the rules. Frank learned the truth about what had been happening for the past four years of his son's life only from the juvenile court after the boy was picked up for petty theft. By that time, Tom had a serious drug problem.

It's not pure folly that makes the authoritarian approach so widely practiced. Authoritarian parents recognize the drug problem and the need for high standards. The problem is not the standards, but the process by which they are established—one that deprives children of understanding and self-respect. Authoritarian parents attempt to *control* the behavior of their teenage children when they should be helping them learn to think and make their own decisions. Limits are important, but children need to have room within the limits to make some choices. They need an opportunity to explore and think for themselves and to talk with adults who listen.

Recent studies have shown that parents who rely heavily on obedience, even when motivated by the best of intentions, actually harm their children. One study found that the ability to reason is impaired by parents who believe that children learn best when they "just listen to what they are told" and obey whomever is in authority. This approach to child rearing squelches curiosity and stunts a child's ability to think. Children in such families are distractable and uncreative, have little intellectual curiosity, and do poorly on tests of basic intellectual skills.[4]

16

OVERPROTECTION

Another response to the drug problem, somewhat related to the authoritarian approach, is parental overprotection. Overprotective parents shield their children from the harsh realities of the world. Like authoritarian parents, they attempt to control the lives of their children, but the method of control is different. Whereas authoritarian parents use rules and punishment to try to tame the "animal" energy of their children, overprotective parents present themselves as allies. They see the world as a threat, communicate this fearfulness to their children, and then rescue them from dealing with reality. These are the parents who, instead of helping their children understand difficult homework assignments, actually do the work for them.

The overprotected ten-year-old girl who goes to summer camp is frightened her first day and calls home to be rescued. Her parents drive about a hundred miles to pick her up that evening and take her home. She never learns coping skills.

Although most teenagers will eventually feel their oats and try to break free from the overprotective nest, the likelihood of parents maintaining control is greater with this method than the authoritarian one.

The big problems come later in life. When parents do all the thinking and decision making, children never have an opportunity to think and make decisions for themselves. As young adults, they have to face the harsh realities of the world without any preparation. They lack experience, and panic in stressful situations.

EMPOWERMENT

In our drug-oriented society, children need the powerful support of their parents. However, too often our ideas about power are limited to the cruder and more forceful manifestations, such as raised voices, threatening gestures, popping veins, and pounding fists. There is a better way. Parents can have a powerful influence over their children without going to these extremes. The alternative is cooperation. It is not power over other people. It is power sharing.

Parents, by virtue of age, knowledge, experience, and material resources, have greater power than their children. You can use this power to protect your children and at the same time to strengthen and empower them, that is, assist them in becoming stronger, smarter, and more competent in their own right. That's what we are talking about in this book. A helpful way to think about empowerment is in terms of a transfer of power.

TRANSFER OF POWER

Transfer of power refers to parents using their own power to help their children become strong individuals. This process is best understood by considering the entire span of child development, from birth, when an infant is totally *dependent*, to approximately age eighteen (varying in different cultural groups), when the goal is to have helped the child become an *independent* young adult.

The parental role is most clear at the extremes of the continuum. With infants, parents have total responsibility. With young adults, parents recognize the need to allow their children to make their own decisions and to take responsibility for their own lives. Parents are available for support.

In between the extremes, the parental role is more difficult to define. Parents continually assess the readiness of their children to assume responsibility. As children grow older, parents gradually relinquish control. It is a transfer of power, with children gaining ever more freedom and responsibility. The philosophy is one of trust. Children will make mistakes, but that's part of learning. All along parents provide ongoing guidance and support. In this process, children are empowered and become more mature and responsible.

Even babies need respect and a measure of independence. For example, they should be given an opportunity to fall asleep alone or to struggle to reach a toy. Parents who believe that their babies can't be happy without Mom and Dad in their presence deprive their infants of the opportunity to form relationships with friends, babysitters, and other relatives.

As children begin to understand language, parental decisions should be explained. Young children are given options and allowed to make some choices. Older children are allowed to make increasingly important decisions on their own and are consulted about other ones.

At a certain age a child is allowed to cross the street at a major intersection, to have a say-so about bedtime, to date, to drive the family car. At a certain age an allowance is given, a child is allowed to take public transportation. No formula clearly states when to give these responsibilities. Variations occur because of the unique individual involved and the particular set of circumstances.

One important difficulty for parents in managing a successful transfer of power is that the process itself is uneven. In particular, the child's demand for freedom, and his ability to cope with it, accelerate greatly during the teenage years. Suddenly, many young adolescents seek independence and a significant role in making decisions that affect their own lives. The challenge for parents is to respect the drive for independence by providing learning opportunities, yet to maintain legitimate limits.

Empowering children through the transfer of power is a delicate process in which parents try to challenge their children, but with challenges that are appropriate. Two major pitfalls are permissiveness and overprotection.

In the previous section, it was pointed out that many parents try to "protect" their children from drugs but go overboard and "overprotect." Similarly, some parents overprotect their daughters from boys. Consider the example of a girl who was not allowed to date. When she left home at age eighteen, unprepared for the social pressures that lay ahead, someone likened it to "throwing her to the wolves."

Rather than saving this girl from teenage males with overactive hormones, it would have been far better if her parents had empowered her—giving her freedom, responsibility, and support. This would have meant allowing her to go on dates with a curfew as a teenager and providing her an opportunity to discuss the different situations that arose. She would have learned from her parents' guidance and supervision. Gradually the curfew could have been extended, and less discussion would have been necessary. By the time she became a young woman, she would have been ready to handle the responsibilities on her own.

An entirely different set of problems is created by the other extreme of child rearing—permissiveness—in which freedom is given without adequate support or at a level that a child cannot yet handle. Under these circumstances, children fail and feel bad about themselves.

I know a mother and father who decided to let their ten-year-old daughter pick her own bedtime. To their dismay, every night she was watching "The Tonight Show." It put her in a good humor before bed, but left her tired and grouchy in the morning. The parents hoped she would realize what was happening and go to sleep earlier, but

19

she kept her late bedtime for almost three weeks. Finally, the parents realized they had given the girl freedom that she was not yet ready to handle. Fortunately, they had the presence of mind to take responsibility for the error so that the young girl didn't blame herself for failing. They explained their mistake to their daughter and selected a reasonable bedtime. The girl was relieved when they took back control.

ROLE MODELS

As you will see in the following chapters, preventing drug abuse is part of the transfer of power, whereby you teach your children important life skills and positive attitudes so that they can make wise decisions on their own. One important way that you teach is by example.

I remember being eight years old and standing next to my father at the sink. He would lather up his shaving cream and I would do the same. Then he would start shaving and I would rub my face with a plastic shaver. At the end he applied witch hazel to his face and to mine. It is a very fond memory. Aside from enjoying the company of my dad, I also was learning what men do from my role model and teacher.

All children learn the same way I did. We watch what our parents do and then copy it. Even now, more than thirty years later, I still shave with a safety razor—the way my father taught me—although long ago he switched to electric.

Because parents teach by example, their drug-taking behavior will certainly influence their children's.

When Mom is grouchy and says, "I can't get up in the morning without my cup of coffee," the children take notice. When she savors a cigarette after dinner, they notice that, too.

When Dad has a drink to "chill out" after work, the kids see it happen. They watch what he drinks, why he drinks, how much he drinks, and how he behaves afterward.

When parents reach for medications at the slightest ill feelings and don't even read the labels, children get a message.

When parents drink alcohol or smoke pot to self-medicate against stress, children notice. And they notice when their parents take Valium or Xanax as tranquilizers.

20

It's not just drug-taking behavior that parents teach by example. Children notice how parents have fun, how they deal with stress, how they cope with problems. Children notice how parents deal with peer pressure.

In drug prevention workshops and books, these harsh realities are sometimes sanctimoniously brought to the attention of parents who then believe that they have to be saints to save their children. I have heard speakers say, "How do you expect to help your kids if you yourself . . . ?"

Because most of us are not saints, many parents feel guilty and worry that one false move will ruin the lives of their children. Although expecting perfection is unfair and unrealistic, there is no escaping the reality that children learn by observing their parents. And if you want to do a good job of helping your children steer clear of drug abuse, you will want to set a good example.

As you read the next chapter about drugs, think about your own drug use.

If you or your spouse has problems with drugs, it will be important for you to make personal changes, for yourself and for your children.

As you read the following chapters about the positive attitudes and life skills that strengthen children and prevent drug abuse, think of where you stand with these attitudes and skills. It will be an opportunity to consider such issues as: how you cope with stress; how you find outlets for good times, excitement, and recreation; and how you respond to peer pressure.

Remember, you are living in a drug-filled and sometimes troubled world, just as your children are. You're not immune from the same problems and pressures that affect them. You need the same life skills they do and may discover some deficiencies of your own.

Many people have the ability to love others but have trouble giving that same love and concern to themselves. Maybe it takes reading a book for your children's sake to stumble upon areas of personal concern that can make your own life better. If that is so, then consider it a gift from your children. Helping them grow to be strong and competent people is an opportunity for you to grow, too.

As you read on, remember that the threat of drug abuse is no match for the power of parental love and education. You can take action to prevent drug problems in your children before they occur and to solve them if they already exist.

2

DRUGS AND THEIR USE, MISUSE, AND ABUSE

Sometimes I begin a lecture with a riddle. I tell the audience that a standard definition of a drug is any substance that can produce physical, emotional, or mental changes in people. Then I say I'm thinking of a particular substance—a white powdery one—that can produce emotional changes. It can change the way a person feels.

"What substance is it?" I ask.

"Cocaine," someone says.

"Good guess, but that's not what I'm thinking about."

"Heroin," someone else says.

"Another good guess, but sorry, that's not what I'm looking for."

Usually by now an audience member guesses right, but if not, I give the answer anyway: sugar.

They get my point that it is sometimes difficult to distinguish between food and drugs. Then I ask if anyone in the audience is a chocoholic. Those who regularly seek a chocolate "fix" probably have a vague understanding of addiction, although most of them don't realize that chocolate contains caffeine, an addictive drug.

"What about coffee?" I ask. "Is it a drug?"

To further complicate matters, I suggest they consider the classification of alcohol. What is it? The body burns it as a fuel. In that sense it's a food. In another sense, because people use it to get high, we think of it as a drug. But in very large amounts, alcohol is a toxin. It is poisonous.[1]

What I'm trying to do in these lectures is to promote open-mindedness in thinking about drugs. The topic is so emotional that people tend to get locked into rigid thinking. They have opinions, usually strong ones. But they confuse opinion with fact. Usually they are overcommitted to their opinions and underinformed about drugs.

Even when people start with identical information, they can reach entirely different conclusions. This happens often in everyday life— the topic doesn't have to be drugs. Consider a husband and wife who have been married for sixteen years. They each know their income, their expenses, and how much money they have in the bank. They agree on the facts. But she wants to go to Europe with their savings, and he wants to spend the money on practical household repairs, such as a new roof. He wants something tangible, to last a long time. She says they will have a lifetime of memories from their trip abroad, and they can leave a bucket under the leak. It's all a matter of how they choose to interpret the facts about their financial situation. It's a matter of what is important to them. The same is true in drug discussions. Facts are only part of what people consider in forming their opinions.

This chapter will prepare you for drug discussions with your children. It gives an overview of how drugs, in general, affect the body. It gives additional information about the specific drugs most often used by children. Also discussed are the stages of drug use—from experimental to dependent—and the signs and symptoms of a drug problem.

But before getting to the facts, let's look some more at people's opinions. Below is an exercise that will help you clarify your own thoughts about the use, misuse, and abuse of drugs.

GOOD DRUGS AND BAD DRUGS

People make their judgments about the use, misuse, and abuse of drugs on the basis of facts, values, and interpretations of the facts. What is acceptable to one person may not be acceptable to another.

Opinions about drugs vary in different cultures and in different historical eras. Early Muslim sects used coffee in religious rites, but had prohibitions against alcohol. It was the opposite in Europe. When coffee was first imported in the seventeenth century, the Roman Catholic Church opposed it as an evil drug. Yet wine was used as a traditional sacrament in Catholic masses.[2]

Attitudes about drugs change over time within a given culture.

When tobacco was introduced into Europe, it provoked such strong opposition that authorities in some countries sought to impose the death penalty for its use. Soon tobacco use was widely accepted and even encouraged in the belief that it made people work more efficiently.[3]

In this country, alcohol has a checkered history. It was legal until prohibition in 1920, when the sale and manufacturing of alcohol became illegal. After thirteen years, alcohol again became legal, and it remains so today. It may be legal, but alcohol probably brings more distress to more people than any other substance.

Within homogeneous groups, such as a nation or religion or ethnic group, there tends to be more agreement than there is *between* different groups. Those in the same age group are usually more in agreement with each other than with the overall population, creating what has sometimes been called a "generation gap."

But even among similar people (all teenagers, all parents, all Christians, all Jews, all school administrators, all teachers), there are great variations about what is considered good and bad. Within a single country, various groups may have different opinions about particular drugs. This is evident in the United States with marijuana. Although many people strongly condemn its use, others use it freely and believe it should be legalized.

Different judgments about drug use are well demonstrated in an exercise I sometimes conduct in workshops, called "Use, Misuse, and Abuse." It challenges people to clarify their own opinions. It helps them see that other people have different ideas. It also helps them learn to differentiate facts from opinions. You can do this exercise at home as I present it here in this book.

As you read the drug situations described below, ask yourself whether they constitute the use, misuse, or abuse of drugs. In workshops, after describing a drug situation, I ask for a show of hands. Invariably, opinion will be divided among the three options. After the vote is in, I ask for an explanation. Why was it an example of drug use? Why misuse? Why abuse?

Let's start with an example involving a hardworking man who comes home from the office and has two cocktails every night after work. If his wife is there, they drink together. If not, he drinks alone. He says it relaxes him. He enjoys the feeling. Is this use, misuse, or abuse?

Think about it yourself and then read some of the responses from workshop participants below. First, what is your opinion?

Now, here's what other people have said:

"I'd say it's use because he uses it to relax."

"In my opinion, it's misuse because there are better ways to relax without using booze."

"I disagree. I think it's abuse because it sounds like he needs it. He does it every day after work and even does it alone."

"Yeah, but nobody is hurt by it. He's at home. He doesn't drive drunk. I'd say it's use."

"But it's not good for his liver. I'd say abuse."

"Wait a minute. Some medical studies say it's good to drink in moderation to relax. I'd say it's use."

"But there are better ways to unwind. In my opinion, it's misuse because it's a habit. He can't go without it."

How about this example? A woman wakes up cranky every morning. She uses a coffee machine with a clock that turns on automatically at the designated time. Her family steers clear of her until she has had her two cups. Is this use, misuse, or abuse? What's your opinion?

Here is what other people have said:

"I'd call it abuse because she has to have it every day."

"It's use because it's only two cups. It's kind of a nice luxury."

"I agree. Some of us drink coffee at the office. Others drink it at home."

"It sounds like misuse to me. She's probably not addicted because she could stop. But she uses it to wake up every day."

"I say it's abuse because she is cranky unless she has the caffeine. Her mornings sound like they focus on coffee. Therefore she is dependent on it."

How about the twenty-year-old college student who smokes marijuana occasionally on weekends? He enjoys himself, never gets into trouble, and behaves quite well when under the influence.

"It's abuse because marijuana is illegal."

"It's illegal to speed on the highway and people do it all the time. I don't see that as abuse. I'd say in this situation it's drug use because it doesn't harm anyone. It just helps him relax. If he harmed someone, I'd call it abuse."

25

"It's just for fun. I'd call it use. It's not any worse than drinking a beer."

"I'd say it's abuse because it's bad for his body, especially his lungs."

"It's misuse because it keeps him from finding drug-free ways of enjoying his weekend."

One of my favorite vignettes in the "Use, Misuse, and Abuse" exercise is the example of a woman whose physician knows her well and has essentially given her an open-ended prescription for Valium. He told her to take the medication only when she is under a great deal of stress and not at other times. She held to the agreement and used the medication on only three occasions during a full year.

Most audience members call it use, but a few will disagree.

"I think it's misuse. Any time you use drugs to deal with problems you are misusing them."

"I think it's drug abuse. Taking tranquilizers only masks feelings. I think the woman should feel her feelings and learn to deal with reality. She could learn to tolerate stress or how to change her situation so she feels better."

"I agree. It's abuse. She could learn yoga or find some other way to relax."

These opinions inevitably bring out the doctor-can-do-no-wrong people:

"It's just use. The doctor prescribed it. She takes the pills only when she's under severe stress. Only three times. It's not like she's hooked on them."

Then I start teasing: "What if she takes Valium five times per year? Seven times? Fifteen? Twenty? Forty? Sixty? Where do you draw the line?"

Here's a wild one to think about. What would you call it when a sixty-three-year-old woman tries cocaine once—only once. Her granddaughter thought she was "cool" and gave it to her. The older woman hardly felt the effects at all. She said it was maybe like drinking one martini.

"I'd say it's use because she is just trying it once. No big deal."

"I'd say it's misuse because by trying it, she is approving of what her granddaughter is doing."

"It's abuse because it's a dangerous drug."

26

"But no one was harmed."

"Maybe she *was* harmed. Drugs are more dangerous with old people."

How about the person who smokes a pack of cigarettes every day, enjoys it, and has no desire to quit?

How about the parent who smokes marijuana infrequently for recreation and lets a teenage son try it once at home?

How about the thirteen-year-old who sneaks one beer with a friend?

The differences that emerge in the "Use, Misuse, and Abuse" exercise make it abundantly clear that people can arrive at different conclusions about drug situations. And so I sometimes tease an audience of adults: "If you can't agree with each other, how do you think you'll ever be able to agree with your children?" Then I get serious and talk about the importance of husbands' and wives' discussing their values with each other and reaching a common understanding so that they are not giving their children mixed and confusing messages.

Some of the biggest differences I have observed when doing this exercise occur with groups of both parents and teenagers. Parents are often very adamant about the drugs they fear their children might be using, especially marijuana. And the children come down harder on alcohol, their parents' drug of choice. The exercise helps the different generations understand each other's point of view better.

The more you and your spouse think through your own opinions about drugs, the better prepared you will be to address the topic with your children. With teenagers in particular, with whom discussion and dialogue is the main source of parental influence, you will want to be informed with facts and clear about your opinions—what they are and how you formed them. Your ability to reach conclusions about drug use, through systematic analysis, will serve as a good role model.

In forming opinions, most of the factual information falls into several main categories, listed and described below. These categories give reasons for opinions and a basis for comparing differences of opinion. Too often, we have opinions because we *know* they are right, but can't discuss the reasons in an articulate manner. By using the categories described below, you can demonstrate good reasoning to your children

27

while also giving them a framework for systematically thinking about drugs.

EVALUATING USE, MISUSE, AND ABUSE

Below are nine categories for evaluating drug use: drug pharmacology; legality; quantity, frequency, and length of use; changes in patterns of use; methods of use; setting; personality, age, and health of user; reasons used; and effects of use.

Drug Pharmacology

The pharmacology of the drug itself has a bearing upon opinions about use, misuse, or abuse. Important considerations include:

- Does the drug create dependence? How easily?
- What is the potency of the drug?
- How does the drug affect the body? The mind? A person's health? A person's behavior? With small doses? With large doses? With prolonged use?
- What drugs are being combined? Some drugs combine in a synergistic way, meaning that the total effect of a combination is stronger than adding the effects of each drug taken independently. In other words, $1 + 1 = 3$. A good example is Valium and alcohol. When they are combined, the potency of the two is far greater than might be expected if they were combined linearly, $1 + 1 = 2$.

You don't need to be an expert in pharmacology to talk about drugs with your children. On the other hand, it is important to be informed. Later in this chapter you will find basic information about specific categories of drugs.

Legality

Legality is an issue when evaluating the use, misuse, or abuse of drugs. The possession or sale of some drugs is legal, while with others it is not.

Legality also has a bearing on other considerations in drug use.

For example: How accessible is the drug? What does it cost to procure the substance? (Illegal drugs are sold at inflated prices. Heroin is a good example. When the opiates, of which heroin is one, were made illegal in 1914 under the Harrison Narcotics Act, the cost of the drug greatly increased. In order to support an expensive habit, most users of this substance had to commit crimes and engage in a criminal lifestyle.)

Legality also has a major bearing on another consideration: drug purity. When drugs are manufactured in clandestine laboratories, or acquired through underground channels, the consumer has no way to evaluate purity. The drugs may be contaminated. Also, the consumer cannot reliably estimate the potency. Most drug dealers "cut" their drugs, meaning that they adulterate them in order to gain greater profit from sales. Because the consumer cannot reliably estimate the potency or chemical composition of street drugs, nor the presence of contaminants, there is an increased risk of overdoses and "bad trips."

Quantity, Frequency, and Length of Use

How much of a drug is used? Is it one beer? One six-pack of beer? One case of beer? Is it one gram of cocaine?

Body weight is a factor in evaluating the amount of a drug dose, as is age. Children and elderly people are more sensitive to drugs and will have more pronounced responses.

How often is a drug used? This is the frequency question. What is the interval between doses? One case of beer over a week? A six-pack every night? Smoking marijuana once in the evening? Smoking all day long?

Another consideration: What is the length of use? Has the person been smoking cigarettes for a month, a year, ten years, or more? Is the use experimental? Is it habitual? (You will find more on how to evaluate this when we discuss the stages of drug use later in this chapter.)

Changes in Patterns of Use

Has the pattern changed? Is the quantity increasing? Is the frequency increasing? Is it remaining the same? Increase in quantity and frequency could indicate that *tolerance* has developed (more drugs are needed to create the same effects). Increase in frequency could indicate the development of dependence and an effort to avoid a *withdrawal syndrome*, the body's negative reaction to not having the drug. Change isn't necessarily negative. A person might be using drugs more often without necessarily suffering any adverse effects.

Methods of Use

How is the drug administered? Is it inhaled, smoked, sniffed through the nose (snorted), injected under the skin? Do you eat it? Drink it?

Drugs that are swallowed tend to be slower-acting, whereas injected drugs enter the bloodstream immediately. The same drug can have very different effects depending, in part, on how it enters the body. For example, the effects of cocaine are influenced by the method of administration, whether it is snorted, injected, or smoked.

Illegally injected drugs may involve the use of contaminated needles, which carry the considerable risk of spreading AIDS and other infectious diseases.

Setting

One very important consideration in the use, misuse, and abuse of drugs is the setting, that is, the physical and social environment. Use that may cause problems in one setting, let's say drinking beer at work, may be entirely acceptable in another, such as at a ball game. The critical questions are:

Where is the drug used? At home? At work? While driving? At school?

When is the drug taken? First thing in the morning? After work? During work? Before going to bed? On weekends?

With whom is the drug taken? With colleagues at work? With fellow students? Alone? With a spouse?

Personality, Age, and Health of User

Drugs affect people differently. The way they affect a person is related to the psychological state of the individual, what he wants the drug to do, and what he expects it to do. This is sometimes referred to as the "psychological set," the way in which an individual's mind is set to respond to the effects of the chemical. If there is anxiety associated with use, it is possible that a drug can create panic or that the pharmacological effects are muted. Attitudes play a part in determining drug effects.

A single cocktail can make one person funny and charming, another person bitter and angry, a third one sleepy, and a fourth one sad.

In a classic experiment, subjects were told that they were drinking alcohol but were actually given a placebo (an inactive substance). After consuming the beverage, they behaved as if they were under the influence of alcohol. Their expectations, not the drink itself, influenced their behavior.[4]

In evaluating drug use, health problems should also be considered. Certain chemicals interact negatively with existing health problems, such as drinking alcohol with a liver problem.

Reasons Used

Why is the drug used? People use drugs for medical reasons, to have fun, to avoid boredom, to relax, to cope with stress, to fall asleep, to escape reality, to suppress feelings, to release feelings, to generate extra energy, to create excitement, to satisfy curiosity, to defy authority, to be accepted by a particular social group, to alter consciousness, and for many other reasons as well.

Most drugs can have varied uses. For example, alcohol is used for almost all the reasons listed above. Codeine can be used medically as a pain killer or recreationally to get high.

In evaluating drug use, one consideration is whether a drug is the *only* way a person has to satisfy a particular need. If this is so, there is greater risk of becoming dependent on the drug to meet that need.

The age of the user is important, too. At certain ages, people have particular developmental tasks. For example, teenagers are learning about romantic relationships in preparation for adult loving relationships. If they cope with the anxiety of dating by getting high all the time, they will not succeed in maturing properly. They will become chronological adults but remain emotional adolescents.

Effects of Use

The immediate effects of a drug depend upon a variety of factors, such as the amount taken, the psychological set, the setting, an individual's biochemistry, an individual's level of tolerance and physical dependence, and the way the drug enters the body.

The relevant questions are: How is a person's physical and emotional health affected by the use of the drug? How does the person behave under the influence of the drug?

For the use of drugs over an extended period of time, the important questions about consquences are: How has a person's life been affected by drug use? Have there been positive effects? Have there been adverse effects? Has drug use caused problems at work? Behavior problems at school? Grade and achievement problems? Has it caused conflict in relationships with friends? With family?

Has drug use become the only way, or one of many ways, to avoid boredom? To deal with depression? To have fun? To deal with stress? Has it given a person more energy at times when it is needed? Has it depleted energy? Has it caused health problems? Financial problems? Legal problems? What will the effects be if use continues at the same level? What if use increases?

Is the user *aware* of how the drug is affecting him or her?

What, then, constitutes misuse and abuse of drugs?

One way to think about *misuse* is as taking drugs in potentially harmful ways, for example, combining drugs that could create dangerous interactions or taking excessive amounts of a substance. Drug misuse would include the unintentional or inappropriate use of prescription or over-the-counter drugs.

One way to think about drug *abuse* is in terms of health—whether drugs have damaged the body or mind or interfered with personal growth, development, and fulfillment. A pamphlet from the the National Institute on Drug Abuse used this definition: "Drug abuse is the use of a drug for other than medicinal purposes which results in the impaired physical, mental, emotional, or social well-being of the user."[5] Another consideration is whether drug use interferes with community-accepted standards of behavior.

Clearly, judgments such as these depend on personal values. Some say if a drug is illegal, it's abuse. Some say misuse. Some say legality is irrelevant, that our society's laws are not necessarily rational and that individuals must take their own counsel. Regardless of interpretation, being aware of the above ways to think about drug use at least provides a framework for reasonable discussion.

ADDICTION, DEPENDENCE, AND TOLERANCE

The concept of addiction is a controversial one. In Roman law to be addicted meant to be bound over or delivered to someone by a judicial sentence. It meant a form of legal slavery. For instance, a prisoner of war would be bound over to a member of elite Roman society. In sixteenth-century England, the meaning was the same. It was said that a serf was addicted, or bound over, to a landowner. But a new use of the term emerged. Previously a legal term," addiction" came to be used more loosely to describe any form of bondage. For example, one could be addicted to a person, a vice, or tobacco. *If you are a slave to something*, then you are addicted to it.

The medical theory of addiction that developed over the years was much more narrow than the general use of the term. A drug was said to be addictive if it created both tolerance and a withdrawal syndrome, which are explained below.

Drug *tolerance* is a physical or behavioral condition that develops in users of certain drugs, under certain conditions. It describes the need to increase the amount of drug taken in order to achieve the same effect. In other words, after using certain drugs for a while, the user must take larger amounts to achieve the same effect. The body is able to tolerate more of a drug without being affected. Some drugs are quicker than others to create tolerance.

The other component of the medical definition of addiction is that an addicted person will experience a physical reaction when the drug is withdrawn, suffering from what is known as a *withdrawal syndrome*. The most common symptoms are vomiting, chills, nervousness, and muscle tremors. They may persist from a few days to a week. Only certain drugs, such as opiates (for example, morphine, codeine, and heroin) and depressants (alcohol, minor tranquilizers, barbiturates), create a withdrawal syndrome. With some drugs (e.g., alcohol, barbiturates), under some conditions, withdrawal is dangerous and reduction of doses should be gradual and medically supervised.

In recent years it has become clear that the narrow medical definition of addiction is too limiting. An individual can be a slave to a drug for psychological as well as physiological reasons. Anyway, with some drugs it is difficult to determine whether the addiction is physical or psychological in nature. Often they occur together.

People psychologically dependent on a drug feel that the drug is necessary for their well-being and have a compulsion to seek and use

33

it. Drug use becomes the center of their lives. Attempts to discontinue use lead to extreme anxiety or depression and can cause physical reactions such as insomnia, restlessness, headache, irritability, and appetite loss.

Because of the difficulty in distinguishing psychological and physiological reasons for the compulsive use of drugs, it makes sense to think of addiction in more general terms, encompassing both motives. To avoid confusion, some people now use a different term—*dependence*—to describe a person's psychological or physical need to have a drug.

The distinction between physical and psychological dependence is important in ensuring that the withdrawal process is handled safely. And with modern treatment, physical withdrawal can be handled with a minimum of discomfort and risk. The major task in overcoming any drug dependence is dealing with the psychological dependence— the perceived need for a drug.

Broadening the definition of addiction, or using the concept of dependence, helps avoid misunderstandings in which drug users say, "No problem with this drug—it's not physically addictive." Any drug has the potential to be abused and many of them can cause dependence. Psychological dependence is no easier to avoid or overcome than physical dependence.

THE DRUG USE CONTINUUM

Most teenagers who use drugs do not develop lasting problems. But some do, and the problems can be devastating. One way to think about drugs is in terms of four stages, or levels, of use along a continuum. The first stage is experimental use, the second is regular use, the third is harmful use, and the fourth is dependence. Drug use can stop at any stage.

Many people experiment with drugs just to see what they are like. The vast majority stop at either stage one or two. Only a small percentage of drug users develop serious problems in important life areas—family, school/work, friends, the law, psychological/emotional health, personal finances, and physical well-being—and move on to stages three and four.

Most parents do not want their children using alcohol or other drugs. However, their response to drug use should be different according to the stage of use. With experimental use, they would want to have an honest, open, and serious discussion. With dependence, they would want to seek professional help.

If a child is in stage one or two of drug use, most parents want them to stop. However, they must at least do what they can to prevent the use from progressing into stages three and four.

Although most parents want their children to completely avoid drug use, at a minimum, delaying initiation can provide some protection against harm. Statistics show that the earlier drug use begins, the greater the risk of eventual problems.[6] This makes sense: Young children have less maturity than older children and less experience with self-control.

Stage One: Experimental Use

Children in this stage are curious and want to try drugs to see their effects. They are also responding to peer pressure. They may try to attain a drug or simply use it when it becomes available. Once their curiosity is satisfied, they may discontinue use, or take a drug when it becomes available again, or move to stage two and begin to seek drugs.

Stage Two: Seeking the Mood Swing

Aware of the effects of drugs on their mood, children at this level integrate drug use into their lives. More time, money, and forethought go into drug use. However, usage remains casual, mainly in social settings, and does not interfere with normal functioning on a daily basis. Individuals in this stage experience drugs as mostly positive. They feel good when under the influence. Adult "social drinkers" fall into this category.

Stage Three: Harmful Use

In this stage, drugs have become a preoccupation. Children use drugs to cope with problems of living. Daily functioning is affected. Responsibilities are neglected. Their school performance deteriorates. They may miss school, embarrass themselves in public, mistreat friends, and lie to cover their misbehavior. They may steal money to pay for drugs, get in trouble with the law, or begin to experience negative physical effects.

Many of these children spend their time with drug-using friends, often discarding old ones. A central focus of activity with these friends is acquiring and using drugs. These children may believe that they could stop using drugs, but generally will discontinue use only for brief periods of time and then resume again with the first motivating event, whether it is stress or "a great party."

The guilt associated with the misbehavior in this stage will damage self-esteem, contributing to more stress and possibly leading to increased drug consumption.

Family members often rescue their children during stage three. They take over responsibilities neglected by their drug-using children and lie to protect them in school or at jobs. This is called enabling.

Stage Four: Dependence

This is the extreme of harmful use. Drugs dominate the lives of people in this stage, who feel compelled to use them. Drug use takes priority over many normal and necessary daily activities. The dependent person is isolated and alienated, feels very bad about himself, and uses drugs to "medicate" against these feelings. Physical, psychological, and social functioning is severely impaired, although the physical consequences may not be as obvious in youths as in adults. The bodies of dependent people are accustomed to the drugs. Drug use at this point probably provides little or no pleasure because the substances are taken as an escape from discomfort, or from the pain of withdrawal. Chances of staying in school or maintaining employment are marginal. An apathetic, secretive, and noncaring attitude prevails. Some dependent people realize that they have lost control. Others continue to insist that they could easily stop, although all the evidence indicates otherwise.

HOW TO TELL IF YOUR CHILD IS USING DRUGS

Casual drug use by children in stage one or two will be very hard to recognize, unless your children tell you about it. Recognizable signs of drug use come late in the chain of events, usually during stages three and four.

In order to know if your children are using drugs, you need a baseline: you need to know their normal behavior. Then you watch for substantial changes. Some of the changes may be normal and healthy. Some are problematic. Of the problematic changes, only some will be drug related. Regardless of cause, if your child has experienced important negative changes, you will want to address them. They need your attention.

Below is a list of the signs and symptoms that *could* indicate drug use, or possibly other problems.

School:

- Increased absenteeism and tardiness to classes
- Drop in grades
- Behavior problems in school
- Negative attitude about school

Social life/friends:

- Dropping out of old activities
- Dropping old friends. Making new friends, who are drug users
- Strange-sounding phone calls, with covert communication about drugs

Emotional life:

- Basic mood changes: was outgoing, now withdrawn; was withdrawn, now outgoing; was relaxed, now fidgety
- Incidents of inexplicable mood changes—euphoria followed by tenseness and edginess
- Caring less about everything—school, sports, other activities

Family:

- Very secretive (do not confuse with a need for privacy)
- Estrangement from family
- Less responsible at home
- More conflict at home

37

Physical effects:
- Red eyes
- Deterioration in personal hygiene
- Weight loss (for certain drugs)
- Sleep disturbances
- Fatigue or hyperactivity

Also, there are various types of *physical evidence* that suggest possible drug use:
- Drug paraphernalia
- Use of incense (possibly to cover smell of marijuana smoke)
- Beer or liquor supply unaccountably diminished
- Money or other valuables missing
- Prescription drugs of family members disappearing

A note of caution: Some of what are called signs of drug use can be caused by a variety of reasons besides drugs. Some can possibly be normal teenage behavior.

I once had parents bring their daughter to my office, convinced that her bloodshot eyes were proof positive of drug use. The poor girl was suffering from allergies and wouldn't go near alcohol or any other drug for all the tea in China.

Many changes that alarm parents may simply be part of normal adolescent development. Most teenagers begin to find new friends, spend less time with their families, and challenge adult values.

Behavior changes can be caused by problems unrelated to drug use, because emotional, family, and relationship turmoil is quite common at this age. The changes are, however, cause for consideration and worthy of your attention.

TYPES OF DRUGS

Sometimes it seems like you would have to go to medical school for five years and then live around a school yard for another couple of years in order to begin to learn about all the drugs that are available. And then you would have to have an incredible memory.

When I first entered the field of drug prevention and counseling I was overwhelmed by the dizzying array of names and nicknames for the drugs. But I've been in the field long enough now to say two things that you will probably find reassuring: (1) There is a sensible way to organize the multitude of drugs into categories, so that to be an informed person, you don't have to know details about every single substance. By knowing the types of substances, you have a basic level of understanding of all drugs. The categories make logical sense and are therefore relatively easy to comprehend and remember. (2) You don't have to be all-knowing about drugs to be helpful to children. You just need to be informed and know where to look if you ever need more than a basic understanding. In the following section you will find plenty of information to begin working with your children to prevent drug abuse. Most of the pharmacological and historical information was gathered from sources 7, 8, and 9. If you want or need more detailed information, you can refer to these sources, or to a wide variety of other publications on the topic available in most bookstores and libraries.

Most drugs that are abused fall into six basic categories: stimulants, depressants, narcotics, hallucinogens, cannabis, and inhalants. I add anabolic steroids to the list because they have become another drug that is abused.

The easiest way to remember drugs is by the purpose for which they are taken.

Keep in mind that drugs are used to modify moods and behavior. Start with this assumption. We live in a busy, rushed society with many pressures and many stresses. In order to meet the demands of the society, people take certain drugs to speed themselves up. These are called *stimulants*. You can see how that would help people keep up with all the pressures.

One effect of living under stress is that it creates tension and anxiety. To relieve these feelings, people take drugs that slow them down and also help them forget their troubles. These are called *depressants*. In slowing people down, one of the first actions of the drugs is to slow the part of the brain that controls inhibitions. So another effect of depressants, in low doses, is to help people get loose and have fun.

Other drugs that slow people down are called *narcotics*. These drugs can be very potent. However, because of their potency and the dangers associated with them, they are only infrequently used by children, in part because of their danger and inaccessibility.

Another problem with our high-pressure society is that many people focus so much on success and making it that their fantasy life and imagination are shut down. It makes sense that they would want a drug that radically alters their perceptions and imagination, or, in the lingo of the recent past, "blows their minds." Therefore we have the *hallucinogens*.

Cannabis, of which marijuna is the major derivative, is in a category of its own. Sometimes its effects resemble those of a stimulant and sometimes those of a depressant. Like an hallucinogen, it can also alter perceptions. Because of its wide range of activity, it is a popular drug.

Inhalants are not widely discussed, but they are important drugs for parents to be aware of. These are volatile substances such as glue, gasoline, and nitrous oxide that children sniff. They give users the effect of being light-headed or drunk. Used for other than their intended purposes, these substances have very significant health risks. These are the easiest drugs for children to obtain and therefore "the drugs of choice" for very young children.

Returning to the theme of a hurried and competitive society, we see that intense competitiveness has entered the sports world. Therefore we have drugs known as *anabolic steroids*. They are hazardous to the health of athletes, yet frequently used because they give a competitive edge. They are starting to be used by young children.

So there you are: a simple way to remember drug types. Those that speed you up (stimulants); those that slow you down and loosen inhibitions (depressants and narcotics); those that alter perceptions (hallucinogens); those that give a broad range of effects (marijuana); those that even young children can easily obtain to get "drunk" (inhalants); and, finally, those that give athletes a competitive edge (anabolic steroids).

These types of drugs are discussed below in a little more detail, and a select group of specific drugs—those favored by children—is examined.

Stimulants

These are drugs that speed up the central nervous system. They usually reduce appetite and make a person feel less tired, more alert, and more energetic. Some people respond to these substances by feeling happy. Others feel anxious and jittery. In taking certain stimulants, people feel stronger and smarter, as their bodies are pushed beyond normal capacity. The logical aftereffects of such a demand on the body is to feel sluggish and tired.

Some stimulants are plants found in nature and others are chemicals created in laboratories. Cocaine, caffeine, nicotine, and amphetamines, sometimes called "speed," are all stimulants. Another type of stimulant is called a look-alike. These drugs are made to look like speed, have similar effects, and are sold legally. Diet pills are among these. The major ingredient in many of these drugs is caffeine.

Cocaine. Cocaine is a stimulant derived from the leaves of the coca shrub, which grows in South America. For nearly 5,000 years, Peruvian Indians have chewed on the leaves of this plant for the mild stimulation it provides as well as the appetite-suppressing effect. They have done this without apparent damage to their health.

The drug did not become a health hazard until 1860, when European scientists succeeded in extracting the cocaine alkaloid from the coca leaf. At first this product, cocaine hydrochloride, was hailed by physicians as an excellent anesthetic. It was used in cough medicines, nasal sprays, and a variety of other medications. It was an ingredient in many teas, extracts, and wines and in the original recipe for Coca-Cola. Sigmund Freud promoted cocaine as a treatment and substitute for morphine addiction. The problems of overdose and dependence became evident only over time. Federal legislation outlawed the drug in the early part of this century.

Cocaine is still used legally as a local anesthetic. Illegally it is used to create a rush of euphoric excitement. It is sniffed through the nose (known as "snorting"). Cocaine is also water soluble and can be injected into the bloodstream. And it can be altered to a substance suitable for smoking.

Cocaine increases the pulse rate, raises blood pressure, and gives feelings of energy and euphoria, promoting better performance on certain mental tasks. Fatigue is decreased. Occasional users who snort cocaine sometimes have a stuffy or runny nose from the drug.

One serious danger under any circumstances is overdose. In large enough quantities, multiple seizures can occur. Cocaine can trigger sometimes fatal cardiac arrhythmia or respiratory paralysis.

Cocaine smuggling is a billion-dollar business. Pure cocaine is "cut" (diluted) with various adulterants. With a street drug, the user can never be sure of the purity or concentration of the substance.

41

Because of the intense pleasure of cocaine, people can become highly dependent upon it. With serious dependence, users report preference for cocaine over food, sex, family, and friends. Chronic excessive use eventually leads to depression and flattened emotions. Some people use cocaine almost continuously in order to avoid coming down and the depression and fatigue that would ensue.

Regular users of high doses of cocaine are restless, irritable, and anxious. They may have difficulty sleeping, which can lead them to use other drugs such as alcohol, marijuana, sedatives, and heroin in order to compensate.

Chronic users of cocaine clearly experience withdrawal problems, including intense anxiety and depression. Even after the initial depression subsides, an ongoing emotional numbness known as "the coke blues" can persist for months.

In extreme cases, longtime users of high doses of cocaine may become paranoid or hallucinate and suffer from what is called "cocaine psychosis," a state that resembles schizophrenia.

Each means of administering cocaine has its own set of risks. Snorting causes nasal membranes to crack and bleed and may destroy the septum (the cartilage separating the nostrils).

One danger of injecting cocaine is the same as the danger of any drug that is taken by injection: the risk of unsanitary needles causing hepatitis, AIDS, or other infections.

One type of smokable cocaine, known as crack, is a less expensive form of the drug sold in tiny chips that give the user a five-to-twenty-minute high. Because it is smoked, it reaches the brain in less than ten seconds. A euphoric high is followed by a crushing depression, creating a cycle of ups and downs that reinforces craving. Dependence can develop within a few weeks of first use. Although a single dose does not cost much, the high is brief and the need for more and more of it becomes very expensive. Crack users are energized, active, and often paranoid in their quest for the drug. As a group, they pose a serious threat to society.

Caffeine. Caffeine is probably the world's most popular drug. It is a bitter, crystal-like substance found in coffee, tea, cacao, and kola plants. It was named after the coffee plant, from which it was first isolated in 1821. It is also an ingredient in many over-the-counter medicines, especially cold remedies and cough syrups.

Arab goat herders discovered coffee around A.D. 850 after observing the energy of their goats who had eaten the berries of a coffee plant. Coffee was introduced to Europe and America during the sixteenth and seventeenth centuries and was a very popular drink during the Renaissance, when many artists claimed it provided inspiration and insight.

Caffeine is a natural component of kola-nut extract used in cola and other soft drinks. Additional caffeine is added to these beverages. Caffeine is also found in the cacao tree, from which we get chocolate.

Body temperature and blood pressure increase after using caffeine. Other effects include decreased appetite and delayed sleep. In some people, intake of more than 250 milligrams of caffeine can cause nausea, diarrhea, sleeplessness, trembling, palpitations, headache, and nervousness. An average five-ounce cup of brewed coffee contains 100 milligrams, a twelve-ounce cola drink between 30 and 46 milligrams. One tablet of No Doz, an over-the-counter stimulant, contains 100 milligrams. Tolerance may develop with the use of 500 to 600 milligrams per day (about five to six cups of coffee). Caffeine intake has also been related to higher risk of certain types of cancer and to peptic ulcer disease.

The use of caffeine by young children is a serious health concern. Young children consume most of their caffeine from soft drinks. Based on body weight, they consume it at a level near those that are known to cause central nervous system impairment in adults.

Nicotine. European sailors and explorers arriving in the New World found the Indians carrying rolls of dried leaves that they ignited and inhaled. They tried this drug, tobacco, liked it, and soon were addicted to nicotine, the chief active substance. Sailors who smoked tobacco craved the drug and carried the leaves and seeds with them, spreading the tobacco plant around the world.

At first use, most people do not like the taste of tobacco. But they learn to enjoy the energy rush. Smoking cigarettes causes an increase in heartbeat, a rise in blood pressure, and a drop in skin temperature. It is hard on the cardiovascular system. Smoking first stimulates and then reduces the activity of parts of the brain and nervous system. Some regular smokers experience a loss of appetite and an increase in metabolic rate, and many experience a decrease in physical endurance due to a decrease in their lungs' ability to exchange oxygen.

Cigarettes are a causal factor in coronary heart disease, vascular disease, chronic lung diseases such as bronchitis and emphysema, and

43

cancer of the lungs, larynx, mouth, and esophagus. They are also associated with other forms of cancer and many other health risks. A smoker has ten times the risk of getting lung cancer as does a non-smoker. Respiratory infections are more common and more severe in smokers.

Smokeless tobacco is also a health threat. Absorbed through the lining of the mouth, nicotine from chewing tobacco enters the bloodstream more slowly than from cigarettes. But the average blood concentration of nicotine in regular users of smokeless tobacco is the same as in smokers.

Smokeless tobacco is associated with increased risk of several types of cancer, including lip and gum cancer and cancer of the esophagus. Prolonged use causes discolored teeth, bad breath, and gum disease. It interferes with the sense of taste and smell.

Young males between eighteen and thirty are the typical chewers or "dippers" of smokeless tobacco. This is probably why tobacco companies use sports stars to promote it in advertisements.

The use of nicotine is likely to produce dependence. More than half of all adult smokers would like to stop. But nicotine is an extremely tough habit to break. Withdrawal symptoms include anxiety, irritability, lethargy, and weight gain due to a change in metabolic rate.

Amphetamines. Amphetamines were first synthesized in the nineteenth century but were not widely used medically until the 1930s, when the drug was introduced as an ingredient in decongestant inhalers. Drug companies saw the stimulant properties of amphetamines, as did thrill seekers, who used the drug recreationally and started calling it "speed." Amphetamines became a medical wonder drug of sorts, enabling users to go for long periods of time without sleep and rest. For the next forty years, amphetamines and two closely related drugs, dextroamphetamine and methamphetamine, were widely prescribed as antidotes for depression, lethargy, and fatigue and, especially in the 1960s and 1970s, as diet pills.

As health hazards were identified, fewer amphetamines have been produced and prescribed. But clandestine labs now produce both the drug and look-alikes with the same effects.

Amphetamines can be injected or taken in pill form. They increase heart and breathing rates and blood pressure. They decrease appetite. They may cause dry mouth, sweating, headache, blurred vision, dizziness, sleeplessness, and anxiety. Users report feeling restless, anxious, and moody. Higher doses intensify the moods. Extremely high doses can cause a rapid or irregular heartbeat, tremors, loss of coordination, and even collapse. Amphetamine injections increase blood pressure and can cause death from stroke, high fever, or heart failure.

In long-term users, speed exhausts the body. Tolerance develops and more of the drug is needed for the same effect. Addicts feel that the drug is essential to normal functioning, and take it to avoid the down mood. Possible problems of long-term use include malnutrition (and diseases associated with it), skin disorders, ulcers, sleeplessness, weight loss, and depression. It's a tough habit to break, with strong withdrawal symptoms.

Large amounts of speed over a long period of time cause "amphetamine psychosis," in which the user suffers from hallucinations and delusions. People who become paranoid from the drug may also become violent.

Depressants

Depressants, sometimes referred to as "downers," slow down the mind and body. In our rushed and hurried society, they are a chemical way to calm down, relax, and fall asleep. Side effects include slowed reaction time and sometimes slurred speech. These drugs are most familiar in certain forms: alcohol; Valium, Xanax and other minor tranquilizers; barbiturates, e.g., Nembutal and Seconal, and sleeping pills.

They depress the central nervous system, slowing heartbeat and respiration. They sedate people and are sometimes known as sedatives.

Depressants, including alcohol, are especially dangerous in combination because they combine with each other synergistically. In other words, if you combine two of these drugs, you get more than twice the impact.

Depressants lead to both tolerance and physical and psychological dependence. Withdrawal from dependence on a depressant can be very dangerous and should be medically supervised.

Barbiturates. The first barbiturate, phenobarbital, was introduced in 1913. Barbiturates are still used for medical purposes, including seizure control. They are, however, very dangerous because overdoses can be fatal. Sometimes people accidentally overdose, taking a small

45

amount at first but then, being groggy, taking more and losing track of how much they have consumed.

Tolerance develops quickly with barbiturates, and the amount needed to induce sleep can eventually equal the lethal amount. Withdrawal from barbiturates, as from all depressants, is serious and potentially hazardous. Symptoms include restlessness, insomnia, and anxiety. Withdrawal can result in convulsions and even death and therefore should be supervised by a physician, who will administer other drugs and/or gradually reduce the dose. It is dangerous for a dependent person to suddenly stop "cold turkey."

Benzodiazepines. Another class of depressants is benzodiazepines, the best known of which are the minor tranquilizers Valium and Librium. These are among the most widely prescribed drugs. Although introduced by pharmaceutical companies as a miracle cure for anxiety, they are simply another type of depressant, carrying the same risks of adverse effects and dependence. Too often they have been prescribed as the remedy for the stress and difficulties of everyday life.

Methaqualone. Methaqualone, another depressant, sometimes known as Quaaludes or "ludes," has an effect similar to alcohol. Small amounts are calming and relaxing. Larger doses create the slurred speech patterns, slowed reflexes, and poor judgment often associated with drunkenness, and they carry the same risks with driving an automobile and cause the same type of hangover. Manufacturers have suspended production of this drug because of the danger of misuse and abuse. However, Quaaludes can still be obtained through illegal channels.

Alcohol. This depressant is one of the most popular and widely abused drugs in the world. It has been around since earliest recorded history. Alcohol forms naturally when fruits or juices ferment in warm places. In the fermentation process, microorganisms that live on the skin of the fruit feed on the sugar, making the alcohol.

From the beginning, alcohol was used for medicinal purposes, at celebrations, and in religious rites. The alcohol used in beverages is grain alcohol. Its chemical name is ethyl alcohol.

Nondistilled alcoholic beverages include wine, beer, and hard cider. Distilled alcohol, known as spirits, dates back only a few hundred years, when wine was heated and then cooled, with the vapors being

46

condensed in another container. The initial idea was to concentrate wine into a smaller volume to make it easier to ship overseas. Then water would be added. However people found they liked the taste and effect of the distilled beverage; this led to the production of scotch, bourbon, rum, gin, and vodka.

The Eighteenth Amendment to the Constitution became law in 1920, forbidding the manufacturing and sale of intoxicating beverages. It was repealed by the Twenty-first Amendment in 1933.

Alcohol is a depressant that slows down the central nervous system. Small doses generally produce good moods and feelings of energy and warmth. They lower inhibition and reduce anxiety. People seek this pleasant effect, but many have difficulty staying in this pleasurable range and take too much. They go from the pleasant zone into the trouble zone.[10]

The effects of the drug vary greatly according to the amount of alcohol in the blood, the personality of the person drinking, and the mental set and setting in which the drug is used. The same dose affects people differently. It also appears that there are individual differences in the body's ability to metabolize alcohol. For some, this means fewer unpleasant side effects, increased preference, and possibly greater risk of addiction.

The effects of excessive amounts of alcohol are apparent in drunken behavior: slurred speech, impaired coordination, and sometimes misbehavior. Another serious risk is that the drug produces a subjective experience of competence and alertness that does not match reality. Alcohol slows the body, slows reaction time, and diminishes judgment. Yet it may increase confidence in performance. This false confidence is one reason that people drive or take other risks under the influence of alcohol.

Another effect of excessive drinking is a hangover. Consuming additional alcohol relieves the immediate effects of a hangover, but can contribute to a developing dependence.

One of the problems of alcohol is its social acceptability. It is advertised extensively, sold widely, and given as a gift. It is served on airplanes, at theaters, at ball games, and even in some work settings. It's a drug that's hard to avoid.

Tolerance develops with alcohol as with all the depressants. It is estimated that about one in ten drinkers, or approximately 20 million Americans (including over 3 million teenagers), are alcoholics. Alcoholism wreaks havoc in the life of an individual and his or her family. It is costly to society in terms of both treatment and the link of this drug to crime and automobile accidents. Withdrawal from a serious drinking problem causes major emotional and physical distress and can even be fatal.

The long-term dangers of alcohol include cirrhosis of the liver, which is a common result of overuse. Alcoholics may also suffer brain and nervous system damage. Used during pregnancy, it can cause fetal alcohol syndrome, a condition involving irreversible physical and mental birth defects.

Narcotics

Some people think that all illegal drugs are narcotics. However, only certain types of drugs, those derived from opiates, or synthetic copies of opiates, are actually narcotics. The origin of the name is the Greek word *narcos,* which means sleep. These drugs relieve pain and make a person drowsy. They slow a person down and create feelings of euphoria. They are most familiar to us as the pain-killing drugs that dentists and doctors prescribe, such as codeine, Demerol, morphine, and Percodan. The illegal drug heroin is also a narcotic. Narcotics can cause physical dependence and are not widely used by children.

Hallucinogens

As the name implies, these are the drugs that create hallucinations—imagined voices, visions, or feelings. Hallucinogens also change perceptions of time, experience, and distance. The effect can be mild or intense depending on the drug and the dose.

Some hallucinogens are produced by the plant kingdom, such as mescaline from the peyote cactus and psilocybin from a species of mushrooms referred to in the drug culture as "magic mushrooms." The practice of incorporating hallucinogenic mushrooms in religious ceremonies dates back to 1500 B.C. in Mexico and Central America.

One risk with hallucinogens is of "bad trips," when users become anxious and panic about their altered state of consciousness. Another problem is flashbacks, when the effects of the drug recur, sometimes long after use, creating panic.

*   *   *

LSD. One of the more widely used hallucinogens, lysergic acid diethylamide (LSD; acid), was accidentally synthesized in 1943 by Swiss chemist Albert Hofmann, who was working for Sandoz, a pharmaceutical company. Four years later Sandoz made the drug available for two purposes: to aid in releasing "repressed material" in psychotherapy and "to induce model psychoses of short duration." American psychiatrists were interested. The CIA was also interested in this drug that could possibly drive people crazy.

In the 1960s many of the human guinea pigs in tests of LSD found that they liked their experience on acid and spread the word, thereby promoting recreational use of the drug. Alarmed lawmakers made possession of LSD illegal.

PCP. Another hallucinogen, phencyclidine (PCP; angel dust), first synthesized in the 1920s, was hailed in the early 1960s as a nonnarcotic anesthetic agent with analgesic properties. But it was found to produce too many adverse side effects and human applications were made illegal. Its only legal use now is as an anesthetic for nonhuman primates. In the late 1960s people started using this "elephant tranquilizer" for recreation. Its extreme potency and unpredictable effects make this drug particularly dangerous.

Inhalants

These are volatile chemicals that produce intoxication when inhaled or sniffed. Sniffing makes a person feel drunk and creates a wide range of emotions, sometimes funny, happy, or fearful. Inhalants include glue, gasoline, nitrous oxide (used by dentists), fingernail polish, typewriter correction fluid (such as White Out), fumes from spray cans (certain paints, deodorants, and hairsprays), water-based Magic Markers, and butyl nitrate (sold in small glass bottles in "head shops"). Most of the substances sniffed are commercial preparations that are safe when used as directed for their intended purpose. But they are very dangerous, even fatal, when abused.[11]

Sniffing can cause stomach aches and fainting. With prolonged use, sniffing can harm the nerves, liver, and kidneys. It can cause brain damage. Some children suffocate from inhaling fumes from bags. Some people suffer heart failure from sniffing.

Marijuana

The most popular of all illegal drugs, marijuana (pot; grass), is the crushed leaves and stems of the hemp plant (*cannabis sativa*). The intoxicating ingredient is delta-9-tetrahydrocannabinol, commonly referred to as THC. The current crop of marijuana has been cultivated to contain much more THC than in the past, and therefore it has far greater potency. Sinsemilla, the Spanish word for "seedless," is marijuana in which the grower disrupts the growth cycle of the plant so that seeds do not form, leaving a high concentration of THC in the leaves. Normally, the THC would go toward producing seeds.

Hashish is made by taking the resin from the leaves and flowers of the plant and pressing it into slabs. It contains more THC than marijuana.

People take marijuana to get high, to relax, and to alter their consciousness. It can loosen inhibitions and put a person in a dreamy state. The drug induces a faster heartbeat and pulse rate. Reddening of the eyes, dry mouth, and dry throat also occur with use.

Marijuana reduces the ability to do things requiring concentration and therefore poses risks when users drive cars. Some users, frightened of the effects of the altered consciousness, panic when they are high, making their experience unpleasant.

Because it is a drug often used by children, one risk is that they will use it in school and it will therefore interfere with their academic success. Another risk is that it will be used to self-medicate against anxiety. Used as a crutch, it prevents children from learning to cope through their own strength, without the use of drugs.

Longtime users of large amounts of marijuana develop psychological dependence. They may be high so much that they have problems with relationships, work, and school.

Marijuana smoke irritates the lungs and can contribute to lung cancer the same way that tobacco does. Smokers inhale deeply and hold the smoke in their lungs. Many marijuana smokers also smoke tobacco, thus combining health risks.

Much of the research on marijuana has been conflicting. The tentativeness of the discussion is reflected in the following excerpt from a pamphlet published by the National Institute on Drug Abuse (with my emphasis added):

"Some research studies *suggest* that the use of marijuana during pregnancy *may* result in premature babies and in low birth weights.

50

Studies of men and women who use marijuana have shown that marijuana *may* influence levels of some hormones relating to sexuality. Woman *may* have irregular menstrual cycles, and both men and women *may* have a temporary loss of fertility. These findings *suggest* that marijuana *may* be especially harmful during adolescence, a period of rapid physical and sexual development."

The "amotivational syndrome," in which a person seems to lose ambition, has been attributed to marijuana. Opinion differs on whether it is drug induced or whether the drug is just a contributing factor. However, "burnout" is a nonmedical term, developed by users of marijuana themselves, to describe people who have smoked heavily over a prolonged period of time. A burned-out person is slow, dull, and inattentive.

Anabolic Steroids

Drug use in athletics has a long history. As early as 1865 there were reports of swimmers and cyclists taking drugs. In 1904, U.S. Olympian Tom Hicks collapsed after winning the marathon. He had taken highly poisonous strychnine in combination with brandy. In the 1954 weight-lifting championships, U.S. weight-lifting physician John Ziegler learned of the Soviet use of testosterone. He then developed Dianabol, the first anabolic steroid in the United States.

Steroids are a synthetic form of the male hormone testosterone. Although available as a prescription drug for certain medical disorders, these drugs are easily attainable in most gyms and widely abused. Coupled with exercise and a high-protein, high-calorie diet, they produce a state of euphoria, diminished fatigue, and increased bulk, power, endurance, and aggressiveness in both sexes.

The use of anabolic steroids is laden with risks. Misuse of these drugs has been associated with personality changes and mood swings, infertility, abnormal liver function, increased cholesterol level, high blood pressure, premature cessation of bone growth, bleeding ulcers, jaundice, and premature death. More muscle and tendon injuries are apparent among users.

Taken by healthy men, steroids shut down the body's production of testosterone, causing men's breasts to grow and genitals to shrink.

Large doses in women trigger masculine changes, such as lowered voice, increased body and facial hair, changes in sex drive and menstruation, and increased aggressiveness.

51

With the enormous dangers inherent in their use, why do athletes take anabolic steriods? Apparently many athletes will do anything for a competitive edge. In 1967, when 100 runners were asked if they would take a drug if they knew it would help them win the Olympics, but would kill them in a year, more than half said they would take it.[12]

The use of anabolic steroids by males is probably also a response to this society's preoccupation with physical appearance, and the desire for the muscular look.

THE SCARE APPROACH

In the 1950s, through the 1960s, and into the early 1970s, children were exposed to much of the information about the dangers of drugs. The idea was that this information would serve as a deterrent and scare children away from drugs. However, these programs failed to decrease drug use, and in some instances actually increased it by arousing curiosity about the "forbidden fruit." Another problem with these programs was that some of them gave false and exaggerated claims of danger, which led to a loss of credibility and eventually the counterargument, also inaccurate, that "drugs are harmless." A third reason these programs failed is that information about drugs can be ignored or denied. Such knowledge is not potent enough to counter the needs or desires that motivate drug use. This is clearly evident with tobacco. Look at the number of adults who smoke tobacco despite what is known about the health risks.

The failure of informational approaches to drug prevention does not mean that children should remain uninformed. Recent thinking is that the information should be given, but not exaggerated, and that it should be supplemented with other programs. The modern approach to preventing drug problems includes providing reliable drug information but also recognizing the *motivations* for drug use and teaching skills and attitudes that provide alternative ways of meeting the needs that would otherwise be met by drugs.

Now that you have a solid base of information about drugs and their use, misuse, and abuse, the next two chapters are about how you can teach the attitudes and life skills that empower children to meet their needs without drugs.

3

THE EMPOWERING FAMILY

Paul, age twenty-three, had a serious cocaine problem when he came to me for help.

His wife, Janet, had just kicked him out of the house. She was tired of the lies, hostility, and extreme moods. Although Paul was making a substantial income selling electronic equipment on commission, he was in debt, constantly borrowing to pay for cocaine and lying to Janet about where their money was going. He was also in danger of losing his job. Regardless, Paul had great ambitions about saving enough money to return to the university, earning a business degree, and becoming the success that everyone had expected him to become. But the way things were going, it was pie-in-the-sky.

Paul came from a high-achieving fmaily. His father was a respected physician and his mother an engineer for a computer company. His older brother studied law at Berkeley and his younger sister excelled in high school and was class president.

To all the world, Paul seemed like a bad apple, an irresponsible young man who was hurting everyone he loved. Most people had no idea of the underlying causes of his drug abuse, the seeds of which were planted during childhood. Paul, like many young children, never had an opportunity to learn the attitudes and life skills that could have protected him against drug problems. In the course of therapy, we uncovered some of the roots of his early drug use.

Paul had been successful in elementary school, had friends, and seemed to thrive. Good report cards were rewarded with praise, but recognition for school achievement was about all the encouragement that he received. He remembered wishing that his mom and dad would spend more time with him but feeling guilty about this because he knew they were "important people."

In junior high he started to have minor academic problems, in part because of the turbulence of adolescence.

"We expect more of you than this," he remembered hearing his father say sternly. And Paul was frightened. He had been doing his best, didn't know what was wrong, and didn't know where to turn for help. In the next few months his grades continued to decline slightly. His father again pressured for better results, established stricter homework rules, and limited Paul's social time. But Paul didn't understand the cause of his school problems and therefore didn't know how to solve them.

He remained unhappy, confused, and scared. He was angry that his parents were not more supportive. He couldn't cope with his father's pressure, which only seemed to make him more tense and caused greater decline in his schoolwork. Paul felt hopeless about reversing the downward trend and gaining his father's approval. As his confidence dwindled, he clearly remembered having one particular thought:

"Dad thinks I'm a bad kid. He should see what the other kids do. If he wants to see bad, I'll show him bad."

Soon he started drinking alcohol and smoking pot, and so his drug problem began. Some would say that this was teenage rebellion, and certainly there was an element of that. But something else was happening. He was under stress and didn't know how to cope. Drugs were an escape, a release from parental pressure. They were also a way to express anger toward his dad and, most of all, a way to feel good instead of discouraged and scared.

WHY CHILDREN USE DRUGS

Paul used drugs for the same reason that many adults use them—to "solve" problems, to escape from pressure.

Linda, age fifteen, had a similar motivation: "I get high because I hate school and my parents drive me crazy. Instead of feeling bad, I feel good."

In general, most reasons that teenagers use drugs are the same as those that motivate adults.

"I smoke pot for fun," said John, age fourteen, to his parents. "Everything's more fun when I'm high. I love the feeling."

"All the kids drink," said Brian, age fifteen. "I'm no different from my friends. Only the schoolboys [bookworms] and the nerds don't drink."

In terms of motivation, the words of these children are consistent with what common sense indicates and scientific studies have shown: Children use drugs for three main reasons.

For positive experiences. Children want to feel good and have fun. They are seeking sensations. They want to alter their consciousness, have bursts of energy, or even experience hallucinations. They want something new, exciting, risky. They are curious. They dread boredom.

To relieve stress. Drugs provide an escape from reality, a mood-altering experience. Children use drugs to relax or to stay calm in tense situations. Drugs are a way to cheer up or avoid feeling bad.

Drugs are also used to improve performance by relieving tension. For example, in a dating situation, teenagers take drugs to lower inhibitions and relax. In a school situation, teenagers use them to calm jittery nerves before taking exams.

In response to social influences. Many teenagers use drugs because they consider it "cool." They want to belong and be accepted by peers. Another social influence is adults. Children see adults using drugs and imitate them in order to be more adultlike.

The mass media, which often portray drugs as glamorous, are also an important influence. Advertisers use the media to promote the use of legal drugs, particularly alcohol, suggesting that getting high is part of the good life.

PREVENTING DRUG PROBLEMS

The public is aroused, and rightfully so, about convenience stores conveniently selling alcohol to minors. Our government officials are very busy at least *talking* about a war against drugs and issuing sanctions against drug-producing countries. Sometimes it's tempting to see the whole problem as "out there" where the drugs are manufactured and sold, and not "in here" where they are consumed—at home, in our country, in our community, and in our families.

We can eliminate one or many of the sources of drugs, but as long as the demand remains, the supply will be forthcoming. And the demand is based on *real needs*. Children turn to drugs to meet these needs. Until they find other ways, and choose to use them, they will continue using drugs. Therefore, any effective effort to prevent drug abuse must identify the needs that are met by drugs and help children learn healthier and less risky alternatives.

There are many ways to have fun, excitement, pleasure, and adventure in life without drugs. There are many ways to minimize stress and alleviate tension without drugs. There are many ways to socialize with other people and be part of a group without conforming to a drug-using norm. Children who are empowered to meet their needs in these ways, without drugs, will be far less likely to abuse drugs than will those who lack the necessary life skills.

What I'm describing is not a quick fix to the drug problem. It's not a "war on drugs" that sounds powerful and impressive. However, with consistent effort parents can prepare children to resist drug abuse. Drug prevention is child promotion. It's more than saying no to drugs. It's saying yes to children.

This chapter is about helping children learn positive ways of meeting their needs—helping them learn to enjoy life, solve problems, cope with stress, resist peer pressure, and form positive relationships. Your home is the classroom. The curriculum is a set of positive attitudes and life skills. The lesson plan is to establish a home climate that empowers children.

THE CURRICULUM

The curriculum of life skills and positive attitudes that allow children to resist drug abuse has four major components: self-esteem, clear thinking, problem solving, and relationship values and skills. The rationale for this curriculum is explained below.

Self-Esteem

At the top of the list is high self-esteem. It is the foundation upon which children develop.

Children with high self-esteem are less likely to abuse drugs because:

56

• They respect their bodies and won't damage them by harmful involvement with drugs.

• They respect themselves and want to achieve their goals. They won't engage in activities, such as using drugs, that could be detrimental to their success.

• They feel competent and confident. They are willing to take and meet challenges without needing drugs to feel secure.

• They know their strengths and are motivated to work hard to attain their goals. They feel good about success. They minimize failure and therefore reduce the need to rely on drugs to hide the pain of failure.

• They feel lovable and won't feel as much pressure to conform in order to win approval, as children sometimes do, by taking drugs to be accepted by peers.

• They know and respect their own feelings. They will take their own needs seriously and learn to meet them, and won't have to rely on drugs for feeling good.

Clear Thinking

Children who think clearly are less vulnerable to drug abuse because:

• They can evaluate experiences and learn from them, thereby gaining mastery and self-esteem.

• They are thoughtful in formulating their own values and opinions, including those about issues such as drugs. They are less likely to make bad decisions.

• They have a sense of how the world works. They can think through the advantages, disadvantages, benefits, and consequences of various ways of behaving and make good choices. They can make good things happen in their life and don't have to rely on drugs to feel good or to kill pain.

• They have good judgment in choosing friends, selecting those who will not be negative influences.

• They can think through the short-term and long-term effects and risks of using drugs.

Problem Solving

Children with problem-solving ability are less vulnerable to drug abuse because:

- They can identify and solve problems that could cause stress.
- They can plan to make good things happen in their life: to attain goals, to create positive situations, and to avoid bad ones.
- They approach decision making systematically, not impulsively or haphazardly. They are less likely to make bad decisions about drug use or behaviors that could lead to drug use. They are more likely to attain their goals.
- They can figure out positive ways of coping with stress. They don't need drugs to take away their pain.

Relationship Values and Skills

Children with positive relationship values and skills are less likely to abuse drugs because:

- They have respect for others and therefore behave respectfully.
- They have the ability to make friends and maintain good relationships. These friendships will contribute to their well-being, reducing the need to take drugs to feel good.
- They will not select negative peers out of loneliness and needing to belong.
- They have independent minds and are not necessarily followers of the crowd. They are assertive enough to go against peer pressure.
- They have the ability to communicate feelings and therefore work out differences with family members and peers.
- They have the ability to solve relationship problems with friends and family members and do not need to use drugs to escape difficulties.

Now that we have described the curriculum, we will talk about the lesson plan, which is also the description of an empowering family.

GIVING STROKES AND ASKING FOR THEM

At first glance, the lesson plan for building self-esteem seems obvious—good, down-home, mushy love. Involvement. Openness. Close contact. You've read it over and over again: Praise your children. Hug them. Kiss them. Tell them that you care. Show it. Unfortunately there is a problem in the love department, a set of culturally accepted rules that keep families from freely sharing their affection.

The problem has been called the "stroke economy" by psychologist Claude Steiner. Strokes are defined as affection in any form. They are compliments such as:

"You're a great kid."

"You're very smart."

"You did a great job."

"I love you."

They are also physical expressions of affection such as kisses, hugs, and pats on the forehead.

All people need strokes to survive, just as they need food, shelter, and water. If strokes were freely shared, everyone could feel loved and appreciated. But we have accepted a set of rules, the stroke economy, that limits the free exchange of strokes and leaves almost everyone emotionally deprived.

Two of the most destructive rules are: (1) You can't give the strokes you feel, and (2) You can't ask for the strokes you want.

Typical reasons for not giving strokes include:

- The other person doesn't care about what I feel.
- I would look foolish giving compliments.
- If I give one, then I'll have to keep on giving.
- If I gave compliments freely, it would cheapen their value.

Because of these reasons and others like them, we learn to withhold affection.

An equally damaging rule is that we do not ask for strokes because:

- It would put the other person on the spot. It's too demanding.
- The other person will think I'm needy or weak.
- I shouldn't need anyone else's attention. I should feel good without it.
- If I have to ask, the other person won't be sincere.

Children who are not getting enough strokes cannot develop self-esteem and will go to great lengths to get attention, sometimes even getting into trouble just for recognition. Their logic is simple: "If I can't get attention by being good, then I'll get it by being bad."

Stroke-deprived children are emotionally needy and vulnerable to peer pressure. They will conform and do what the in-crowd is doing, including using drugs, in order to be accepted by their peers.

In an empowering home, parents have to overcome the rules limiting the free exchange of strokes. Besides promoting self-esteem, freely exchanging strokes helps to promote positive feelings within the family. This builds goodwill and is the basis for other important aspects of family life, especially for dealing with problems, negative feelings, and constructive criticism.

You may want to review your own stroke practices in your family. Consider these issues:

The importance of expressing deep affection and respect. These feelings often go unstated. Do you say sweet things such as "I love you" and "You're great"? These are much-needed affirmations.

The importance of physically expressing your love. Do you give physical strokes, such as hugs and kisses?

The tendency to detract from appreciation by attaching a secondary and unneccessary message. Do you give pure uncontaminated strokes? Beware of these forms of contamination:

A stroke combined with a demand: "I think your schoolwork has been great. Now keep it up."

A stroke combined with criticism: "You might not be good at math, but at least you're a creative person."

A stroke combined with a criticism from the past: "You never were so sweet to Grandma before. You used to ignore her. I like the change." (This would be better stated as: "I really like how sweet you were to Grandma during your last visit with her.")

The tendency to focus on only a narrow range of "worthy" behaviors, such as good report cards. Do you try to keep a broad vision of what you appreciate in your children? In giving strokes, try to be expansive in what you appreciate, praising diverse qualities and actions of your children, such as cooperativeness, intelligence, creativity, effort, productiveness, imagination, warmth, humor, friendliness, special competencies, physical appearance, emotional strength, physical prowess, and joyfulness.

The tendency to give, but not to ask. Do you ask for the strokes you need from your children? This sets a good example. Also, it is a way to teach children the importance of giving as well as receiving affection.

Showing interest in and paying attention to what your children feel and think. Do you take your children's emotions and opinions seriously? Are you a good listener? Do you empathize with what your children feel? Do you ask for their opinions?

Part of the lesson plan for self-esteem is to break the rules of the stroke economy and to freely exchange affection in your family.

BUILDING SELF-ESTEEM WITH UNCONDITIONAL LOVE

The connection between the love of parents and self-esteem in children is widely understood. But it's important to discuss a certain type of love that is absolutely crucial to the empowerment of children and therefore to the prevention of drug problems, that is, unconditional love.

This quite simply means that no conditions are placed upon your love. You show your affection and it remains constant. It is irrevocable. It is not: "I love you *if* you . . ."

Unconditional love means: "I love you no matter what, even when you have problems at school or at home and even when I'm angry at you. I will not withdraw my love under any circumstances."

This type of love is the building block of self-esteem. When children feel loved unconditionally, they are able to love themselves. Unconditional love promotes two other components of self-esteem: self-acceptance ("I'm fine the way I am") and self-confidence ("I can be successful at what I do").

Unconditional Love and Self-Acceptance

In an environment of unconditional love, people are free to be themselves, to say what they think and feel without fear.

In contrast, children who are worried about losing their parents' approval hide their inner thoughts and feelings, especially the negative ones. "If I get angry," they fear, "my parents will stop loving me. I'd better not let anyone know what I *really* think or feel." Under these conditions, hurt, anger, and other emotions fester beneath the surface and create stress in the family.

One of the best way to show unconditional love and to teach self-acceptance is to encourage and respect openness by asking children for their opinions and asking them what they feel. Even as adults, most of us have had the experience of feeling something we couldn't

61

quite allow ourselves to say. Children need extra encouragement, or permission, to speak out. This permission can be a very simple but loving statement: "What's the matter? What are you feeling? It's okay to tell me, whatever it is."

Anyone who had this encouragement as a child remembers it fondly.

Later in this chapter, you will read about communication methods that you can use in your family and teach your children, so that even negative emotions, suspicions, and criticisms can be expressed and handled constructively.

Unconditional Love and Self-Confidence

The "I love you no matter what" attitude of unconditional love promotes self-confidence in children—the sense that they can be successful in meeting all challenges.

Throughout the years, you want to help your children strive to accept new challenges and learn from them. The learning process inevitably involves mistakes and setbacks, but unconditional love provides security. You never waver in your affection. You trust in your children's ability to gain competency. Children who are not trusted in this way are afraid of making mistakes and losing their parents' approval.

Sometimes children need gentle encouragement to take challenges and lots of support to persevere, just as we adults do. The first time nine-year-old Peter was allowed to take a bus across town with his best friend to go to a movie, they transferred at the wrong place, got lost, and were an hour late returning home. In some families, Peter might have been ashamed about what happened and punished. He might have feared criticism and invented a story to explain his tardiness. Instead, he and his parents openly and lovingly discussed the experience. His parents showed him a map and helped him learn more about the bus routes. Their confidence helped Peter maintain his own confidence that he could eventually master the transit system in his city. Self-confident children believe in themselves, learn from their experiences, and master the challenges they face. They are not defeated by setbacks.

I cannot overstate the importance of unconditional love that allows children to go to you when they are having problems, or you to go to them to offer help, not punishment and not a threat. Most of the adolescent drug abusers I have counseled had school or other problems *before* they began using chemical substances. They didn't know what to do. They didn't turn to their parents for help. They turned to drugs.

When children are having problems in school, or anywhere, the message of unconditional love is: "You can make mistakes, have problems, and suffer setbacks, but I'll still be here for you." It's tragic if children feel they must hide their difficulties from their parents, because if they do, where will they get the support they need?

Unconditional Love and Constructive Criticism

The attitude of support and unconditional love is reflected in the way that criticism is expressed. Ideally, criticism should be of a child's behavior, not his basic character.

When Susan left her dolls and other toys scattered throughout the living room, her mother harshly criticized her character: "Susan, you're a little slob. Go pick up your stuff and put it in your room."

It would have been far more constructive to say: "Susan, you left a mess. You left your toys scattered around the house. Please remember that you are supposed to put them away after you use them. Please put them away now."

The latter response allows Susan to maintain her self-esteen while being reminded of her responsiblities.

Seven-year-old Katy has a mom who helps her learn from mistakes without attacking her character.

Katy went to a friend's house after school and forgot to call home. Her mother was frightened and tracked her down. Her mom did *not* say: "What a stupid and irresponsible thing you just did." Instead, she said: "I was frightened and upset that you didn't call. You're supposed to call to let me know what you're doing. Why didn't you call?"

"I forgot," Katy answered. "I was so excited about seeing Sandra's new dog, I just forgot. I'm sorry."

"I expect you to call in the future," her mom said. "What do you need to do to make sure you don't forget even when you're excited about something?"

"I don't know, Mom."

"Why don't you think about it for a while and we can talk later."

At dinner Katy volunteered a solution: "Mom, I think I need to be *doubly* careful to call when I'm excited and having a great time. I'll remember next time."

"Good for you, Katy."

When nine-year-old Matt's academic performance declined suddenly, his mom didn't respond with punishment. She didn't accuse him of being lazy or stupid. Instead she showed unconditional love and asked him what was happening. He was upset and said he couldn't concentrate in school.

"Why not?" his mom asked. "Is something bothering you?"

"No."

"Are you sure?"

"Well, I don't know, maybe."

"Is it the divorce?"

"Yeah, I think so. Things have gotten worse. Dad doesn't take me on weekends like he used to."

"And that's pretty upsetting, right?

"Yeah."

"And it's been on your mind?"

"Yeah."

"And you think it's affecting you in school?"

"I think it is, Mom. I've been having trouble concentrating."

This discussion clarified at least part of the problem. Matt's mother needed to help her son deal with the divorce and his dad. Then she needed to see what else was contributing to the school problem. If Matt had fallen behind in his schoolwork, he might need help catching up. Once the problems were addressed and he did catch up, he would undoubtedly go back to his previous level of school achievement.

As you can see, unconditional love is an alternative to responding to every problem with blame, punishment, and harsh criticism. It is based on trust in the idea that children can learn from experience and often leads to problem solving, which is another part of the lesson plan for empowerment.

Think about unconditional love in the teenage years, and you can see that children who are certain that they are loved will be the ones who are willing to discuss alcohol and other drugs with their parents. Because they are not scared, they will be able to benefit from adult wisdom and experience.

Preemptive Unconditional Love

One way to show unconditional love is to refrain from blame and put-downs. A related way is to take *preemptive* measures that prevent children from blaming themselves for events they did not cause. By preemptive measures, I mean something done *before* problems occur in situations which, if ignored, could cause problems.

For example, children tend to blame themselves for an alcoholic parent. "If I had been a better child," they think, "my dad wouldn't be drunk and he wouldn't treat me this way." Children also tend to blame themselves for a divorce. They have seen their parents fighting, sometimes over them, and believe they have caused the conflict.

With preemptive unconditional love, children are reassured. In counseling, I suggest to divorcing parents that they each make statements such as the following to their children:

"You are not responsible for the divorce at all. It is entirely the responsibility of your mom [or dad] and me. We were not able to work out our differences. You are not to blame at all, and we will both continue to take loving care of you."

BUILDING SELF-ESTEEM THROUGH MASTERY AND SUCCESS

After talking about unconditional love, it may seem like a contradiction to talk about the need for success and achievement in self-esteem. But there is a connection. Unconditional love is a good starting point. But success and competency also contribute to how we feel about ourselves. Constant failure detracts from self-esteem.

To promote self-esteem in children, it's important to arrange conditions to maximize mastery and success in school, at home, with friends, as a community member, and in the special interests of your children, whatever they may be.

This means giving freedom and responsibility and providing challenges. It means encouraging them to take challenges, to set attainable goals, and to achieve them. In the transfer of power, you don't want to push too hard, but you also don't want to underestimate what your children can do.

As you will see in this chapter, mastery of the other parts of the curriculum for empowerment—good clear thinking, problem solving, and positive relationship values and skills—will contribute to your children's success and therefore their increasing self-esteem.

CLEAR THINKING FOR EMPOWERMENT

Thinking is a skill that requires cultivation. With sufficient practice and experience, all children can become good thinkers. They won't necessarily become Einsteins, but certainly individuals with good judgment, prepared to make wise decisions of all sorts, including decisions about drugs.

As a parent, you have enormous opportunity to promote thinking skills and to support your children in gaining an understanding of the world. You can help them feel confident about their thinking, learn to focus their thoughts, define a thinking task, and carry it out successfully.

In empowering families, the home atmosphere is conducive to thought-provoking conversations, with topics ranging from the most philosophical to the most personal. There is a feeling of "Let's talk." Anything that interests a family member is discussed. It could be a critique of a film that everyone saw or a brainstorming session about where to go on a family vacation. In these conversations, everyone is urged to formulate an opinion and express it. No subject is taboo, not even a family crisis such as illness, divorce, or the loss of a job. No one is punished or criticized for sharing their personal thoughts.

Aside from the considerable educational benefits of these discussions, when it's time to talk about drugs with teenage children, it helps to have had a long-standing history of openness.

In discussions at home, it is not so much *what* children think that matters. The essential idea is that they are encouraged to think, to form opinions, to listen to other opinions, and to practice logic. They need a chance to think for themselves and, through dialogue, to see a variety of different ways of looking at an issue.

You can promote discussions in your home with your own personal openness and by asking thought-provoking questions. Many of the questions will arise spontaneously, in keeping abreast of each other's activities:

- "What do you think of your new teacher?"
- "What's happening with Kenny's brother [who is spending a year as a foreign exchange student]?"

Questions can be about local community issues and current events:
- "What do you think of the new highway they're building nearby? How do you think it will affect us?"

- "What do you think about the upcoming elections?"

You can also be more playful and gamelike in your questioning, such as:

- "If you could visit any country in the world, where would you like to go? Why?"
- "What are your five favorite things to do for fun?"

Thought-provoking conversations are an important link to the formation and clarification of values. By focusing on value-laden topics such as religion, sex, grades, proper behavior with grandparents, and, of course, drugs, you help your children think through their values.

Another important topic for discussion is media presentation of drugs. As families watch television programs together, it is a good opportunity to point out ways that alcohol and other drugs are sometimes romanticized, as in the cheerful, sexy, festive scenes that are used to sell beer. Media awareness of this sort is excellent preparation for dealing with negative social influences.

Clear Thinking about Goals

In your discussions, it's important to help your children learn *how* to think, but not tell them *what* to think. For example, in a discussion about school, you might be tempted to talk about the importance of good grades. But children benefit more if they are drawn out and given a chance to reach their own conclusions. Ask them, "What would you like to achieve in school? What are your ambitions?" Then ask them why. Afterward, you can add your own ideas and opinions to help expand their thinking.

Children raised in a supportive and thinking environment will feel good about themselves, have self-confidence, and understand much about the workings of the world. Without being pressured, they will choose to strive for positive achievements. They will want to be loving and contributing members of a family. They will want to succeed in all aspects of life.

Family dialogue can also be used to encourage children to think about the future. For example, ask directed questions such as: "What do you want to be when you grow up? What do you need to do to achieve these goals?"

The ability to think about the future helps children make wise decisions, especially important later in life, when drugs are the issue.

Drugs feel good when used, but children need to be able to project into the future and see the dangerous long-term effects.

Clear Thinking about Rules

One goal children strive to achieve is to be loving, responsible, contributing, and respected members of their family. Their responsibilities include, for example, calling home when they are supposed to, returning home at the designated time, and handling a fair share of household duties. Success earns them praise and gives them a sense of importance, belonging, and self-esteem. It feels good to be part of a cooperative and respectful family.

This doesn't mean that children are little angels. They need rules, limits, and controls. They often want to stay up past their bedtime. They want to ride their bicycles to places they are not allowed to go. They may want to go out in the evening when you believe their safety is at risk. Part of their learning experience includes gaining an understanding of the reasoning behind rules, learning to accept reasonable authority, and realizing that they cannot do whatever their impulses dictate. Parents control the behavior of children with clear and consistent rules until children have learned enough self-control to do it themselves.

Open discussions are an important part of the process of setting rules and making agreements at home and of establishing the division of household responsibilities. To promote good thinking, the reasoning behind rules is explained, and, when possible, children are involved in the decision-making process. Children realize that rules are set up to protect them and to help them succeed, an awareness that is important later, when rules are set about drugs and other teenage issues.

For example, setting a bedtime is a great teaching opportunity. Bedtimes are not set, as children sometimes think, to prevent them from watching their favorite television shows. Open discussions help them see that bedtimes are set to ensure that they get enough sleep to be alert in the morning. This awareness promotes forethought and self-control. Children will realize that they may not feel tired at their bedtime, but they must go to sleep to be rested the following day.

Children often perceive rules as obstacles to their happiness. You can help them understand the good reasoning that underlies family rules. Below is an example of two different ways of explaining to a child why he is not being allowed to ride his bicycle to a particular

68

park. The first leaves out important details and doesn't address the feelings of the child:

"No, you can't ride your bike to the park. It's not safe."

The second is much more informative and loving:

"I'm sorry. I wish you could ride to the park. I know you want to go, but there's a lot of traffic on Congress Street and I don't think it's safe. When you're older and have more experience, I'll let you ride to the park. Meanwhile, you can ride in our neighborhood, and we can take some longer bike trips together, too."

Clear Thinking about Consequences

One of the best ways to help children learn good thinking skills is in nature's way—allowing for cause and effect, or, as psychologists put it, teaching through natural or logical consequences.

Let's say that your son consistently forgets to bring his lunch to school. This is an open invitation for you to rescue him by hopping in the car and delivering it yourself. You won't get a tip like the pizza delivery boy would, but your son would see, as he probably wants to, that you care and that you will do things for him. He also would see several other facts: (1) You believe he can't be responsible for himself, and (2) He doesn't need to be responsible because someone will bail him out.

A better alternative is to make an observation: "I notice you've been forgetting your lunch a lot lately." Then ask a question: "What do you think is going on?" Finally, offer problem-solving assistance: "What can you do to remember to bring your lunch?"

This shows that you care. You noticed a problem. It also shows that you believe your son is capable of remembering and does not need to be rescued.

If he continues to forget to bring his lunch, you resist the temptation to deliver it. Instead, you explain that you respect him too much to treat him like a baby and that you know he is capable of remembering. If he forgets again, he'll have to buy his own lunch with his allowance or go hungry.

The natural consequences of forgetting: He will be hungry for a day; he will quickly learn his lesson. In many situations such as this, nature will work wonders. You can let children learn for themselves.

Sometimes children "forget" as this boy did, or break rules of one sort or another, as an "experiment." They are not bad kids. They are curious children, trying to find out how the world works. This boy might be wondering: "Will Mom really not bring my lunch? I'm going to find out." Once he finds out, he'll probably start remembering.

Sometimes we have to help nature along. Either the natural consequences are too severe (you don't let your child cross a dangerous intersection to learn by natural consequences) or the lesson is too complex. The supplement to natural consequences is logical consequences. These are consequences that logically fit with the problem behavior.

For example, one mother drove her two children to school to save them from a very long bus ride across town. Her ten-year-old son began picking on his five-year-old little sister, consistently ruining the trip for everyone. Mom warned against such nastiness and said she refused to go to the trouble of driving him around town if he would not be respectful of his sister. This was a logical consequence.

The boy persisted in his bullying behavior. Next day he was on the bus, an hour and a half each way. He learned fast. That was the last time he bullied his sister in the car.

A good example of combining natural and logical consequences involved a girl who was not doing one of her household responsibilities, emptying the dishwasher. First her mother asked her what the problem was and tried to solve it through discussion. That didn't work. The natural consequence of the continued misbehavior was that other family members became angry at the girl. They expressed their resentment in a disciplined and constructive way. That didn't help. Finally, the mother said there would be some logical consequences:

"You'll have to do your own laundry this week. I don't feel good about doing it for you when you won't do your share around the house."

Then she added, and this is very important:

"This is not the way I want it. I would prefer cooperation. But when you don't do your share, I eventually grow weary of doing mine. I want you to learn about being responsible. I look forward to the near future, when I hope you'll do your share of the chores and I can feel good about doing mine."

A week of doing her own laundry helped the girl better understand the importance of sharing household responsibilities. Afterward, she did a much better job of emptying the dishwasher.

As you can see, children are not helped by being spared rules or by being protected from the consequences of misbehavior. They need the rules and limits to learn self-control. They need the consequences to learn from experience. It builds judgment.

As children get older, self-control and good judgment are important life skills that protect against drug abuse. Children who are good thinkers about consequences will see the risks of using drugs.

In using rules and consequences, the idea is to take the meanness out of child rearing. Children can learn all the valuable lessons they need without being mistreated, threatened, or severely punished. Natural and logical consequences are educational.

SETTING UNPOPULAR LIMITS

Some parents who themselves grew up with authoritarian parents who set harsh rules and used severe punishment may tend toward permissiveness. "I don't want to be like my parents," they think, so they avoid setting limits and making rules, or, if they make them, fail to follow through with enforcement. This is a serious mistake. Children who grow up in such an environment will tend to be out of control. They need parental control in order to develop inner control.

I worked with a single mother in therapy whose eleven-year-old son, Peter, was very bright but doing poorly in school. His grades were near failure because teachers subtracted credit for homework that wasn't completed. Peter said he was too tired to do assignments at the end of the day, after practicing with the soccer team, doing his household chores, and eating dinner. A very reasonable discussion with Peter didn't seem to help. Mother was not persuasive enough to convince him to take control over his school destiny. I suggested that soccer participation could be made contingent on the completion of homework. It would not be punishment, but if Peter was too tired to do school assignments, the time that would have gone to soccer would be better spent on homework. Mom would essentially be saying that school has a higher priority than sports. When I suggested this, she said to me: "I want to be a good mom. I don't want to deprive him of anything."

"Tell him that," I said. "It's great you feel that way, that you don't want him to miss anything. You want him to play soccer. You don't want to take it away from him. But if he doesn't do his homework, you will need to do it, to protect him from failing in school."

Mom did lay down the law and miraculously Peter found that he had the energy to do his schoolwork every day after soccer practice. Mom used her authority with love and firmness and helped her son develop much-needed self-discipline.

There is an art to maintaining parental authority with grace. When you have to establish a "bottom line" that your children find objectionable, you can let them know you're sorry they're disappointed, that you don't like disappointing them, but that under the circumstances you find it necessary.

PROBLEM SOLVING

Clear thinking, as discussed above, encourages children to pay attention to their thoughts and opinions, to develop their reasoning ability, and to reflect on their experiences. Problem solving is a special type of clear thinking. It involves an attitude of accepting problems, rather than ignoring them. It also requires the skill of identifying problems and of finding solutions.

Problem solving is as basic to the prevention of drug abuse as learning to swim is to drowning prevention. Children with problem-solving ability know how to:

(1) have fun;
(2) prevent negative stress;
(3) cope with stress and frustration;
(4) find friends with positive lifestyles;
(5) deal with negative peer pressure.

Parents tend to think of problem solving as it applies to existing problems with their children. For example, it could be misbehavior at home, a bad report card, poor eating habits, or trouble getting along with friends.

But problem-solving abilities should also be used to plan for success. That is, children are given an opportunity to set ambitious goals for themselves and then to use problem-solving skills to devise a plan to attain these goals.

Problem solving also has an important place in prevention. That is, the problem to be solved is how to prevent future problems. For example, you can help your children with problem solving *before* they enter a new school by discussing what to expect and how to handle it. Similarily, *before* the family moves, you can talk about potential problems concerning the new home and neighborhood. And you can prevent potential drug problems by discussing drugs *before* your child has been exposed to and tempted to experiment with them.

Another type of problem solving is early intervention. For example, you might notice that your son is not socializing with other children. Before he feels depressed about the isolation, you can bring the problem to his attention and help him make some changes.

I had a personal experience as a child that I think illustrates how parents can help with early intervention. During the summer between third and fourth grades, I transferred to a new school. The children in my new school had learned tumbling in physical education the previous year. In gym class, I was frightened when we lined up to do foreward somersaults. I don't remember the exact details of what happened, only that I came home and explained that I was very upset because I couldn't do what everyone else was doing. My parents went into the "you can solve this problem" mode. I can still remember my mother saying, "You can do anything you want to do."

That weekend we moved some mattresses into the attic and they gave me lessons. I practiced in the safe confines of my own home. Instead of dreading my return to gym class, and fearing humiliation because I couldn't tumble, I proudly went back, convinced I could master any challenge and solve any problem. My parents had done a good job of early intervention.

Teaching Problem Solving

One way that children learn about problem solving is by observing their parents. It's a good idea to make a self-evaluation of your own efforts as a role model: How do you approach problems? Do you set a good example by taking a positive problem-solving approach to family life and other problems of day-to-day life? Do you ignore problems, hoping they will go away? After problems are identified, do you use a systematic problem-solving approach or do you respond haphazardly or impulsively?

I found it interesting to do therapy with a family in which the oldest son had an impulse-control problem with drugs. He didn't go looking for drugs, but if they showed up, he couldn't turn them down. His parents had a similar impulse problem, not with drugs, but with their credit cards. They never met a home improvement item or electronic appliance that they didn't want to buy. They never heard about a vacation adventure that they didn't want to take. However, they were in debt and forever digging themselves deeper. In their therapy sessions, we had some excellent discussions about how to face problems and how to resist temptations.

Another important assessment you can make as a parent is whether you observe and address problems that are occurring in the lives of your children. Also consider whether you encourage your children to take a problem-solving approach. Problem solving is an activist way of life. If your child is having problems in school, this shouldn't be ignored. If your child seems moody and upset, find out what's happening. If your child doesn't seem to have friends or is having problems with peers, talk about it. If your child can't openly discuss his feelings, help him learn to do this. Children need support in recognizing and solving problems.

You provide this support both by serving as a good role model and by teaching your children to understand and to use the problem-solving process. This process is described below and illustrated with an example.

(1) Look for indications of problems.
(2) Assess the cause of the problem.
(3) Pick the goal.
(4) Identify available resources that could be used to attain the goal.
(5) Now that the goal is clear and the resources are defined, think of all the possible alternative solutions.
(6) List the pros and cons of each possibility.
(7) Choose the best action or best combination of actions.
(8) Make an action plan and carry it out.
(9) Evaluate the outcome and revise the plan as needed.

This process was used by the Sherman family shortly after they moved to a new home in a different city during the summer. In late August, the parents noticed an indication of a problem—their seven-year-old son, John, was agitated. They assessed the source of the problem and found that he was nervous in anticipation of his first day in a new school.

John and his parents set a goal of making it easier for him to get a good start. His parents were an available resource. His new friend who lived down the block was another available resource. John and his parents brainstormed a list of possible actions to take and evaluated the pros and cons of each of them. Then John decided what to do. He had his parents take him to the school building before school opened to make it feel more familiar. He talked with his new friend to find out more about the school. He arranged to walk to school the first day with his friend. He discussed his fears with his parents and got reassurance. John carried out the plan successfully. He gained a valuable lesson in coping with stress and taking control over his own life.

Problem Solving about Behavior after School

Two problems concerned Mrs. Bowen about her nine-year-old son, Paul. First, he spent almost all of his allowance on junk food. Second, every day after school he came home to watch television alone instead of playing with friends. When Mrs. Bowen returned from work, she would find Paul in front of the television munching Hostess Cupcakes surrounded by empty potato chip packets. At dinnertime, it was small wonder that Paul had no appetite.

Mrs. Bowen started with her own problem solving, listing all the alternatives. She had several. She could ignore the problem and hope it would go away of its own accord. She could punish Paul or lecture him. She could tell him what to do. She could try to control his behavior by cutting his allowance (no money for junk food) and disconnecting the televison. Or she could talk it over with Paul and invite him to think it out for himself, which is what she finally did.

Over the course of several weeks, mother and son had excellent discussions about nutrition, exercise, and friendships. Mrs. Bowen realized that Paul had some favorite shows he didn't want to miss and that part of the fun was snacking. But Paul began to understand the importance of changing his lifestyle and even started to joke about "couch potatoes." He said he wanted more friends but that he was shy and didn't know how to make them. He asked his mother for advice. One suggestion he liked was to join a basketball team, which he did, thereby getting more exercise and cutting down his television time. Mother and son also figured out ways that Paul could have friends sleep over on weekends. Gradually Paul cut back on junk food and began to save his allowance for, in his own words, "better things."

"After all," he said, "I get free food at home. Why should I waste my allowance on junk?" Mrs. Bowen had helped her son with problem solving and laid the groundwork for a healthier lifestyle.

Problem Solving about Boredom

Mr. and Mrs. McClain had recently read an article linking boredom and drug abuse in which a young teenager was quoted as saying that she used drugs for fun and that getting high was the only way she knew of to "entertain" herself.

When the McClains' eleven-year-old daughter, Karen, said she was bored, they became alarmed and brought her to my office. I reassured the family that this was a problem that could be easily solved. The parents resisted the temptation of criticizing Karen or lecturing her about all the wonderful things you can do in the world. They also decided against serving as her social director. Instead, they helped Karen brainstorm her own list of fun activities. Then they helped her implement them, including making arrangements for the piano lessons she wanted and transporting her to various recreational activities. They calmed themselves down and empowered Karen to find joy and pleasure in life.

Solving problems about how to have a healty lifestyle, as Paul did above, and about how to overcome boredom, as Karen did, are constructive measures toward the prevention of future drug problems.

POSITIVE RELATIONSHIP VALUES AND RELATIONSHIP SKILLS

The best place for children to learn positive values about relationships and important relationship skills is at home, with the family. Most of these values and this knowledge are acquired in day-to-day living, when children are given positive attention, unconditional love, encouragement, support, and affection. If parents are calm, respectful, and patient, children will learn to be that way. If families are cooperative in sharing the work around the house, children will learn to be cooperative. Thus all of the skills we have talked about earlier in this chapter help children learn to value positive relationships and to maintain them. The same can be said in reverse. The good relationships you have with your children will provide many opportunities to teach the other life skills.

The home climate of an empowering family is one of close contact and openness, allowing for great involvement in the lives of your children. Part of a close relationship includes keeping up to date with routine discussions of everyday events. These discussions occur after school, after work, at the dinner table, before bedtime, and during other special times together. You talk about your day and your children talk about theirs. It's a gold mine of opportunities to help your children gain greater awareness of themselves and the world around them.

When your daughter says she's bored or your son says he was chased home by bullies, you can teach problem-solving skills.

When your child is worried about an exam or has had a very frustrating day, you can teach coping skills.

When your child heard about crack for the first time or wants to know about AIDS, you can teach thinking skills.

On countless occasions you can increase self-awareness and self-respect by encouraging and praising your children.

Inevitably, conflict will occur in *every* family, even with the very best of relationships. People have differences. Conflict is normal. To minimize conflict and to resolve it when it occurs, good communication and negotiation skills can be practiced at home and taught to children.

Using a few basic relationship skills at home and teaching these skills to your children can enhance the quality of family life and will provide a strong foundation for your children's relationships with others. These skills—expressing resentments and other negative feelings, communicating suspicion, expressing constructive criticism, and negotiating differences—are described below.

Expressing Resentments and Other Negative Feelings

In my lectures and counseling, I recommend a simple fill-in-the-blanks sentence for the communication of resentment and other negative emotions within the family. The sentence goes like this: "When you did (A) I felt (B)." With this format, (A) describes an observable action. For example:

"When you left dirty dishes on the kitchen counter . . ."

"When you didn't help clean the garage yesterday . . ."

"When you left your books and papers and school materials on the living room floor . . ."

"When you raised your voice to me while we were watching television this morning . . ."

In the first phrase, the idea is to be as specific as possible to facilitate understanding. Instead of saying, "When you waste electricity," make the meaning more specific, such as, "When you leave your bedroom lights on after leaving the room . . ."

The second part of the sentence—(B)—describes one or more feelings:

". . . I felt annoyed."

". . . I felt resentful."

". . . I was very angry and hurt."

Putting it together, you end up with a sentence such as this: "When you left dirty dishes on the kitchen counter, I felt annoyed."

In using the recommended format, you want to be careful not to insert judgments in either part of the statement. In the above example, judgments could wrongly have been used in either the first or second phrase, as illustrated below:

"*When you acted like a slob*, I felt annoyed."

"When you left dirty dishes on the counter, *I felt you were being a slob*."

Note that in this last statement, even though the words used were "I felt," what followed was a judgment, not a feeling.

Another precaution is against exaggeration, especially the use of words such as "always" and "never." These extreme words often make a description of a behavior inaccurate. For example, before saying, "You *always* come late to our family meetings," think of whether that person has been on time even once.

The elegance of this format for expressing emotions is that the resulting statement is indisputable. It describes how a person felt when a particular event occurred. It is not a judgment about the event or the person. In a cooperative household, people want to know the impact of their actions and don't want to make others feel bad unnecessarily. In families and other close relationships, the respectful communication of feelings is often preferable to an argument, lecture, or demand.

Communicating Suspicion

One very important, but seldom discussed, communication skill is the communication of suspicion. When people are lacking information about a situation, they creatively fill in the gaps with their intuition and imagination. When they imagine something negative, they are said to be suspicious. Once suspicious, one option is to assume that the intuition is correct. This can cause serious problems. For example, a parent might punish a child for something he never did. Another option is to assume the suspicion is wrong. But this causes problems, too, because the suspicion lingers until it is disproven. I recommend a third option for dealing with suspicions: Withhold judgment until more information is gathered. Thus, suspicions are stated tentatively to help determine their veracity.

Many misunderstandings in families can be avoided by an agreement to check out suspicions. Very important questions will come to the surface. It's not uncommon, for example, for parents to say: "I don't believe you've told me everything. Have you?"

Also, children will have their own suspicions: "Since you won't let me go away with my friends for the weekend, I think you believe I use drugs or that I might do something crazy. Is that true?"

The temptation in responding to suspicions such as these is to be quickly reassuring and possibly to deny hard-to-admit realities. This would defeat the purpose. The ideal response to a suspicion is to find the validity in it, even if it is just a kernel of truth:

"Son, I don't think you use drugs and I don't think you would do something crazy. But frankly, I think that if you went with your friends, there might be pressure to drink alcohol and experiment with drugs. I don't think you're ready yet to handle that pressure."

The boy might be disappointed to hear this, but at least there is now greater understanding and the possibility of further dialogue.

Expressing Constructive Criticism

Those of us who have not yet attained perfection—even if we deceive ourselves and think we're almost there—can most definitely benefit from constructive criticism. That's how we learn. Children learn from the constructive criticism of their parents. It is equally true that adults benefit from constructive criticism, sometimes even from children. Family members need a form for communicating their critical thoughts in a loving and supportive way.

The tone and purpose are crucial. The purpose is to build each other up, not to tear each other down. The tone therefore should always be loving, in the spirit of unconditional love, as described earlier in this chapter. Name calling and put-downs are inappropriate.

Constructive criticism falls into two basic categories. One type is about issues that affect the rest of the family. For example:

"You said you would pull the weeds in the front yard, and you haven't followed through."

"When you were on the phone with Grandma, you sounded impatient with her hearing difficulties."

"I've noticed that you haven't been returning the keys to the car after you've borrowed them."

A second type of criticism is about the well-being of the person criticized:

"Son, you seem to rush through your homework at night. I'm concerned about whether you're learning your lessons when you rush this way."

"I've noticed that you don't make arrangements to see friends on the weekend. Is it difficult for you to do this? Can I help you? Do you want to talk about it?"

"You don't seem to be getting any exercise lately, especially since you stopped riding your bicycle to school. I think physical activity is important. What do you think?"

Criticism of any sort is most constructive when it is specific. Generalizations are supported by specifics that clarify the meaning:

"You haven't been very nice to your younger sister lately. This morning when she asked for help, you said, 'Get lost.' You don't have to help her, but you could at least be polite in turning her down."

Constructive criticism is best expressed in humble terms, acknowledging that other people may have a different view of reality: "This is how I see things. How do you see them?"

To avoid misunderstandings, differentate fact from opinion:

"Twinkies and all those sugary foods you eat almost every day have little nutritional value and lots of calories [fact]. I think you eat too much of that stuff [opinion]. What do you think? [What's your opinion?]"

By calling an opinion an opinion, you allow room for differences of opinion. This promotes dialogue and understanding.

Negotiating Differences

One of the best ways to promote good relationships within families is to cooperatively settle differences through negotiation. This is based on the premise of equality, that all family members have an equal right to have their needs met and that everyone will make an effort to take care of each other. Good communication starts with everybody stating their desires. Then, differences are settled by negotiation. Solutions can be compromises (we'll meet each other halfway), trade-offs (you get your way this time and I get my way next time), and creative solutions (let's find a brilliant solution that satisfies everyone).

In negotiation between equals, people try to meet each other halfway. But parent/child negotiation is not between equals. Parents have the ultimate authority and sometimes have to lay down the law. Still the process of negotiating should be based on mutual respect, and the goal is to empower children by giving them ever more say-so in decisions about their lives.

With younger children, negotiating might involve giving them opportunities to participate in particular activities under specified conditions:

"You can play with your friends as long as you are home and washed up in time for dinner at six o'clock."

"You can stay up late and watch the television show tonight as long as you take a nap during the day and finish all your homework."

Family discussions about the division of housework roles should include active participation by children, who should be allowed to state their preferences and lobby for them. Similarly, children should be involved in discussions about family vacations and recreation.

If you want a more detailed discussion of communication and negotiation skills in family life, I suggest you read *A Guide to a Happier Family* (J. P. Tarcher, 1989). I admit some prejudice in this recommendation, because I wrote this book, together with my parents, brother, and sister-in-law.

THE EMPOWERED FAMILY AND REPORT CARD WARS

Because school problems often precede drug problems, this chapter concludes with an example of how parents can empower children in school situations, and how empowerment contrasts with the ever popular carrot-and-stick approach.

We start with the carrot. In some families, report card time is almost like "Wheel of Fortune," played for cash rewards. Two A's equal an evening of miniature golf. All A's earn a trip to Disneyland. What, no sports car? That will have to wait until a varsity letter is also earned.

The intention of parents is to encourage excellent school performance. Eager schoolchildren work hard for their cash prizes. But ask them why they strive for good grades and the answer is, "To get a trip to Disneyland."

What's the real message? "Good grades are important to Mommy and Daddy." School seems *very* important to parents, but there is little understanding of why it might be important to children. Bribed youngsters don't recognize the inherent joy of learning, or learn that mastery of schoolwork is a fine feeling in itself.

This reminds me of something I have heard teenagers with a marijuana or alcohol problem say about their parents: "*They* [my emphasis] should be happy that I don't use cocaine."

It's the same confusion. Whose life is it anyway? The satisfaction of school success is first and foremost for children themselves. The pain of drug problems may be heartbreaking for parents, but first and foremost, it is the child's life that suffers.

The reward, or carrot, approach to school success not only confuses children about the joy of learning but also creates three other problems. One is that monetary rewards begin to lose their appeal as other factors become more important to children. Another is that some children begin to resent the bribery: "If my parents *really* loved me, why would they show their appreciation only when I get high grades?" A third is that it creates an extra burden of pressure. Children vying for parental rewards and approval are sometimes scared by the pressure. Overanxious, they have trouble in school.

A better way to motivate children is to allow them to discover for themselves the joy of learning and the good feelings that accompany school success. This is easily accomplished in a home that encourages clearheaded thinking. Children's natural excitement about education is encouraged by parents who ask them what they learned in school during the day. Children recognize that they are engaged in an important activity—gaining knowledge and mastering skills.

You can ask your children how they feel about grades. Most of them, without being bribed, will say that they want to achieve good grades. Better yet, let your children bring it up themselves spontaneously. Children love it when their parents listen to their exuberant reports.

In open discussions, children sometimes reveal doubts about their own ability. This is an opportunity to encourage them and to give them whatever support they need for school success, such as teaching them study skills or helping them understand subject matter or arranging for a tutor.

If there are problems in school, you can help with problem solving. School, like any other type of work, sometimes can be boring or frustrating. Children sometimes have to endure bad teachers. When children are oppressed, discouraged, or frustrated, you can help them learn to cope. This, like mastery of the subject matter itself, is an inherent reward that money can't buy.

With the carrot-and-stick approach to education, when the rewards have failed and school grades are substandard, the other side of the equation—punishment—comes into play.

"You haven't done your homework, therefore you can't play with your friends this weekend." Punishment such as this misses a very important learning opportunity. A child could be asked why he didn't do his homework. It could turn out he had a good reason. For example, it could be that he doesn't understand the consequences of missing assignments and falling behind in class. Rather than punishing a child, the empowering parent wants to help him learn to think clearly about the effects of his action so he can self-motivate to make changes.

When grades decline in school, "report card wars" are fought in the trenches of many American families as the punitive force of parental punishment is pitted against the cunning maneuvers of their children.

A ten-year-old boy forges Mom's signature on a bad report card. Four months into the school year, Dad steps into the picture: "Where's your report card, son?"

"Well, Dad, the computer broke down. There won't be report cards for a few more months still."

"I'm gonna call the school."

"I don't feel well, Dad."

"You're busted, son."

The sad truth is that children who are having difficulties in school often are afraid of their parents . . . usually with good reason. When parents discover low grades, the response is a punitive one: "You can't go out weekends. You can't socialize. You won't get your allowance for a month."

Such a response essentially pits the parent against the child. Generally, the assumption is that the child has been lazy, that is, he or she hasn't been doing enough homework. More effort is needed. Grades will improve if adequate parental pressure is applied. Therefore, part of the punishment is loss of autonomy: "You will come home directly from school and do three hours of homework every day." In other words, the parent says to the child: "You are unmotivated. I'm going to make you work harder."

What is lost in this interaction is the fact that children themselves, given an opportunity, would very much like to succeed in school. They might not know how to do it. They might not feel that they can do it. They might be discouraged. They might give up. They might even hide their discouragement by claiming that school is boring. Children need help, not punishment. They need problem-solving assistance.

Parents who take a punitive approach to a poor report card fail to tap a child's inner motivation for success. They fail to help a child understand the real reasons for substandard academic performance.

A much better response to poor grades is to be on the same side as the child: "I imagine you feel pretty discouraged about your report card. Let's talk it over and figure out where the problem is. I'd like to help you improve your grades."

Usually a discussion between parent and child, in a loving atmosphere, can uncover the underlying problems. Sometimes the answer can be found simply by asking a child what he or she thinks the problem is.

A child might know exactly, for example, "I get scared when I take tests." Often the child doesn't know. In these circumstances, parents can help by asking questions such as these: "Do you have trouble concentrating when you do schoolwork? Which subjects cause you problems? How do you study for exams?"

It might be found that children are upset about something, even a problem at home, that is distracting them from concentrating. They may need help in developing study habits (such as finding a quiet place to do homework and picking a time to work without distractions). They may not understand how to prepare for tests. They may have lost confidence in their own ability.

Solutions will not necessarily be simple, but identifying the real cause of poor grades is at least the first step of problem solving. It's a far cry from engaging in report card wars . . . and a whole lot more constructive.

4

WORKBOOK FOR EARLY
DRUG PREVENTION

The roomful of children have been primed for a guest lecturer: me. I walk into the third-grade classroom, look around, and then ask, "Who in here has ever taken drugs?"

A wave of nervous giggling spreads through the room, followed by silence and eventually a protest about such a silly question. "Of course we don't use drugs," they say.

"You don't?" I reply, pretending shock. "What about aspirins? Haven't any of you ever taken one? What about cough medicine?"

Everyone laughs.

"I bet you use other drugs, too. Who in here ever had a Coke or Pepsi, even once? Raise your hand."

All hands are up, including mine.

"What's the drug in cola drinks?"

Usually someone in the class knows about caffeine.

The children are smiling, amused and interested, a good way to begin a drug discussion. Too often such discussions begin with a drum roll, setting a nervous tone. Look at the embarrassment and resulting dishonesty that we have in parent-child discussions about sex. We can avoid the same pitfall with drugs if we lighten up and confront the issue with a little less pomp and a lot more grace.

I know about the drum-roll approach to drug information from firsthand experience, as I'm sure many of you do. I remember those scary drug movies we were shown in school, with innocent teenagers, intoxicated by marijuana, jumping out of tenth-story windows. And

I can picture those sinister men who came into playgrounds armed with needles to stick into the arms of little children.

For me it was lots of smoke, but no fire. They could have been showing *Invasion of the Body Snatchers.* It seemed as unreal to my experience, but far less entertaining.

Those sorts of lessons in school did nothing to prepare me and my generation for having meaningful drug discussions with children. At worst, they promoted overly serious, rigid, and agonized encounters.

This chapter is a workbook of sorts, which should be used in conjunction with the curriculum and lesson plan for preventing drug abuse presented in the previous chapter. It will be most useful for working with younger children and preteens.

As you know, part of the lesson plan is to teach drug information. So the first part of the workbook covers that topic. But I assure you— the approach is gentle and nonhysterical.

The other part of the lesson plan is to teach positive attitudes and basic life skills. As you saw in the last chapter, children need self-esteem and the ability to create positive experiences in their lives *without* drugs. They need to learn to cope with stress when it occurs, *without* drugs. And they need to know how to make good friends and resist negative peer pressure. The second part of this chapter is filled with activities you can do with your children to help them master these challenges.

STARTING DRUG DISCUSSIONS

When you discuss drugs with young children, I recommend talking in very relaxed ways and using spontaneous situations to broach the topic. Many opportunities present themselves in everyday life.

One such opportunity is following media exposure, for example, after viewing a television commercial, television show, or film production involving drugs.

Simple questions are all it takes:

"What did you think about the movie? Do you think it was an accurate protrayal of how drugs might affect someone?"

Or simple observations made in a humorous, rather than "scare the children," tone:

"Sure looks like everyone has a great time at the Silver Bullet Bar (or whenever Spuds McKenzie is around). I think they leave out some details, like the guy who is smashed and breathing sawdust on the barroom floor. And the guy who jumps in his car to go home to his wife and children after downing a six-pack."

Another opportunity for drug discussions is in the context of real life experiences, for example, when a friend or relative becomes intoxicated at a party or in your home. Casual discussions about drugs can take place at the dinner table as part of the normal flow of conversation:

"I've been reading in the newspaper about real young kids using drugs. Do you ever hear about kids using drugs in your school? I'm curious."

The tone is very important here. The parent is not cross-examining the child. Rather the spirit is one of interest and involvement. It's all part of what happens in close families. It's part of getting to know each other.

In that same spirit, your bright and alert children might ask you: "If drugs are so harmful and dangerous, why do you drink wine with dinner and beer during the football games?"

This is a good, thought-provoking question. Children have a way of keeping you on your toes. I'd answer by saying:

"Some drugs are legal and can be taken safely by adults. Taking drugs is like flying an airplane, or better yet, taking parachute jumps. It requires maturity. Adults are supposed to have enough maturity to make good decisions about drug use. Truth is, not all of them do."

Hopefully, you can honestly say that alcohol, as you use it, doesn't harm you. However, if you have a drug or alcohol problem, face it; your children have raised an important issue. If you want to do everything you can to help them, you'll have to confront your own problems.

In most families, if people aren't censoring their thoughts, discussions about drugs will occur spontaneously. However, if you find some barriers in your family, or if you want to add a new dimension to your discussions, you can play a word-association game. In this game, all family members write the first five thoughts that come into their minds about alcohol, tobacco, marijuana, and cocaine. Then you talk about whatever thoughts occurred to you. This is a good way to break the ice and to get an idea about your children's attitudes and current level of knowledge. With this game, your children also get insight into your thinking.

WHEN TO START

At workshops and lectures, parents often ask when they should start to talk with their children about drugs. They are referring to alcohol and illegal drugs such as marijuana.

I explain that drug education begins at a very young age, shortly after children begin to master the language. But it doesn't begin with discussions of pot and alcohol. It starts with the precursors, which are discussions about what we put, and don't put, into our bodies. Teaching about poisons, such as ammonia and other dangerous cleaning agents that are kept out of the reach of children, is part of the discussion. Teaching about nutrition, what foods and which combinations are healthy and which are not, is another part. Ideally, nutrition discussions begin before little kids overdose on Twinkies. They are part of an ongoing dialogue about what is a balanced diet and how food helps your body grow and stay healthy.

One of the first opportunities to talk specifically about drugs with children is when they are taking medication, whether it's a cold remedy or a prescription drug. You can inform them about different types of medical preparations, such as pills, ointments, sprays, drops, liquids, and shots. You can talk about the directions and precautions printed on the bottles or containers. Explain that a person takes only the right amount at the right time and that misuse can mean that benefits are lost, or worse, that harmful and sometimes dangerous reactions can occur. Children need to know that they should take medicine only when it is given to them by you or another responsible adult. These early discussions make it clear that people have to be fully informed in order to decide whether to take drugs, how much to take, and how often. At some point, you can explain about prescription medicines: that they are taken only under a doctor's supervision and only by the person for whom they are intended.

Even as you have these discussions with your children, you can reflect on the examples you are setting. It wouldn't be a good idea to go rummaging through the medicine cabinet every time someone has the slightest medical symptom. This gives the appearance of casualness about taking drugs. Also, a good argument can be made for staying away from vitamins shaped like cartoon characters and medicines sweetened to taste like candy. These "medicines in disguise" could confuse children. Taking vitamins is not a recreational activity. Taking medicine is not the same as eating candy.

The ideal time to start talking about illicit drugs is before age ten. Preteens are old enough to think about many adult subjects, yet still young enough to accept parental guidance. Usually they have not used illicit drugs and will agree with you that cigarette smoke is gross and stinks up a room and that people who drink alcohol sometimes get obnoxious. Most children under ten think that the idea of smoking pot is "icky."

By fourth grade some children report that alcohol is a big problem for their age group. By sixth grade, many children are already beginning to feel the pressure to drink. It makes sense, therefore, to start discussions early, when you and your child are more likely to agree about non-use. It is easier to reinforce a non-use norm than to try to change someone who has already decided that drug use is acceptable.

Another important reason to have discussions at this young age is because children's expectations about drugs are established early, and positive expectations go hand in hand with future use. Many children who drink expect that alcohol will improve their functioning. Some of the expectations are inaccurate, such as, "It'll help me think better while taking an exam." Other expectations correctly identify potential benefits ("It'll make me more relaxed, funnier, and braver at parties") but don't recognize the risks, such as addiction, public embarrassment, or failing to learn to cope with social situations without drugs. Therefore, long before children actually begin to drink or use other drugs, it's important to talk with them about what they believe happens when the substances are used. You can clear up some of the widespread myths.

KEEPING YOUR COOL

The unpanicked approach to drug discussions can take place even when you are a little shocked about how the topic arose. I'm sure my dad was a little shocked many years ago when I first discussed tobacco with him.

I was in fifth grade. A friend of mine had stolen a few cigarettes from his mother. We smoked them in his "clubhouse," a shack in his backyard.

The filter broke off the cigarette that I had puffed on. (I didn't even know what it meant to inhale.) My friend said that I would catch tuberculosis because the cigarette had no filter.

89

"What about nonfilters?" I asked.

"That's different," he answered. "You get tuberculosis from smoking filter cigarettes when the filter breaks."

In terror, I confessed my terrible wrongdoing that night, hoping I could still be saved. My father reassured me about my particular health concern and then asked what I thought of cigarettes. "Pretty gross," I said. He agreed. He said my mother and he didn't smoke because "we think they're gross, too," and if I ever wanted to hear more details about why they didn't smoke I could ask. That incident is one of many reasons that I don't smoke now, so many years later.

I suppose my parents could have punished me. But I didn't need to be punished. My father helped me think through the issue of tobacco in a way I could understand. He showed me I could talk with him about drugs without fearing the consequences. Nothing was taboo. The message was: "Glad you could share that with me. Let's talk it over." If there's a problem, "Let's solve it together."

WHAT TO SAY

The most important message to communicate to children about alcohol and other drugs is that these substances are not for them to use. This message should be communicated unequivocally. You can acknowledge that many children in this country do use drugs and that perhaps their parents have not explained as clearly as they should have about the potential dangers. But you want it to be clear: Drugs are not for children.

Does this mean when a child asks to taste your wine at dinner you have to deny the request? In my opinion, that's being a little too rigid. Of course you'll use your own values to decide what to do, but a taste, out of curiosity, is very different from the experimental use of drugs for the mind-altering effects. You can give a taste, but still make it clear that only adults have the option of really drinking alcohol. As you may recall from your own experience, most children who try alcohol find the taste to be unpleasant.

Much of what you choose to discuss with young children will be determined by your own values, the interests of your children, and the flow of the dialogue. Below I have highlighted some of the most important material you will probably want to include in a thorough "intro to drugs" discussion. The quantity of information presented here couldn't effectively be communicated in one or even several sittings. Consider it as part of the curriculum for the preteen years.

BASIC DRUG INFORMATION

You'll want to define "drug." As mentioned earlier, one definition is: substances that produce changes in the mind and body. A few examples will illustrate this: People use drugs to make a headache go away, to clear a stuffed nose, or to change their moods.

Sometimes, however, people take drugs for one purpose, but they experience side effects. For example, cold tablets relieve cold symptoms, but they also make you drowsy and thirsty.

Some drugs, you can point out, are accepted for use in our society and others are not. Just because a drug is legal does not mean it is harmless to your health. For example, tobacco and alcohol can be very dangerous.

Why do people take drugs? This is an important issue to address. Let your children provide their own answers at first. They probably know many of the reasons. You can add others: to feel good, because their friends do it, for fun, to be popular, to escape, to forget bad things, to sleep, to stay awake, to cure diseases, to relax, to not feel nervous.

Your bright children might take notice: People use drugs to make friends, to feel good, or to not feel bad. So what's the problem?

The answer, in my words, goes like this:

"Sometimes people do benefit from the use of drugs. But drugs are very powerful substances, and their use is laden with risks. In some people, under some circumstances, drugs can create serious problems, even ruin their lives. Drugs are often not a good way for people to meet their needs.

"I'll help you learn a variety of very healthy ways to meet your needs, so that you can have a great life. Then, when you're an adult, you can make your own decisions about using mind-altering drugs.

"Meanwhile, in this family, we'll be sticking with medically indicated drugs for your physical health."

This provides an opportunity to introduce the concepts of abuse, dependence, and tolerance.

ABUSE, DEPENDENCE, AND TOLERANCE

Even very young children can understand the concept of abuse if it is presented in a simplified form. Ask them what they think it means. They might have heard of child abuse. They may have ideas such as "being mean to a friend," or "when you kick the cat."

Young children don't understand drug pharmacology or, in that sense, drug abuse, but they can be prepared for such an understanding by putting "abuse" into terms that make sense to them, such as *ice cream abuse:*

"What if I had one dip of chocolate ice cream after dinner? If it was real good, should I have another dip? How many? What if I had six dips and got so sick I threw up? How about two dips right before dinner?"

This gives children an idea of abuse, meaning excessive—too much, taken at the wrong time, something that is bad for you.

This same reasoning can be carried over to alcohol: "What if I had one beer with dinner? What if I had six and drove a car?"

This shows that abuse is dangerous to oneself and potentially to others.

The concept of drug dependence can also be introduced to children in an age appropriate manner.

"Some people," you tell your children, "take drugs to feel good. But if this is the only way they know how to make themselves feel good, then they will *depend* on the drugs. They will *need* them to feel good. Their whole life will center around drugs and nothing else. In extreme cases, they'll forget about their jobs and family. The drugs will control them."

You can explain that drugs sometimes make things too easy: "It would be like my doing your schoolwork. It would make it easier for you, but you wouldn't learn anything" (or "my making your beds," "my selecting the clothing you wear every day," or whatever activity your children are learning to master).

"That's why," you continue, "it's important to learn to enjoy life and feel good about yourself. So your happiness won't depend on drugs. Kids get in serious trouble when they start to depend on drugs. They never learn how to make friends, entertain themselves, or solve their own problems. In that sense, drugs keep them weak."

The concept of tolerance—that you need more and more of certain drugs to attain the same effect—can be understood by children. A good way to illustrate this is to use the most recent thriller movie that children have been seeing, one they went back to see several times.

"Do you remember the thrill you got the first time you watched *Friday the 13th?* When you went back the second time, did you get the same thrill? How about the third time?

"Sometimes drugs are like thriller movies. You want that same feeling, so you keep going back for more. But you're never satisfied like you were the first time. When this happens with drugs, it's called tolerance. People keep coming back for that same effect but find themselves disappointed unless they take larger doses.

"With thriller movies, sometimes kids look for scenes that are ever more gruesome. One distinction, however, is that drugs that are safe in small amounts may become harmful and dangerous in larger doses."

SPECIFIC DRUGS

Elementary schoolchildren are generally interested in an overview of the categories of drugs and, in simple terms, their effects. You might want to use the types of descriptions I presented on pages 38–52, explaining, for example, that stimulants speed up people, making them peppy, while depressants slow them down and allow them to relax.

In this discussion, highlight some of the special risks of each category of drugs and begin to talk about specific substances. It's not a matter of lecturing. You'll have to find "teachable moments" to instruct in these matters.

In addition to discussing the obvious abused drugs, such as marijuana and cocaine, I believe it's very important to discuss tobacco. Tobacco is highly addictive, a serious health risk, and frequently one of the first substances used in a drug-using career. Caffeine is another drug worthy of special attention because it often slips through the cracks. Some children drink coffee. Most children consume soft drinks without full awareness of the effects of caffeine.

Other drugs worthy of special notice are anabolic steroids, used by athletes to improve performance and by a subculture of males to look more muscular. Sterioids are dangerous. One good way to approach this topic is in the context of the question: What price would you pay for success?

In these discussions about drugs, alcohol merits *very* special attention because of its ubiquitous presence in our society. Children will see people under the influence of this drug and should be informed about its effects and dangers. As part of understanding the world in which they live, children should be informed about alcoholism.

Among the first dangerous drugs accessible to young children are inhalants. They should be discussed at home. Your children may have friends who try to encourage them to sniff the fumes of inhalants, such as airplane glue, in order to feel "drunk." Warn against inhaling fumes for recreational purposes. Sniffing is a very unhealthy and dangerous practice. It could even be fatal.

In discussing marijuana, a little historical perspective will help your child understand the confusion surrounding the dangers of this drug. Because the dangers were terribly exaggerated at one point in the past, there was a reaction by some people, who claimed that pot is harmless. But it is not. Let your children know that marijuana can cause serious problems. Marijuana smoke is bad for the lungs. And let them know that many children, teenagers, and adults misuse marijuana to escape from their problems. Also make sure they realize that although marijuana is widely available, it still is illegal, and that, like alcohol, it can be hazardous if used before driving an automobile.

DRUG DANGERS

To keep your credibility, it's important not to exaggerate the truth about drugs. You can explain that many poeple use alcohol, and even illegal drugs, carefully and without significant harm. They don't become addicted. They don't overdo it. But you also want to make sure that your children are well aware of the hazards and risks of drugs, and that they are not confused by some of the many myths. The following is some material you might want to cover.

Addiction

Explain that *no one* thinks that they will become dependent on drugs when they first start using them. Everyone assumes that drugs are safe. However, people should pay attention, because some of them are wrong.

94

One way that addiction sneaks up on people is when drugs are used to fend off "down" feelings. For example, stimulants give the body an immediate shot of energy for a short period of time, but eventually fizzle, causing the body to feel fatigued from overwork. Sometimes people take additional stimulants when the effects are disappearing so they won't get tired right away. Eventually, they are taking more and more drugs to avoid the down feeling. Similarly, some people try to mask the effects of a hangover by drinking more alcohol.

Children are often misinformed about alcoholism. Many don't realize it's a drug addiction. They don't know that millions of children and teenagers are alcoholics and that someone can be an alcoholic without drinking every day.

In discussing addiction, if you or your spouse are hooked on cigarettes, short of breaking the habit, the next best action is to admit you made a terrible mistake. You're addicted. Say that you shouldn't have started smoking in the first place and that you regret what you've done. If you have made unsuccessful attempts to break the habit, tell your children.

Immediate Effects

Research has indicated that young children are much more concerned with the immediate negative effects of drugs than the long-term effects. Still, talking about long-term risks is important because it's part of helping children learn to think ahead to the future. But surely it is also important to discuss the more immediate ill-effects of drugs. Thus, for preventing the use of tobacco, you might mention these negatives:

- Your hair and clothing smell bad.
- You get bad breath.
- Your teeth get stained.
- You go crazy when you're stuck in nonsmoking buildings.
- You can get in trouble if caught smoking at school.
- It can be an expensive habit.

This information will be of more concern to most children than facts about all of the serious health hazards.

Illegal Drugs

Aside from the obvious legal risks, children should know that illegal substances present other hazards. For example, it is impossible to accurately determine the potency and purity of street drugs. Many of them contain adulterants. Some relatively mild drugs, such as marijuana, may be laced with more potent substances, such as PCP.

Drunk Driving

This should more generally be called driving while intoxicated, because safety can be compromised by other substances besides alcohol, including marijuana and legally prescribed medications.

It is hazardous to "drug and drive."

Children should be told never to accept rides from someone who is intoxicated by alcohol or any other drug. They may need special training in how to refuse rides.

Alcohol is a factor in half of all highway deaths. It impairs judgment and slows reaction time. Because of the enormous danger of drunk driving, it is worth discussing some of the pharmacology of alcohol so that children realize it is absorbed into the bloodstream directly from the stomach without being digested and that it is slow to leave the body (most of it is eliminated slowly by the liver). You can dispel the myth that a cold shower or a cup of coffee will sober people up. The only benefit is that it buys time and keeps them from getting on the road sooner.

Overdoses

Explain about the serious dangers, including the risk of death, of taking too much of certain drugs. This applies especially to cocaine and the depressants, and to other drugs as well. Children should know that depressants combine synergistically, multiplying the effects. They should be aware that the risk of overdose is greater as a person gets high and loses track of how much he has already consumed.

What's Normal?

Many children have an exaggerated idea about how many of their peers are actually using drugs. Consequently, they think of drug use as "normal." You can use current statistics that frequently appear in the newspaper to clarify the actual situation.

Now that we have discussed drugs, we turn our attention to the other part of drug prevention and health promotion—building positive attitudes and teaching life skills. These skills and attitudes flourish in the type of empowering home atmosphere described in the previous chapter. Below are some specific activities you can do with your children to further empower them. You might want to use all the activities, or choose the ones that would be most useful in your own family. I think you'll find that this workbook helps keep you and your children on the right track.

LIFESTYLE: FEELING GOOD AND HAVING FUN

Children use drugs to feel good. Therefore part of health promotion/ drug prevention is helping children find ways to engage in fun and rewarding activities and helping them feel good about themselves without drugs. Below are some activities that promote these goals.

Activity One: What I Like about You

Purpose: To increase the amount of affection that is expressed in the family and to increase self-esteem.

What to do: You and your children get together and discuss *only* what you really like and love about each other. The only requirement is honesty. You have a homework assignment to compliment each other at least twice a day all week. At the end of the week, you talk about how it feels to give and receive compliments.

Activity Two: Role Models and Pride

Purpose: To increase self-esteem by identifying with a positive role model.

What to do: You and your children search for and read a book in which the main character, the hero, is someone your child can identify with. For instance, the character could be someone struggling with a situation similar to your child's—perhaps a kid brother, or a tough time in school. Or the character could live in your type of neighbor-

97

hood or come from your religious, ethnic, or racial background. Discuss the problems that the hero faced and how they were overcome.

Activity Three: Kids Just Wanna Have Fun

Purpose: To help expand your children's ability to create and enjoy pleasure.

What to do: You and your children have a discussion about fun. On paper, they list all the things they like to do and ones they think they might like to do, but haven't yet tried. You help them figure out how to do activities on their list. Also, you help expand their list by making additional suggestions.

In expanding the list, think of broadening their interests. The idea is not to push your children against their will but to encourage new activities. If all their activities are quiet and alone, suggest some adventurous ones that involve friends or family. Think about calm fun and exciting fun. Think about indoor and outdoor activities. Think about activities that involve creativity, such as music and art, and ones that involve imagination, such as reading or playing with dolls. If your child is very serious, buy a subscription to *Mad* magazine. Make sure physical activities are on the list. If they are not, talk about it. Make sure creative hobbies are considered, such as sewing, woodworking, and cooking. Consider after-school activities and various clubs, such as the Scouts, YMCA, YWCA, and 4-H.

If certain fun activities on the list are potentially dangerous, such as rock climbing, discuss the risks and safety precautions that you know about. This is a good way to begin to discuss risk taking, an important topic because the urge to take risks can contribute to drug misuse and abuse.

Activity Four: What I Like about Myself

Purpose: To increase self-esteem. To show that feeling good about yourself includes allowing for imperfection, growth, and learning new skills.

What to do: Ask your children to name five things they like about their personality. For example, tell what you're like as a person. (I'm generous and loving, I have a great sense of humor, I'm a good friend, I'm loyal.)

What do you like about your body and physical self? (Nice eyes, pretty hair, physically strong, good weight, good at basketball, dressing in style.)

What things do you do that make you feel good about yourself? (Paint, act in school plays, dance, play piano, play soccer, play with friends, get along with my brother.)

Tell me something you did today that makes you proud of yourself. How about something you did yesterday? Something you plan to do tomorrow, or soon?

Sometimes a child will respond with frustration: "I can't think of anything I like about myself." If this happens, offer encouragement: "I know many good things about you. Try hard. I'm sure you can think of some."

If the difficulty persists, you can help by making suggestions yourself, but also take note. This is a self-esteem problem. Think about how you could give more love, compliments, support, and opportunities for success to promote greater self-esteem.

Part of promoting self-esteem is allowing for imperfection and planning for improvement. While working on the list of what they like about themselves, children sometimes spontaneously discuss problems. If they do, introduce another part of the exercise—writing a list of "What I Want to Improve about Myself." The next activity in this workbook will help them achieve their goals.

If frustrations don't occur spontaneously, the second part of this activity, "What I Want to Improve," can be done after the first is completed.

Activity Five: Go for It

Purpose: To help children learn to set short-term and long-term goals and to make plans for attaining them.

What to do: Tell your children about some of your own goals and what you're doing about them. Explain how planning is beneficial. Ask them to write down their dreams and goals. Help them clarify realistic objectives. Show how long-term goals can be broken into short-term objectives. (Example: One boy wanted to be like his older brother, who played on the high school basketball team. He could practice shooting baskets and other basic skills in elementary school. He could join a league. He could jog to get in great shape. He could go to a basketball summer camp.) Help your children set up action plans for attaining their goals.

Activity Six: Telling the Truth

Purpose: To help your children appreciate and accept themselves and their feelings. To encourage them to accept challenges. To open up communication in the family.

What to do: You present the following incomplete sentences (and/ or others you may consider meaningful for your children) and give them an opportunity to provide their answers. You can do many of them at once or a few at a time, on different occasions. It's important to listen with unconditional love, as described in the previous chapter. Do not dispute or criticize what is said.

I feel good when I . . .
I feel hurt when I . . .
I find it hard to . . .
I like myself because . . .
A good decision I made this week was . . .
I feel sad when . . .
I feel scared when . . .
I feel frustrated when . . .
I feel loved when . . .
I feel left out when . . .
I feel best with our family when . . .
I feel best with my friends when . . .
I get angry when . . .
What I most want to tell you [Mom and Dad] is . . .
I'm worried that . . .
My biggest gripe at school is . . .
My biggest gripe with my best friend is . . .
When I think about my schoolwork, I feel . . .
My one wish is . . .
My biggest goal is . . .
My strongest feeling about my brother [or sister] is . . .
I wish grownups wouldn't . . .
The last time I cried was . . .
If I could be doing anything else today, it would be . . .

STRESS AND KIDS

I remember smiling to myself when a ten-year-old girl, Susan, told me in her own words: "I just had the worst day of my life." It was cute to hear those adult-sounding words from the little girl. But I knew it wasn't funny and that stress was as real to her as it is to any adult. Children need to learn to plan their lives to prevent unnecessary stress. They also need to learn healthy ways of coping with unavoidable stress.

Children who feel good about themselves and can plan their time with positive activities will experience less stress. But there's more to it. Some stress is good, such as the stress involved in learning something new, trying out for a school play, or playing in a little league game. However, too much stress is harmful and causes people to feel bad, sometimes even to become ill. Therefore, part of stress management is picking appropriate challenges. Children have a lot to learn about stress. The following activities will give them a good start.

Activity One: Stress, the Pest

Purpose: To help children understand the meaning of the concept. To help them recognize their personal indicators of stress.

What to do: Ask children if they have heard of "stress." They may have some ideas, such as "when things get crazy," or "when I'm under pressure." Explain that stress is the normal response of people to the demands of everyday life. We all have tough times. Even by first or second grade, a child can understand some of the harsh realities of life: Not everyone will like you. Not all days will be good ones. You will have positive and negative emotions.

Another important part of defining stress is to personalize it. Help your children learn to recognize stressful events by asking, "When do you feel stress?" If needed, make a few guesses: "When you have tests in school? When Grandma visits? When you go to Sunday school? When your sister and you fight?"

Fifth-grade children who were asked what makes them feel bad listed the following top five items:

- Spending too little time with their parents.
- Parents arguing in front of them.

101

- Turning in their homework late.
- Having nothing to do.
- Having too little money to spend.

In personalizing the meaning of stress, help your children learn to identify their own physical signs: "Where in your body do you feel stress?" And their own reactions: "What do you do when you're under stress?" If they have trouble identifying the indicators of stress, list some of the possibilities: tight muscles, constricted breathing, whiny, irritable, losing temper, lump in throat, feel like crying, breathing fast, sweaty, feel real hot, heart pounds, tremble, can't fall asleep, sweaty hands, cold hands, feel tired and weak, headache, upset stomach, feel helpless. Explain that by recognizing the signs of stress, people can take care of themselves better.

Explain that some responses to stress are physiological and largely out of our control, such as sweating, but that other responses can be controlled. And some are better than others. Discuss the idea of good and bad responses to stress. Explain that we can do things to help ourselves relax. Or we can do things, such as overeating or taking drugs or throwing tantrums, that only make us feel worse.

Activity Two: Stress-Busters

Purpose: To help your children become aware of positive options for coping with stress.

What to do: Let your children brainstorm ideas about positive ways to deal with stress. You can add to their repertoire. If the following ways have not been listed, you can mention them:

- Distract yourself. Read a book or watch a movie.
- Physical exertion. Go for a walk or swim.
- Uplift your mood. Listen to upbeat or relaxing music, sing along or dance along. Use your imagination to think about nice things. (Nine-year-old Sara was stressed and bored while babysitting her younger sister. I suggested she use her imagination to think pleasant thoughts. She said she concentrated on her favorite things—rainbows, unicorns, and her dollies—and felt much better.)
- Accept your bad feelings and let them pass. Cry and look forward to brighter days.
- Make your body relax. Take six deep breaths or get someone

to massage your neck, back, or feet, or wherever you feel tense. Take a nap. Take a warm bath.

  • Energize your body. Take a cold shower. Splash water on your face. Go outside in the fresh air.

  • Use problem solving: Figure out what's bothering you and do something about it.

  • Get support. Talk about problems with a friend or us [parents]. Ask for help.

  • Communicate feelings. If you are upset with someone, talk it over.

  • Stop doing whatever is stressful. If you are run down and tired, stop pushing yourself. Relax instead. If you feel stressed from boredom or sluggish from watching too much television, then get active. Go get some exercise.

Activity Three: Barbara the Beaver

Purpose: To increase awareness of healthy and unhealthy ways to react to problems.

What to do: Tell a fictional story, such as the one below, based on the story "Albert the Ant" by Jessica Horne. Four characters are stranded on a desert island. One panics, hides under some lumber, and screams in terror (Charlie the Chicken). One blames the other three and chases them around, paddle in hand, trying to swat them in the behind (Brian the Bulldog). One makes believe everything is okay and tans herself on the beach and then hides her head in the sand (Ellen the Ostrich). And the heroine, Barbara the Beaver (for girls), or the hero, Billy the Beaver (for boys), tells his animal friends to "chill out" and starts thinking about what to do. Then she industriously builds a raft with the wood, and paddles them all to safety.

This story is a good example of the fact that sometimes you have to solve problems in order to feel good. It wouldn't have helped if Barbara the Beaver drank beer to forget that they were stranded on an island. Even if Barbara found a good way to relax, for example, taking a nap, it still wouldn't help them to escape. She had to solve the problem in order to feel good. You can use Charlie the Chicken as an example to begin to discuss escapism, that is, people sometimes try to make themselves feel good, but in so doing overlook important problems.

Ask your children about times that they, or you, or anyone in the

103

family, may have behaved like the characters in "Barbara the Beaver."

Suggest that your children act like Barbara the Beaver all week long. Check in with them every day. What happened to Barbara the Beaver today?

Activity Four: Let's Solve a Problem

Purpose: To enhance problem-solving skills.

What to do: Ask your children to identify a problem. For example; they can't afford to buy a particular toy; they are angry at a sister about something; they are being picked on by a kid in school.

Now walk your child through the problem-solving process. First pick the goal. Then identify available resources. Think of all the possible alternatives. List pros and cons of each alternative. Choose the best ones. Make an action plan for success. (You may want to reread the section about problem solving in Chapter 3.)

Your discussion might go something like this:

Child: "There's a great toy I want to buy, but I can't afford it."

Parent: "Oh, I'm sorry to hear that. How much does it cost?"

Child: Twenty bucks."

Parent: "How much do you have?"

Child: "About four dollars. But I'm spending some of that on the movies."

Parent: "I see—that is a problem. What are you going to do to solve it?"

Child: "I don't know. Can you just buy it for me?"

Parent: "That's one possibility. Let's look at all the other ones, too. First, what's your goal?"

Child: "To get the toy."

Parent: "How else could you get it?"

Child: "Like I said, you could buy it for me." (This kid has a sense of humor!)

Parent: "Seems like we covered that one already. What are your other ideas?"

Child: "I could get someone else to buy it for me. I could wait until Christmas."

Parent: "Yeah, good, what else?"

Child: "I could save my allowance, but that would take a long time."

Parent: "Any other ideas?"

Child: "No."

Parent: "What about earning money?"

Child: "That's an idea. Do you have any jobs I could do?"

Parent: "I could offer you some work, like in the yard and washing the car."

Child: "But it takes so long to save money."

Parent: "Is the toy very important?"

Child: "Yeah, I really want it."

Parent: "Maybe you could do a better job of saving your money. Have you ever thought of that?"

Child: "That's a good idea."

Parent: "I'd help you with that."

As the discussion unfolded, the child recognized that he could try to get someone to buy the toy for him or he could save up for it. He decided to save his allowance, to reduce the amount of money he spent on junk food after school, and to wash the car to earn extra cash. That way, he figured he could buy the toy in three weeks.

Activity Five: Decision Making

Purpose: To show that decision making is part of problem solving. To show that many decisions involve weighing pros and cons and also involve comparing immediate and long-term benefits.

What to do: Present imaginary bad decisions children sometimes make, such as the following:

Joan decided to watch television instead of doing her homework. She got in trouble with her teacher.

David ate so much Halloween candy that he couldn't eat dinner. He threw up.

Ginger ran away when she broke a window in the neighbors' house, but they saw her.

Talk about why these imaginary children decided to do what they did. Talk about other options they had. Talk about the pluses and minuses of each option. When Joan watched television instead of doing her homework, the plus was that she had fun. The minus was that she felt bad later about not doing her homework. Also, she got in trouble the next day and had to stay after school to catch up. If Joan had thought carefully about the future, including *all* the pluses and minuses of her options, she might have made a better decision.

Discuss the major steps in decision making: (1) List the choices. (2) List the pros and cons of each. (3) Determine which is best at the present moment, which is best in the long run, and which is best overall. (4) Make a choice. (5) Do it and see how it goes.

Your children will realize that people don't always make the best choices. But if they do step five above and "see how it goes,'" they can benefit from their experiences and learn to make better decisions in the future.

Ask your children what decisions they need to be making these days. (It is important that you give them some freedom to make choices so they can learn from the experience.) Walk them through the decision-making process, using the steps listed above.

Activity Six: Taking Risks

Purpose: To explore the role of risk taking in decision making.

What to do: Write out a list of activities that have unpredictable outcomes, such as the following:

- Perform in a talent contest.
- Try out for the soccer team.
- Sneak a beer when Mom and Dad aren't home.
- Run for class president.
- Steal something from the store.

Ask your children what all of these activities have in common. Introduce the ideas of uncertainty and unpredictability. In the simplest terms, these activities may turn out okay or may turn out badly. You don't know for sure ahead of time. Explain that many decisions involve uncertainty. Give an example from your own life. "I quit my job with a pretty good salary in order to go back to school. I knew that the job I quit didn't pay as much as I wanted to earn. For a while, though, while I was in school, I had very little money. As it turned out . . ."

This helps your children see that even you—a parent—have had tough decisions to make and must deal with uncertainty.

Explain that doing something without knowing for sure how it will turn out is taking a risk. Risks can be very exciting and therefore appealing, but only some of them are worth taking. A good way to make a decision about a risk is to list the pros and cons and also the best and worst possible outcomes. Then you consider how likely it is that it will turn out well or badly. Then you try to decide if the risk is worth taking.

Make the concept real with an exciting example: "Some risks are really dangerous. If you stole clothing from the department store, you'd have a bit of an adventure. You'd also have some new clothing. Those are positives. But you know you can get whatever clothing you need from us [parents] anyway. Then there are negatives. You might feel guilty. And if you got caught in the store, they would arrest you. You might not get caught, but the consequences of the worst possible outcome are very bad. In my opinion, it's a bad risk. There are better ways to find adventure.

"On the other hand, imagine auditioning for the school play. It's a risk, too. You might not get a part. If you didn't, you'd be disappointed, but it's not a very big deal. If you did get a part, it would be terrific fun. That would probably be a risk worth taking."

Discuss why people take risks. Some are an attempt to excel, such as running for class president. Some are for excitement, such as climbing a mountain or using drugs to see if you can get away with it. Some people take risks to be popular, such as kids who take drugs to show their friends they are cool. Some guys do dangerous things to prove they're macho. Sometimes people take risks because of their convictions: "I'm going to say what I really think even though I know my friends won't agree."

Finally, children can be asked to name good and bad risks they have taken recently or in the past.

Activity Seven: Loosening Up

Purpose: To empower children to relax.

What to do: Explain that this is a way they can alter their moods by learning to relax when they are tense. At first you all do it together; then you explain that they can do it alone, without your assistance, whenever they want.

Start by telling them to get in a very comfortable position on a chair. They can take off their shoes if they wish. Loosen all constricting clothing. Then tell them to take a few deep breaths to relax. Imagine

107

they are in the most wonderful place in the world. Then guide them through a relaxation process. You start with the tip of the toes. Tell them to tighten this part of their body as much as they can, then to relax it. Then you go on to the rest of the foot, with the same instructions: "Tense the rest of your foot as much as you can. Hold it for a second or two. Now let it relax." Then you move to the ankles. Then the lower leg, knees, thighs, midsection, rear, stomach, chest, shoulders, arms, neck, jaw, nose, eyes, ears, top of the head. Tense and relax the muscles throughout the body. If any part starts to feel tense again, go back to it, tense up, and then release.

When the whole body is relaxed, talk it over. Ask some questions: "How did it feel? Do you see what power you have to make yourself relax?"

Activity Eight: Stress at Home

Purpose: To improve communication and identify causes of stress at home. To learn problem solving as it applies to home life.

What to do: You and your children make a list of sources of stress at home. Then you discuss how to cope with the stress, by either responding better to the pressure or finding solutions. You make a plan, put it into action, and set a time to discuss what progress has been made.

In the Romanella family, the biggest source of stress was a mad rush for everyone to get off to work and school in the morning. They decided to shift their scheduling—to prepare school lunches and to lay out the next day's clothing—before bedtime. They also all decided to get up fifteen minutes earlier so they could have a more leisurely time together.

A couple of weeks later, they agreed that the scheduling changes had been successful, but that nobody liked waking up early. They went back to the old wake-up time and found the mornings were still better than they had been. The plan was successful.

In the Thomas family, the problem was that a fourth-grade boy, Eric, didn't have a quiet place to study at home. He shared a room with his younger brother, and the only desk in the house was in the living room. When he studied in his bedroom or at the desk, Eric would hear the television blasting. The family decided to establish a quiet time in the house, when no radio, stereo, or television would be on. Eric agreed to do his homework during that period.

SOCIAL INFLUENCE

One reason children use drugs is in response to the influence of others, most notably the media, adults, and peers. Children can be protected against the negative influence of the media by being aware of the downside of using drugs and by developing consumer awareness.

They can be protected against negative adult influence by getting a more complete understanding of what it means to be an adult and of the process of becoming an adult.

They can be protected against negative peer influence by having positive friendships and knowing how to resist peer pressure. The activities below provide a solid foundation for teaching "resistance" skills, that is, the ability to go against negative social influence.

Adults have their problems, too. You often hear about children and peer pressure, but we should recognize that conformity is a problem for all age groups in this culture. Many adults drink, use drugs, and do many other activities just to be accepted by their peers.

Activity One: Media Drug Dealers

Purpose: To increase awareness of manipulation and social influence in sales pitches. To increase consumer awareness.

What to do: After watching commercials for beer and wine with your children, discuss them in terms of the sales pitch.

Also have your children gather alcohol and tobacco advertisements from the print media. Identify the sales gimmick. Look at the key words and concepts associated with drugs: romance, glamour, fun, success. Consider the visual message: What does the picture show? More friends, a happy family? A good time? What are the subtle messages? Who is the target? Whites? Blacks? Hispanics? Young people? Children? Parents? Men? Women? Blue-collar workers?

It is interesting to observe that much of the drug advertising is geared to young people. Most people who smoke cigarettes or drink alcohol begin during their youth. That's when advertisers want to get loyalty to their products. Also, as older smokers and drinkers break the habit or die, the industry seeks replacements. They need young people to be drug consumers. Children need to realize that they are targets.

Examine advertising tactics: the bandwagon approach (everyone's doing it); snob appeal (join the in-crowd); promises (be sexy or popular or happy); feel good about yourself (identify with stars who use the products).

Point out the bias in media advertising. Alcohol is always shown being used on festive occasions, such as birthdays, parties, and weddings. People are always enjoying themselves. Ask your children to think about how alcohol could also ruin or detract from such occasions.

Point out that alcohol commercials are often used for sports and entertainment programs, so that the products are associated with health and good times. Note, too, that the alcohol industry sponsors many athletic events, such as tennis tournaments and bicycle races, probably to attempt to counter the image of their products as unhealthy. Observe that in cigarette advertisements, you sometimes don't find smoke, as if the stink wouldn't permeate a room.

Part of building consumer awareness is explaining that the motivation of advertisers is to sell products and make money. They want people to be consumers, to buy and use their products. They are not interested in your well-being, so you have to protect yourself.

The bright side of what is happening in the media is the recent upsurge of public service announcements (PSAs) supporting children in resisting the temptation to use drugs. But these commercials, too, use sales tactics. To do a balanced job of helping children gain consumer awareness, look at the tactics of the PSAs.

Activity Two: The Age Game

Purpose: Sometimes children smoke cigarettes, drink alcohol, or do other drugs because they are trying to act grown up. This is to help your children find positive ways to grow up.

What to do: With your children, conduct a survey of local rules and laws in your community related to age. Find out when children have to pay full price for movie tickets. Find out how old you have to be to get a learner's permit to drive a car, get a driver's license, drop out of school, get a job, enlist in the military, buy alcohol, buy tobacco, and vote in an election. You can expand the activity to look at the elderly, particularly if the children are close to their grandparents. Find out what the age requirements are for retirement, senior discounts, and Social Security. Discuss the merits and problems of these age issues.

Introduce the concept of maturity. Maturity comes from learning

110

through experiences. Age allows for more experience, but doesn't guarantee maturity.

You can discuss the transfer of power in this context, that is, that you are giving your children opportunities and experiences to be increasingly responsible so that they will be prepared to succeed as mature adults.

Be specific. Tell them what you are allowing them to do that is part of growing up. Give examples of increasing freedom, such as places they can go where they couldn't go before. Give examples of increasing responsibility, such as the household chores, or babysitting duties you have given to them. Tell them about some of the freedom and responsibilities they will have in the future.

Activity Three: Peer Pressure

Purpose: To help your children understand peer influence and pressure and the concept of individuality.

What to do: Tell a make-believe story, such as the one below, about fitting in with a crowd and being influenced by others:

"John is out with a group of friends. They all order Big Macs and he wants a fish sandwich. It's hard for him not to do what everyone else does. Why?

"What do you think John's friends would think if he ordered a fish sandwich? What would they say?"

Discuss influence and subtle peer pressure. When does influence become pressure? Also brainstorm related situations, such as kids all wearing the same brand of jeans or liking the same songs.

Give your children support to be different: "You don't need to do everything your friends do in order to keep friends." Discuss the concept of individuality. Talk about what makes a person unique and special. Pick specific people, friends, and relatives and list their special qualities. Ask your children to list their own special qualities.

Activity Four: The Bully

Purpose: To identify and resist power plays.

What to do: Children learn early, from experience, what a bully is. Talk to them about their definition of a bully and their ideas about standing up to bullies. Talk about how physical violence and the threat of physical violence are often used to push people around. Introduce the concept of power plays, the ways that people try to control others. Children will recognize physical violence as a type of power play. Discuss other, more subtle types of power plays. Give examples such as these:

- Do what I tell you to do or you'll hurt my feelings.
- Do what I tell you to do or I won't be your friend.
- Do what I said to do or I'll call you names. ("You're chicken." "You're stupid.")
- Everyone will laugh at you if you don't do what I say.
- Cool kids do it.

The second part of this exercise is having a discussion about responding to power plays. Strong responses begin like this:

- "I'm going to do what I think is right."
- "I'm going to do what I want to do."

The rest of the answer is: "I'm willing to run the risks and suffer the consequences, whatever they may be. I don't have to explain myself to you or to defend my choice."

In other words, you are teaching your children to be assertive and that they don't have to take a defensive position. They don't have to explain themselves.

Example: "Why don't you want to try drugs?"

The answer is simple: "Because I don't want to," or "Because I don't feel like it."

"Well, give me some reasons."

"I don't have to give you reasons."

Children need to know that they don't have to explain themselves to bullies.

Activity Five: Just Say No

Purpose: To teach assertiveness, especially as it applies to drugs.

What to do: Children who have been raised to be gentle, agreeable, and loving individuals may find themselves with a dilemma when faced with pushy friends who are pressuring them to take drugs or to act in some other way against their own will. Children often confuse assertiveness with aggression and passivity. Assertiveness is an important concept to understand and skill to develop.

Start this activity with a tease. Tell your children that you want them to steal groceries for dinner at the supermarket. Keep a straight face, be insistent, and tell them to try to talk you out of your position. Use a whole series of power plays to back your unreasonable stance:

- "Be brave. Don't be chicken."
- "Give me five good reasons not to do this."
- "Okay, now give me five more reasons."
- "Well, I'm the parent. Whatever I say goes."
- "I think you're a wimp. You need to be more adventurous."
- "If you don't steal the food, I'll subtract the cost of tonight's dinner from your allowance."

After you've had some fun with the argument, you can discuss the difference between assertiveness (which means sticking up for yourself, asserting your rights), aggression (which means imposing force on other people), and passivity (which means allowing other people to control you because you have not acted in your own behalf).

Now change the focus to drugs and assertiveness. Ask your children if they understand about not using drugs. Do they know the dangers? If they know them, then discuss situations that might occur in which a group of children are trying to talk them into drinking alcohol or smoking pot. Ask if they could be assertive and refuse an offer. Ask what they would say and how they would feel about it. If they are nervous about "saying no," you can validate their feelings by agreeing that it is difficult to be different from a crowd.

As a parent, this is an opportunity to promote the value of individuality, of being assertive despite pressure, even when a person very much wants to be accepted by friends. Explain that in the long run, most people respect you more when you hold to your convictions.

Because it is difficult to resist peer pressure, suggest the practice of staying away from people who use drugs and the places where they use them.

Give some resistance strategies, such as using "strength in numbers." If drugs are present, find the other kids who aren't using drugs and stick with them.

Now raise the issue of power plays, situations in which drug users try to coerce their friends into joining them. Several pamphlets published by the National Institute on Drug Abuse suggest these responses to peer pressure:

- "No thanks."
- "I'm not interested."
- "No way."

One good idea is to stick with these basics, over and over again. It's the best answer. Some children have difficulty being this assertive. They find it easier to make excuses or to change the topic. That's fine if it works. But they might find themselves up against one of the classic power plays in which the aggressor keeps the other person on the defensive.

Pushy Child: "I don't get it. Why not smoke pot?"

Defensive Child: "My mom would kill me if she ever found out."

Pushy Child: "You don't have to tell her. She'll never know."

Defensive Child: "I'd rather go to a movie."

Pushy Child: "That's no fun. You're just chicken."

Defensive Child: "I don't think it's safe."

Pushy Child: "Oh, you're chicken."

Defensive Child: "Let's talk about something else."

Pushy Child: "Quit being so scared. Let's just do it."

Defensive Child: "My parents said they wouldn't let me use the car if I ever smoked pot."

Pushy Child: "Don't be a wimp. Quit making excuses."

The pushy child will go on and on unless the other child stops being defensive. An excellent way to stop the power play is to turn the tables:

"I told you where I stand, and I don't want to change my mind. Stop trying to bully me into something I don't want to do. Get off my back."

One option children should always remember is to simply walk away.

I have found that children and parents can have fun role playing imaginary scenes with peer pressure. Invent a variety of situations, involving or not involving drugs, to help your children practice their assertiveness skills. Take turns "pushing" and "resisting." Here's one to start with. Tell your children this:

"Make believe you're part of a group of kids who want to climb a fence and swim in a reservoir at night. You want to convince me to come along. I think it's too dangerous. Try to talk me into it anyway."

Or try this one:

"I want to talk you into stealing a pocketknife at a drugstore. You know you shouldn't, but a group of us want you to do it with us."

HEALTHY LIFESTYLES

The prevention of drug problems is part and parcel of health promotion. You can't have one without the other. Therefore, this workbook started with a section on drug information but also included activities for improving self-esteem, having more fun, minimizing stress, coping with stress, and resisting the negative influence of parents, peers, and the media. An activity that ties it all together, sort of a master activity, is to prepare a healthy-lifestyle checklist with your children. The idea is to get them thinking about their own physical, social, and psychological well-being. It's an opportunity for them to appreciate their strengths, identify their weaknesses, and make plans for improvement.

After your children complete the following checklist, ask them which of their health habits are good. Which ones are weak and in need of improvement? Follow up with problem solving and then help them make an action plan for change. This is an activity that can be repeated from time to time. Here's the checklist:

(1) WEIGHT AND NUTRITION.
Do I eat a balanced diet?
What do I usually have for breakfast? Lunch? Dinner?
Do I eat healthy snacks?
Do I eat too much junk food? If so, which kinds?
Am I in my proper weight range?
Do I eat too much sugar?
Do I drink soft drinks with caffeine? How much? How do they affect me?
(2) REST AND SLEEP.
What is the right amount of sleep for me?
Do I go to bed at my bedtime?
What happens when I don't get enough sleep?
Do I rest when I'm tired?
(3) RECREATION.
What are my favorite activities when I'm alone?
What more could I do alone that I haven't been doing?

115

What do I like to do with friends?

What more could I do with friends that I haven't been doing?

What are my television viewing habits? Do I want to change them in any way?

What do I do for physical exercise?

Do I exercise every day?

What are my favorite hobbies? Do I want to start new ones?

Do I read? Listen to music? Play music?

(4) SOCIAL LIFE.

Am I happy with the friends I have?

Do I want new friends?

Do I want to do different things with my friends that I've never tried before?

How well do I get along with my friends?

Can I go against the crowd?

Do I want to join any clubs, such as the 4-H or Scouts?

Do I tell my friends what I feel?

Are there after-school activities that I might want to do?

(5) ATTITUDE AND HEALTHY STRESS LEVEL.

Do I have a positive outlook on life?

Do I have a sense of humor?

How do I deal with stress?

Do I plan my life so I don't have too much stress?

What is my stress level (high, medium, or low) in school? With friends? At home?

Do I face my problems? Do I solve them.

Can I say what I feel?

(6) HYGIENE.

Do I bathe every day?

Do I take care of my skin?

Do I take care of my hair?

Do I brush and floss my teeth every day?

Do I know how to protect myself and other family members from communicable illnesses?

(7) SAFETY.

Do I practice bicycle safety?

Do I wear my seat belts in the car?

Do I know what to do if I'm home alone?

Do I know where I should not go alone?

Do I know what to do in case of fire?

Do I know what to do with strangers on the street and at
   the front door?
Do I know about poisons, medicines, prescription drugs, and
   illegal drugs?
Do I take unsafe risks?
(8) FAMILY.
Do we say what we feel?
Do we all pitch in around the house?
Can we work out our differences?
Do we have fun together?

Children who grow up in an empowering home environment with
a healthy lifestyle will enter adolescence with positive attitudes and
basic life skills. They will be well-equipped to handle the important
decisions about drugs and other health matters that they'll be facing.
In the following chapters, you will read about the next step—
empowering adolescents through education and dialogue.

PART II

THE EXCHANGE OF INFORMATION

5

OPENING THE DIALOGUE

"How can I find out if my child is using drugs?" That's the question I'm asked most often at lectures and workshops by parents who want to know the signs and symptoms of drug use.

When asked, I wonder if these parents are trying to decide whether to talk with their teenagers. I point out that such a discussion is necessary whether substances are being used or not. In fact, the ideal time for the discussion is *before* drug use is suspected.

I also wonder if parents are trying to decide whether to play detective by snooping through a child's room. I hope not. Such an action could destroy any trust that existed in the relationship. Even if they were to stumble upon a stash of drugs, if good communication hasn't been established, little can be done to solve the problem.

At these lectures and workshops, I list the typical signs and symptoms of drug use, such as excessive moodiness, withdrawal from the family, behavior problems at school, and a change in sleep patterns. (See pages 36–38 for a more comprehensive listing.) But I also warn against jumping to the wrong conclusions. These signs and symptoms can have a variety of other causes, including depression, a reaction to stress, or a reaction to family problems. Regardless of cause, it's important to do something about them. But the point I emphasize most in my comments to parents is that there is only one good, reliable way to find out if children are using drugs—to ask them.

I know that some parents think this is naive: "Sure, ask and expect an honest answer? It won't work."

And sometimes they're right. The *only* way to get an honest answer to a straightforward question about drugs is to have established a very special relationship. It's not always easy. But it can and must be done. If parents fail to establish a family climate that allows an open and honest dialogue, then they won't play a role in their adolescent child's decisions about drug use. The child's peer group will be the sole source of information and discussion.

Open discussions are the best way to know if a child is using drugs. Even more important, they are absolutely essential in preventing drug abuse. It is through discussions that teenagers learn to make wise decisions. It is also through discussions that parents can find out what their children are thinking and help them expand their awareness.

In this chapter, I introduce the "exchange of information process," a way for adolescents and their parents to have a disciplined exchange of views about emotionally charged issues such as the use of alcohol and other drugs.

This process is more than merely exchanging information. But when I first devised the concept about ten years ago and started using it in therapy, I wanted a name that put the focus squarely on the need for parents and teenagers to be *rational*. I was seeing families in which emotions had reached such an intense level that discussions were free-for-alls, devoid of any exhange of information whatsoever.

The exchange of information has five parts:

- You suggest a discussion and children agree to participate.
- You present your thoughts and feelings about drugs.
- Your children present their thoughts and feelings.
- You discuss each other's point of view.
- You reach an understanding and make agreements with each other.

The immediate goal of the exchange of information is that adolescents, assisted by their parents, set high standards of behavior and make wise decisions about alcohol and other drugs. The long-term goal is that they maintain these standards and learn to make wise decisions on their own, without the help of parents.

This chapter focuses on the first stage of the exchange. It tells how you can establish the sort of special relationship that allows adolescents to talk honestly about themselves. A warm and nonthreatening family climate is required. Often, a great deal of work is needed to improve the climate at home before it's possible to engage in a nuts and bolts discussion about drugs.

THE BENEFITS OF THE EXCHANGE OF INFORMATION PROCESS

The exchange of information process gives children a significant voice in setting rules and standards for themselves. Part of the process is parents listening to their children. This worries some parents who are concerned that this sounds too democratic. They worry about loss of parental authority. Perhaps they imagine an arrogant thirteen-year-old son, hands on hips, telling his parents that he plans to use drugs: "We had our discussion. Now it's time for me to make my decision. I think it's okay to smoke pot, so I'm going to do it."

This is *not* how the exchange process actually works. By agreeing to respectfully listen to your children and to strive for mutual understanding, you do *not* surrender your authority.

Although the ideal goal is reaching agreement (yes, it really can be done), parents and teenagers don't always see eye to eye. You still have the final word. You maintain the ultimate power in setting limits and establishing rules, as well you should.

But, you may wonder, if parents are to decide in the end anyway, why have discussions? Why go through the motions? Isn't this just a way of manipulating children?

Definitely not. There are many good reasons for having discussions:

- They provide an opportunity for parents to learn what their children are thinking.
- They provide an opportunity for children to learn what their parents are thinking.
- They increase the chance for mutual understanding.
- They increase the chance of coming to agreements.
- They increase the chance for compliance, even if there is still disagreement.
- By having discussions, parents help their children think through their own decisions.
- By having discussions, parents help their children learn skills that are needed for thinking through decisions on their own.

• Discussions give teenagers a sense of responsibility and thereby contribute to their self-esteem.

• Discussions serve as an excellent way to learn about cooperative, loving relationships.

Agreement, Understanding, and Competence

Parents who use the exchange of information process are often amazed to find that good discussions vastly increase mutual understanding and can lead to agreements when none seemed possible. Children benefit from the input of mature adults. Parents benefit by gaining an understanding of the problems and conditions of the era. Without such discussions, parents are too far removed from their children's lives.

When agreements are made, children who participated in a discussion feel a sense of "ownership" in the outcome and are likely to abide by the terms that they helped to establish.

Even when parents and children do not agree after a discussion, the probability that teenagers will comply with the parental "bottom line" is greatly increased, because children have been treated with respect during the exchange of information process. They were given an opportunity to express themselves. They heard the point of view of their parents and the reasoning behind it. Under these circumstances, adolescents are more likely to abide by parental rules, even if they consider them unduly restrictive.

However, to ensure success with this process, parents must respectfully listen to their children. Some parents have a discussion because they were told that they should, but they show no tolerance for opinions different from their own. They don't realize that listening with an open mind is an opportunity to better understand their children. Even if they aren't swayed by the input, they could at least acknowledge and address the concerns that are raised.

Most of us have had the experience of talking with someone who wasn't listening or with people who, while we talked, were planning what they would say next. We know how bad that feels. Children feel the same way when their parents don't listen or talk down to them.

A good indication of open-minded communication is having a willingness to budge from your starting position. Although parents maintain the ultimate authority, children must have input. If they never have any influence in the rules and decisions that are made in dis-

124

cussions, they will eventually doubt that their parents are really paying attention.

Self-Esteem, Good Reasoning, and Good Relationships

Another set of reasons for using the exchange of information process, and probably the strongest case for it, has *nothing* to do with setting limits or establishing authority. It has *everything* to do with good parenting, parenting that empowers children to grow up as healthy and competent human beings.

As you know, an important part of preventing drug abuse is helping children develop high self-esteem, good thinking skills, and the ability to make good relationships. During the adolescent period, these goals have special meaning. Children are establishing their sense of identity. They are attempting to find answers to basic questions such as: Who am I? What do I believe is right or wrong? Where do I fit into this world? In their younger years, they relied on their parents' values. Now, nearing adulthood, they seek their own answers. At the same time, adolescents are also beginning to develop mature thinking skills—in particular, learning formal logic, the ability to consider all possibilities and all outcomes in complex situations.

Let's look at an example of how a teenager's convictions can be challenged, making a clear sense of identity important:

Six teenagers were crammed into a small car, five of them smoking pot. Fifteen-year-old Sandra didn't want to participate. But her friends passed her the joint and encouraged her to smoke. Sandra's ultimate decision to decline the offer depended upon the strength of her own sense of identity. She was sure about her position, wasn't frightened of losing approval, and held firm in her position. A clear identity was an excellent defense against peer pressure.

Thinking skills are also important in wise decision making. Let's look at how they can influence an adolescent's decision about drugs:

Fourteen-year-old Tim lived in a school distrct that had a serious drug problem. He had done some careful thinking about the issue. Many of his friends used drugs and told him how much they enjoyed it. Tom saw them feeling good, but also noticed that some of them were high almost all the time and getting in trouble. Some had declined dramatically in their school performance. So, although he saw his friends were having fun, he also observed the whole picture and decided the potential dangers of drugs outweighed any interest he had

125

in using them. His clear logic enabled him to make a good decision.

To prepare for encounters with the real world, teenagers such as the two described above need a compass to find their way and answers about how to conduct their lives.

But these answers don't come automatically with age. They require experience, practice, and effort. By engaging your children in the exchange of information process, you give them much-needed experience. You help them forge an identity and learn to think for themselves. You give them a chance to clarify their opinions and values. When it comes to drugs, the best thing you can do for adolescents is to help them learn to think clearly, make good decisions, and choose a healthy lifestyle.

Another benefit of the exchange of information process is that it promotes high self-esteem. Children feel good about themselves when they are respected and taken seriously. This translates into greater internal strength, a stronger sense of identity, and therefore greater resistance to peer pressure.

Finally, the exchange of information process also supports adolescents in another important developmental task: learning about mature relationships—both romantic ones and friendships. By engaging in dialogue at home, children learn communication and cooperation skills that apply to other meaningful relationships. They learn about mutual respect. Without question, the family can be the best learning ground for mutual respect and loving relationships.

BUT WHAT ABOUT PARENTAL AUTHORITY?

In spite of the apparent logic of the exchange of information process, some parents consider it a weak position. Concerned about the decline of parental influence, they want a demonstration of parent power. They say, "We have to lay down the law." They want parents to spell out strict rules and to severely punish transgressions. They believe that fear of punishment will keep children under control and therefore away from drugs. They are very concerned with obedience.

Authoritarian parents usually start their sentences with statements such as these:

"When I was a kid . . ."

"Under my father's roof, we always knew . . ."

"We wouldn't dare . . ."

Many of these parents fear they would lose authority if they involved their children in a discussion. Ironically, it usually works the other way around:

(1) Parents set rules without involving their children.
(2) Children feel that they have been discounted and therefore rebel against the rules.
(3) Parental authority declines because children have *not* been involved in the decision-making process.

In other words, the rules and limits imposed by parents without discussion are perceived by children as obstacles to their well-being. Teenagers disregard parental authority when they feel ignored or unloved or when they don't understand the rationale for rules they are told to obey.

At a workshop, I was explaining the exchange of information process to parents when a father in the audience started talking about how he "ran things" in his home.

"My children know the rules. I tell them what's right and what's wrong. They know they'd better behave."

I was concerned that he might have misunderstood me. I explained that I advocate parental authority and that I believe in rules and consequences for misbehavior. I added, however, that I believed it was wise to include teenagers in the process of establishing rules.

I also explained that there are many different types of power. Rules and punishment are one type. But a parental repertoire should include others, especially the power of education, that is, the power to influence children by teaching them to make wise decisions. I asked if he explained the reasoning for his rules to his children.

"No," he answered. "I don't believe parents need to do that. We are the adults, after all. We know what's best."

I thought about two things. First, adults may know what's best, but somehow they must help their teenage children gain that insight. I also wondered whether this man's children were rebelling, a common reaction to an authoritarian style.

"How's it working?" I asked.

"Great," he said. "All these other parents worry about their children using drugs. I never worry. My kids do as they're told. It's the same way I was brought up. My kids know that if they break a rule they'll be severely, *and I mean severely*, punished."

127

A woman sitting in the audience couldn't stand it.

"You sound just like my father. You're driving me crazy."

Then she told her story:

"When I was a kid I had a father like you. He was always laying down the law. I hated him. The stricter he got, the trickier I became. He wouldn't let me talk on the phone at night, so I climbed out the window and went to a pay phone.

"In fact, it was kind of a challenge. Whatever he said not to do, I did. He gave me ideas about things I never even dreamed about doing. He would boast about how great his kids were—just like you—while we were being real lunatics behind his back.

"I still hate him for it. He has mellowed over the years. Now I have my own children. But I felt so unloved and so untrusted. I felt like I had to fight for my independence. I made mistakes I never would have made otherwise. He made me learn the hard way. I never felt like I had anyone to talk to.

"Maybe the worst thing was, he made me feel that I was a bad person."

The two parents debated one another. The man insisted that he loved his children. The woman said he didn't. If he did, she said, he would trust them.

I believed that the man sincerely loved his children, but I also had a strong suspicion that they didn't *feel* loved.

Parents, such as this father, who rely on strict authority and punishment to prevent drug problems are usually well-intentioned. They take what appears to be powerful action but often discover later, sometimes much later, that their power is an illusion. They huff and puff while their children openly rebel against them or sneak around behind their backs. The children become contemptuous, secretive, and cunning. As parents try to clamp down, their teenage children become more defiant.

Authoritarian parents have a one-dimensional sense of power. They see power as attempting to control the behavior of their children. They don't understand that control power is not only ineffective, but counter to the healthy development of adolescents who are striving for independence.

To quote a knowledgeable friend of mine, "Parents should give away power before it is taken away."

This gets back to the central theme of this book—empowerment.

Parents who involve their children in discussions about rules and limits give away a certain measure of control. They surrender the right to arbitrarily set limits without input. Yet, this is appropriate. In fact, the more teenagers demonstrate responsible decision making, the more they should be granted freedom and responsibility. This is inherent in the transfer of power that occurs throughout childhood. By the time children become young adults, they should be prepared for independence.

The exchange of information process promotes a gradual transfer of power from parent to child. In so doing, it maximizes parental influence by promoting the strongest power that parents possess— the power to influence by education. Children who feel safe with their parents will come to them for help and advice when they need it. They will use the guidance of their parents to make wise decisions.

CONTROL VERSUS TRUST: A TRADE-OFF

Helping a child grow means to gradually give always a little more responsibility than the child has had before. By relinquishing control, parents extend trust to their children, who thereby gain self-esteem.

A mother allowed her teenage son, David, to attend a large party at school. He said there wouldn't be any drugs. She was concerned, however, that a small group of students might bring alcohol or pot. She was making a trade-off. She traded control (she could keep him at home under her observation) for trust (she was going to show confidence in his good judgment). David knew that he should stay away from drugs and his mother trusted that he would do that.

Will David succeed with the freedom and responsibility that have been extended?

The answer to this question depends upon what is meant by success. It is inconceivable that a child (or anyone) would never make mistakes. We all experimented and made mistakes in adolescence. If success means never making mistakes, then extending trust is doomed to failure. On the other hand, if it means doing one's best and learning from mistakes, then trust helps children develop competence. If you believe in children and help them learn from their experiences, they will have their ups and downs but ultimately do just fine.

David went to the party, was surprised to see that drugs were being used, but steered clear of the substances. His mother had given him freedom that he was able to handle successfully. David wasn't even tempted by the drugs. Had he been tempted, he and his mother had the sort of relationship in which they could have had an honest discussion.

DISCIPLINED PASSION

"What? No pounding fists? No threatening gestures? Where's the passion in the exchange of information process?"

These are questions asked by parents who hold strong convictions about drugs and are concerned that the exchange could be as boring as white bread.

On the contrary, success with this method requires passion. Because you care, you *should* have strong feelings and convictions about drugs. The exchange process gives you a rational and disciplined way to express your feelings and a structure for thoughtful and loving discussion of issues that arouse your passion.

Feelings are discussed during the exchange, but carefully. They are described in detail, not acted out. Intensity of feeling is expressed in words rather than gestures. The idea is not to intimidate children, but to let them know what you are thinking and feeling and to let you know what *they* are thinking and feeling.

Below are examples of two different ways that parents communicated their feelings in similar situations. The first is an undisciplined expression of emotion.

When Maria, age sixteen, came home an hour past curfew without calling, her father turned red in the face, yelled at her, and called her "an irresponsible girl." Without even responding, Maria ducked into her bedroom. But her dad threw open the door and angrily told her she couldn't go out for two weeks. Then he left.

Another girl, Marsha, also came home past her curfew without calling. Her father was much more caring and disciplined about what he said. He explained he had been scared that something bad might have happened. When Marsha said she was fine but simply lost track of time, her dad said he was angry and that she would have to be more careful in the future. Marsha apologized, said she could understand his point of view, and promised she would do better next time. Her dad was glad to hear that she understood, but said she would have to wait two weeks for another opportunity to go out on a weekend night.

130

Both parents punished their daughters. Some people might not feel that punishment was necessary in the second example because Marsha admitted her mistake. Regardless, the communication was more effective. Marsha definitely heard what was said. She knew that her father had been worried. She understood that he was angry and why. Marsha's father knew that his daughter had not deliberately defied the curfew, but that she had been careless. He knew she regretted her error. This type of caring and disciplined communication is what takes place during the exchange of information.

In addition to the communication of feelings, the exchange process allows for strong and passionate opinions. After all, we're talking about drugs here, very powerful substances. Children would be short-changed if their parents didn't share their opinions and convictions. This isn't to say that parents have all the answers, although they do have more experience and are responsible for the well-being of their children. In the exchange process, strong opinions are stated, described, discussed, and explained. They are not arbitrarily imposed. It's one thing to have strong convictions and something else to impose them on others.

PREPARATION: A CLEAR POINT OF VIEW

An open and honest discussion with teenagers about drugs is an ambitious goal, requiring a great deal of preparation. The first part of preparation is being sure of your own point of view. This means being informed about alcohol and other drugs. If you are confused or uninformed, you won't be able to help your children achieve clarity. You don't need to become a drug expert, or learn street lingo. The basics of drug knowledge, enough information to engage in the exchange, is included in Chapter 2 of this book.

Be careful of the pitfall of self-certainty, best summarized by the phrase: "If I think it's so, then it must be so." Your point of view is based on three different elements. One part is facts. Another part is interpretation of facts. A third part is values. In preparing for discussions about drugs, it's important to learn to differentiate the three.

Failure to differentiate results in confusion. In a counseling session, I heard this exchange between a parent and child that illustrates the confusion of facts and opinions. The topic was marijuana. First, some

131

facts: Marijuana is an illegal drug that creates a mild euphoria among users. Now the dialogue, with my comments in parentheses:

Parent: "Marijuana is illegal."

Child: "Yeah, I know."

(As you see, they agree on the facts.)

Parent: "It's a very bad drug, I don't want you using it. You understand?"

(Here we see an opinion presented without any factual backup.)

Child: "It's not any worse than the martinis you drink."

(The child is responding tit for tat.)

Parent: "Anyone who smokes marijuana would have to be crazy."

(An opinion presented as fact.)

Child: "I don't agree. I know kids at school who smoke, and they aren't crazy."

Parent: "Well, it's illegal."

Child: "So is speeding on the freeway. You do *that* all the time. Are you crazy?"

In this dialogue, the parent and child agreed about the illegality of the substance. But when the parent began presenting opinion as if it were fact, the child became oppositional and was prepared to argue against *anything* that was said.

Opinions about what is good and bad are almost always subject to debate. The same is true with right and wrong. In a good discussion, people have their opinions, perhaps strong ones, but don't state them as fact. However, they are capable of explaining why they hold a particular opinion. They can say in their own words: "This is what I know is a fact. . . . This is my opinion about the facts. . . ."

Even though opinions and values are subjective, they are still an important consideration in drug discussions and agreements. This is well illustrated by a statement that a father made to his son during a counseling session:

"I'm strongly opposed to teenagers' drinking alcohol at parties. I know that alcohol helps people relax. But if you use it to relax, you won't learn to deal with people. The alcohol will cover your nervousness at parties. In my opinion, it's important to muck your way through tense feelings, to learn how to connect with other kids, and to enjoy being around them without using drugs. I think it's not a good idea to go to parties where kids are drinking. If someone does bring alcohol to a party, I want you to abstain."

PREPARATION: BEING PERSONAL

The effectiveness of the exchange of information is based on honesty and openness, a two-way affair. Parents who want their children to talk openly about themselves should be prepared to do likewise. Your children will be curious about your own history with drugs.

Your point of view will certainly reflect your life experiences. In a counseling session, a father who was a police patrol officer expressed his strong feelings to his daughter about alcohol at parties. He told her that he didn't want her going to parties where alcohol was served. He recognized that his own viewpoint was skewed by his experiences as a police officer:

"You know, because of my work I'm particularly sensitive about legal issues. And because you're a minor, you shouldn't drink alcohol. But the toughest thing for me is that I see firsthand the most horrible results of drunk driving. I know I'm probably supersensitive because of my work experiences. But that's part of who I am. I want you to be able to go to parties, but not to those with drugs and alcohol. I want to be able to relax when you go out. I couldn't relax if you were at a party where drugs were present."

Though his daughter wanted more freedom, the father's ability to articulate the *personal* basis for his point of view helped them understand each other and reach an agreement.

In the course of a discussion about drugs, it's very likely that teenagers will ask you about your own habits and experiences, past and present. You're a role model. There's no escaping it. Parents who haven't resolved their own drug problems, and there are millions of them in this country, will have diminished effectiveness with their children. Sometimes the realization of this influence on children serves to motivate parents to get much-needed help for themselves.

You don't have to have a flawless background to be a good influence on your children. If you've had drug problems, it's important only that you've solved them or are in the process of solving them and that you can explain your experiences. Such candor is appreciated. The more you open up, the easier it will be for your children to talk honestly.

Some parents think that to be effective with their children they themselves should be drug free. They believe they will have to give up their glass of wine with dinner and cocktails over the weekend if they are to ask their children to refrain from indulging. These parents need to realize that there's a difference between a mature adult using substances and a teenager. Furthermore, adults who use legal drugs responsibly provide an excellent role model for future behavior.

PREPARATION: WHAT IF YOU DON'T LIKE WHAT YOU HEAR?

Once your own ideas are clear, another part of preparation is thinking ahead to what your children might say. You may not like what you hear. Your children may be thinking thoughts, or doing things, that make you uncomfortable. Even if they aren't, they still may test your sincerity by saying that they are. How will you respond if you hear something discomforting? Some parents panic about the safety of their children. Others feel insecure about themselves ("I've failed"), which may be translated into resentment and insecurity about their children ("They have failed me"). Will you be tempted to slip into the mode of control power?

I gained insight into this tendency during a workshop I conducted for parents and teenagers at a swanky hotel a few years ago. I asked some of the teenagers in the audience to volunteer to come to the microphone. Then I asked them if they could talk openly about drugs with their parents.

I had done this before. Occasionally one or two teens would say they could talk with their parents, but the majority would say they couldn't. Then I would ask the ones who couldn't talk why this was so. Usually they feared punishment or a lecture of some sort.

On this particular occasion, eight teenagers were on stage with me, *all saying they could talk openly with their parents.* If they could talk with their parents, I wondered, why was I invited to discuss communication problems? Something was wrong.

I probed a little, first asking one child:

"Are you sure you can talk openly about drugs?"

"Yes."

"How about you?" I asked another.

"Yes."

"You?"

"Yes."

I was getting nowhere.

"Can you talk about sex?"

An echo of yesses reverberated. It appeared that these kids had good communication with their parents. It was a rare audience. I began to wonder if I was in the right conference room. But then I figured it out:

"What if you smoked pot. Could you tell your mom?"

"No way! Are you kidding?"

Aha. These kids could talk with their parents about anything, even sex and drugs, as long as they said exactly what their parents wanted to hear. Communication would break down if they said something that their parents didn't want to hear.

The exchange of information process will not work if parents panic. To be successful, it's essential that you accept a child's opinions or actions as the *starting point* for discussion. At times the temptation will be to revert to strict authority, harsh criticism, and punishment. That will mean converting to the ever-so-easy mode of control power. It will probably mean the end of honest and open discussion, too. Momentary control may be gained, but the chance of a significant learning experience will be reduced. In the teenage years, the best educational experiences always involve dialogue.

In preparing for what you might hear, I think it helps to be aware of a certain paradox. I suggest that you imagine the worst possible scenario about a child.

Maybe you will think about a teenage daughter admitting to regular use of cocaine. Pretty terrible, but let's make it worse. Suppose this same girl is also pregnant.

This scenario could get anyone's heart beating rapidly. If you could respond to this situation without panic, in spite of inner turmoil, then your teenagers will be able to talk to you. The ideal response would be something like this, said with affection:

"I love you. I'm on your side. I'm glad you could tell me what has happened. Solving this problem won't be easy, but together we can figure it out."

In other words, if children are certain that you won't panic, that the roof won't cave in on them, then they will feel free to talk. If the lines of communication are open, they will have the benefit of your mature input into their decision-making process. In this way, the disaster visualized above, and other terrible problems, can be avoided.

A cool, calm, and collected parental response to hearing something painful will go a long way toward increasing understanding. Such calmness requires discipline but pays great dividends.

THE SHY CHILD

At drug workshops, some parents have said that their children are very introverted and shy about talking about themselves. They doubted that the exchange of information process would work with them.

My response surprises them. I say that their children *especially* need the exchange. If they cannot articulate their feelings, then they are holding them inside and proceeding without feedback and input from others. These children are isolated, alone. They need support to deal with drug pressures and temptations. They need parents who will help them open up and overcome their emotional barriers.

This doesn't mean the hammer approach. Intimidation won't work. It means parents empathizing with their children about how hard it is for them to express themselves, yet saying that they must learn to overcome their shyness. It is only by bringing their inner thoughts and feelings into "public" view that children can benefit from guidance and support.

Shy children will not open up suddenly. They need encouragement but also patience and, most of all, the feeling of safety. As they reveal their inner thoughts, parents should be accepting and supportive.

If a child is severely withdrawn, the family might need to seek professional help.

THE METHOD: CAN WE TALK?

The exchange of information process borrows from Joan Rivers. The first step is to ask, "Can we talk?" The difference between her approach and this is that she talks regardless of your wishes.

In the exchange format, "Can we talk?" is a serious question. Without consent, it's pointless to proceed.

A discussion should be proposed in a relaxed, nonthreatening way, with enthusiasm rather than anxiety, possibly after the topic of drugs arises spontaneously, or simply as a subject worthy of discussion. You can calmly say, "I'd like us to talk about drugs. What do you think?"

If you're the parent of an eleven-year-old or older child and you haven't previously broached the subject of drugs, you might start by expressing your own desire to "get with it":

"I know that lots of kids begin to drink and use drugs at a young age. Let's talk. I want to know your thoughts and feelings, and I want to tell you mine. How does that sound?"

A child's response to this proposition will be influenced by previous history. An enthusiastic "Yes, let's talk" would be unusual. If your child does agree, you can proceed to the next step—the discussion itself.

One possible response to a proposed discussion is, "No way, I'm not going to talk with you." If this happens, the most important issue is the family climate, not drugs. The question becomes: What can be done to improve the climate so that discussions can take place?

Another common response to the "Can we talk?" question is an unconvincing, "Yeah, yeah, sure, go ahead."

The not-so-hidden message is:

"Get it over with. Give me your usual lecture. Set the rules as usual. I'll pretend I'm listening."

Eager parents take this "Yeah, yeah, sure" literally and begin the discussion. It's a mistake because the child has not really agreed to talk. The best response is:

"It doesn't sound like you sincerely *want* to talk. You're not at all convincing."

This will probably elicit another "Oh, just go ahead" with an implied "Get it over with."

But this "Go ahead" is no more convincing than the initial one. The parent again should resist the temptation to proceed:

"It *really* doesn't sound as if you're ready for a discussion. It sounds more like you want to go through the motions and get it over with. I don't want to have a discussion until I'm sure you want to talk. I want to talk *with* you, not *at* you."

If your child says "No way" about a discussion or persists with an insincere "Yeah, yeah, sure," then you have to work on improving communications before you can discuss drugs.

Behind every "No, I won't talk" is an unspoken reason. To open the dialogue, the obstacles must be revealed and addressed. This means probing for problems. Sometimes it's a simple misunderstanding, sometimes just a minor reluctance to proceed. But be prepared. Asking about obstacles to a dialogue about drugs is an invitation to be criticized.

This is the hard part of opening the dialogue. If you ask your children to honestly say what keeps them from talking, you must be willing to hear their criticism and to make some changes. Sometimes you even have to courageously invite and encourage criticism:

"Why is it that you can't talk about drugs with me? I'm willing to hear your feelings and your criticism. I'll take them seriously. I know you have to feel safe to talk. If I've done anything to keep you from opening up with me, I want to hear about it."

It takes major-league commitment to invite criticism. But the alternative—a poor one—is a closed relationship and diminished influence about drugs and other important decisions.

Some parents worry that accepting criticism from their children means admitting mistakes and therefore losing authority. While it does sometimes mean admitting mistakes, such an admission is a positive step. It shows that you are listening to your children. Also, you set a good example: You want your children to admit mistakes too, so that they can learn from their experiences.

FIVE OBJECTIONS TO TALKING

When parents ask their children why they can't talk freely about drugs, five major reasons are usually given: anger about not being trusted; suspicion about sudden interest in dialogue; doubts that they will be understood; fear that they will be punished; and fear that they will be given a lecture. These reasons are listed below along with a commentary on each and a suggested response.

Objection: "What's the matter? Don't you trust me? I'm probably the only kid in my class who doesn't use drugs. You should see the other kids. But with my luck, I'm the one who has a mom who accuses me. I don't even drink alcohol. You're being ridiculous. I wish you'd leave me alone."

Commentary: Children who are not accustomed to open-ended discussions about personal matters may assume that their parents are suspicious about them. Parents need to make clear the purpose of the discussion and offer reassurance that they are not suspicious (if they aren't). If there is reason to suspect drug use, you can be honest about that, too, yet express an openness about hearing differently.

Response: "It's important that we be able to talk about things like drugs in this family. I'm not accusing you. I'm glad you don't use drugs and that you're doing so well without my input. But there are drugs all around. It must be hard if you're one of the few kids who don't use them. I think these are tough times to be a teenager. I want to be on your side. To do that we need to talk with each other."

Objection: "Why the sudden interest in talking? You never seemed interested in what I was thinking before. Did you read a self-help book or something? No way I'm going to talk with you."

Commentary: This is an understandable response in a family in which personal issues have not been discussed very much. Children will wonder: Why now? Under these circumstances it helps to begin with a little self-criticism.

Response: "You know, with all the news about young people using drugs, I think I've been kind of hiding my head in the sand and shirking my responsibilities by not discussing drugs with you sooner. Not that I suspect you're using them or anything, but simply because I know that drugs are available and I want our home to be a place where you can talk about everything. I want to face this issue together. And by the way, you're right. I did read a self-help book. I want to be the best possible parent I can be. I want this to be the beginning of a positive change. We need to start talking with each other."

Objection: "Don't be silly. I don't want to talk with you. You'd be the last ones I'd talk with. Times have changed since you were a teenager. You wouldn't understand."

Commentary: Times certainly do change. The concern about misunderstanding is probably sincere. But the whole idea of good communication is to break barriers and reach mutual understanding. This point needs to be stressed.

Response: "I'm sorry you see us [the parents] as the last ones you'd want to talk with, because if things were right in our family, we really should be the first. I know we're from a different generation. I know times have changed. That's why we want to have a dialogue. We want to be able to understand the changes. If we don't talk with you, we'll be out of touch. And you know, we do have *some* knowledge and experience. We want to share it with you."

Objection: "Yeah, sure, talk with you and get punished. Forget it. Even if I told you why I *don't* want to talk, you'd punish me."

Commentary: If punishment has been the mode in the family, then teenagers most certainly will expect the same in the future. Even if it hasn't been the mode, children may fear it. You need to reassure your children that you want mutual understanding and won't be punitive. Punishment would not lead to the type of results desired in the exchange of information. You should provide amnesty (or forgiveness) for what has happened to date. Remember: Amnesty doesn't preclude stating a strong point of view and establishing high standards of behavior henceforth.

Response: "I promise that I won't punish you for what you say or what you've done. I know that at times I've lost my temper when you've told me something I didn't want to hear. This time I'll listen to you. I'll take what you say seriously. I promise. But if you're using drugs, I will want us to have a serious talk."

Objection: "I know what you'll do if we talk. You'll lecture me just like you always do. You'll tell me that when you were a kid you never did things like kids do nowadays. Then if I argue, you'll interrupt me and turn stone cold."

Commentary: If you've been preachy in your discussions to date, small wonder your children anticipate more of the same. Remember, the exchange of information is based on dialogue. You need to listen attentively, without interrupting. When you give opinions, instead of lecturing, explain the *reasoning* behind your opinions.

Response: "You're right. I've been preachy at times. It's been a mistake. This time I'll try to share my opinions with you, but I won't lecture. And I'll listen to what you think and feel. Things are going to be different, because I want us to have good discussions. Most of all, you can be sure that I won't panic and throw down some big punishment." (Some parents worry that making this commitment leaves them powerless if they discover their child is harmfully involved with drugs. This again underestimates their ability to influence their children through reasoned discussions.)

IT TAKES TIME

The transition from a closed family to one with open communication takes time. One of the most effective and underused communication methods is backing off and giving space.

When a teenager is wavering, perhaps he or she is thinking, "I don't know if I really want to talk with you yet." This is an opportune moment for backing off.

An effective reply is: "Why don't you think about it a while, and we'll discuss it again in a couple of days."

Sometimes people need time to think in privacy. The whole idea that a parent is willing to *really* listen and won't dish out heavy-duty punishment might take a while to sink into the consciousness of a teenager who expects a parental lecture followed by parental control. The willingness to back off shows that you are going to be respectful.

Patience is a virtue in the exchange of information. Usually that patience is rewarded. Sometimes the discussion will take place right away. In most cases, children will at least begin talking about their hesitations within the first week. Even if dealing with drugs is put on the shelf temporarily, improving the family climate is the most important first step toward parents' having a powerful educational influence on their children. It may take time to build up trust. But it will be time well spent.

Meanwhile you are sure about one thing: Because you love your children, you will persevere in your efforts to open the dialogue about drugs. You would be doing them a disservice if you did anything less. You will continue to work for a dialogue until it happens.

WHEN YOU FIND CIGARETTE PAPERS IN YOUR CHILD'S DRESSER

After explaining the exchange of information process to parents, I like to use role-playing techniques to demonstrate the method.

This is the situation I often present at workshops:

You have done your son's laundry and are putting his shorts in his dresser. You are *not* snooping. To your great surprise you stumble upon cigarette papers. You know that they can be used to roll joints. You've never talked about drugs with your child. That evening after dinner, you ask your son if you can have a personal talk. He stays behind. You want to open the dialogue about drugs. How do you do it?

When I first started using this exercise in workshops, I let parents do the role-playing with each other, one parent playing the role of a parent and another one playing the role of a son. But I noticed that most of the time, the one who played the parent scared the daylights out of the one who played a child, usually by bringing up the issue of the cigarette papers very abruptly. So nowadays I usually ask a parent to play the role of the teenager, but I play the parent.

Realizing that there are a variety of ways to successfully open a dialogue about drugs, I play my part differently depending upon the audience. If the parents tend to be alarmists, I ignore the discovery of cigarette papers. By doing this I emphasize that the issue is opening the dialogue, not building a case based on evidence. I figure if drugs have never been discussed in this imaginary family, I can start a discussion at the ground floor without mentioning the cigarette papers. The drawback of this tactic is that it leaves me, the parent, with a secret, and perhaps also a burning desire to discuss it.

At other times in this role-playing, I take a different approach and discuss the cigarette papers. Below is the transcript of such an interaction I had with a parent who played the role of a difficult teenager. After I asked, "Can we talk?" this is what happened between my "son" and me:

Me: "You know, I was putting away your laundry today when I stumbled upon cigarette papers in your drawer. I really wasn't snooping. I was just . . ."

Teenager (played by a parent): "You what? You were snooping in my room! Damn it, I can't have any privacy. This house is awful. You had no business looking through my things."

Me: "I wasn't looking through your things. I never do that. I was putting away your laundry. That's all."

Teenager: "You creep. You snoop."

Me: "Please, don't get nasty and call me names. I wasn't snooping and I'm not accusing you of anything. I realize you're fourteen years old and we've never really had a talk about drugs. I think we should be talking, and it's my mistake that we haven't. Whatever you're doing, using them or not, we need to talk and understand each other.

Teenager: "Well, I don't want to talk with you. Not after you were looking through my dresser."

Me: "Truly, I wasn't snooping. But I can see you're upset and not ready to talk right now. I'm going to wait a couple of days before bringing it up again. But I do want us to be able to talk."

As you can see, in the role-playing I was self-critical about not discussing drugs sooner. Self-criticism is a powerful tool in developing a positive family climate. It is disarming. When parents are honestly critical of themselves, children feel safer. They feel that they can be more open and admit their own mistakes.

I gave my "child" a few days to "calm down." We then continued the role-playing.

Me: "Son, I want us to talk openly about drugs. You know it's really hard for me to bring up the topic, and I'm sure it's hard for you to talk about it with me. But I want us to have good communication. I love you a lot."

Teenager: "Go ahead, get it over with. Let me hear your lecture."

Me: "I don't want to lecture you. I'm sorry if that's what you expect. I want us each to talk."

Teenager: "Yeah, sure. I'll tell you what I think and you'll punish me."

Me: "I promise I won't."

Teenager: "You say that now. Maybe you won't do anything right away. But who knows, a week or two later when you're mad about something, you'll probably throw it back in my face."

Me: "If I've done that before, I'm sorry. I promise I won't do it now. I want us to reach some understandings. I'll tell you what I honestly think. But I'll also be respectful of your opinions."

Teenager: "That'll be a change."

Me: "Yeah, it will. But it's the kind of change I want to make."

Teenager: "Well, I've tried pot. It's no big deal."

Me: "I'm glad you could tell me that. I want to keep on talking so we can understand each other."

In playing my role, it was difficult hearing that my son had smoked pot. I regretted I had waited so long to talk with him. But I knew that we were making progress. We began talking. We opened the dialogue. And through our discussions, I believed I could have a positive influence.

Once the dialogue is begun, the next tasks in the exchange of information are getting everything into the open and making family agreements. The following two chapters tell how to do it.

6

LISTENING TO EACH OTHER

You could cut the tension in the room with a knife. Mrs. Robbins, home from a workshop on drugs, started a discussion with her son, Mark, who seemed reluctant to talk. He complained that she overreacts to everything. She promised to stay calm but knew it wouldn't be easy because Mark's reluctance made her suspect that he might have something to hide.

"I think," Mark said, "that kids using drugs is no big deal. Lots of kids smoke pot. And I think the reaction of adults to cocaine is *way* overblown."

Mrs. Robbins bordered on panic. She had promised constraint and now wondered if it was a mistake. She sat their quietly as Mark continued.

"But Mom, I'm not interested in drugs. It's just not my thing."

Suddenly, Mrs. Robbins was almost ecstatic, but not quite. She needed reassurance. "Really?" she asked.

"Mom, don't you trust me?"

She thought for a moment. She knew the various signs and symptoms of possible drug use. Mark had shown none of them. Mark had a history of responsible behavior. He hadn't lied to her about anything.

"Yes, I do trust you," she told Mark.

"Then let's drop it already. I want to go do my homework."

Mrs. Robbins knew that many parents would kill to have their kids eager to do homework. So she happily dropped the topic.

Mark had told the truth. He had never used drugs and had no interest in them. But by ending the conversation as she did, Mrs.

145

Robbins missed an important opportunity for a discussion. She could have trusted her son, as he requested, but still talked with him and helped him become more fully informed and prepared for future decisions about drugs.

That same evening, a few houses away, Mr. and Mrs. Jordan, who also had attended the drug workshop, had a discussion with their daughter, Lisa.

"Sure I smoke pot," she told her parents. "What's the big deal?"

Her confession started a long and serious discussion. Lisa explained why she smoked. "Everything's more fun when you're high. I like it. Anyway, it's the same as you guys having a couple of cocktails at night."

The Jordans listened to their daughter and then very reasonably explained their thoughts and feelings. They emphasized the health risks, the risks of addiction, and the possible legal consequences.

The discussion and argument dragged on for almost two hours. Mr. and Mrs. Jordan wanted "success," but not based on a rule they couldn't possibly enforce (Lisa could smoke pot secretly). They wanted "success" based on education. They wanted Lisa to understand the potential harm of using drugs and, on that basis, agree to stop.

After a very lengthy discussion, Lisa finally said she would not smoke pot anymore. Her parents beamed with satisfaction, thinking they had successfully confronted a very tough issue without making threats. They didn't realize that Lisa had grown tired of the endless debate. They hadn't attempted to impose harsh rules, but their desire for immediate success led them into a long and embattled competition of words. Lisa felt the discussion wouldn't end until she agreed with their point of view. So she agreed to give up pot, but never really intended to hold to that agreement.

As you can see with both families, there are many pitfalls in discussions about drugs. Mrs. Robbins missed an opportunity to help prepare her son for future decisions. Mr. and Mrs. Jordan overpowered their daughter with words.

This chapter will help you avoid these and other pitfalls. In the preceding chapter, the first stage of the exchange of information process was presented: opening the dialogue. Once it's open, it's time for the discussion to begin. In this chapter the focus is on parents and children explaining and clarifying their points of view. The emphasis is on promoting openness so that your children can speak freely. The emphasis is also on using communication skills to help your children expand their awareness.

BEGIN WITH YOUR THOUGHTS AND FEELINGS

Someone has to go first in this discussion. Ask your children what they prefer. Probably they'll want you to start, just to get a feel for your position.

Much of what you say will be personal, based on your own values and experiences. My recommendation is to start with a statement that demonstrates open-mindedness about drugs and shows your love. Then continue by sharing some of your beliefs and opinions. Keep your opening statement brief, bearing in mind that this is only the beginning of a dialogue and the first of many discussions. You don't have to say everything.

Most children will have heard "drugs are terrible" statements from radio and television public service announcements and possibly school antidrug programs. They may have heard "drugs are wonderful" statements from friends, siblings, and other sources.

In your opening remarks, I recommend a more neutral "drugs are available" and "drugs are powerful" statement. In this context, you can say that you want to be on your child's side in facing this drug-filled world. One father put it this way:

"I know that anyone who wants to get alcohol and other drugs can get them, even kids. Because drugs are such powerful substances, I think it's important we talk about them. I want to support you.

"Drugs change the way people feel and behave. They can make people feel good or make them feel bad. People take drugs to feel good, but as you may know, they can cause serious problems, too."

I liked this beginning. This parent avoided pharmacological statements. He knew there was plenty of time for that later.

Some children, however, may be curious about drug pharmacology and ask questions. If this happens, Chapter 2 provides basic information to answer many of the questions that might be asked.

Now talk about yourself—your opinions, attitudes, and experiences. You might want to discuss how you have seen people affected by drugs and how you have been affected. Perhaps you might mention how your opinions have changed over the years. I recommend maximum self-disclosure. The more you open up, the more your children will do likewise.

If you have a problem with alcohol or other drugs, it's best to admit it. Hopefully you are working on it yourself. You can talk honestly about how drugs have adversely affected you and how you would like your children to be spared the pain you've suffered. If you're not working on it, don't expect that your discussion about drugs will carry much clout with your children.

In this stage of the exchange of information, one task is to begin to discuss your beliefs about teenagers and drugs. As you speak, make a distinction between facts and opinions. You might say, for example: "My opinion about teenagers drinking alcohol is . . . I base this opinion on these facts. . . . I base it on these observations. . . . I base it on these experiences. . . ."

Be brief. Say a little and give your child a chance to talk. Most of all, right from the beginning, it is important to avoid what I call conversation stoppers. These are threats or extreme statements that cast aspersions on anyone who might think or behave a certain way. These statements abruptly end discussions:

- "Anyone who does drugs has to be crazy." (There goes the mutual respect. If a child has experimented even once, he or she has been put down and may simply clam up.)
- "Anyone who thinks about doing drugs is irresponsible." (This silences the child who has even *thought* about it.)
- "No one in this family would ever even consider using drugs." (A child may wonder, "What am I, chopped liver?")
- "If I ever find out one of my kids has used drugs, I'll turn him over to the police." (Testing a threat like this would be a worthy challenge for a teenager working on a sense of independent identity.)

YOUR POSITION ON DRUG USE

This stage of the exchange is not the time to set rules. In this part of the discussion, you are sharing thoughts and feelings. The rules and agreements are established during the final stage of the dialogue, after everyone has had an opportunity to speak.

My recommendation to parents of young children and young teenagers is an unequivocal no on drugs. Personally, I would say something like this:

"The reason I don't think children should use alcohol or other drugs is because this is a time for you to learn to get high on life, without drugs. It's a time to learn how to cope with stress and how to solve problems, without drugs. It's a time to learn how to make good relationships, without drugs. But if you get high on drugs, it can keep you from developing your own inner strength.

"Anyway, drugs are powerful substances and can be harmful. As you know, even adults make poor decisions about drug use and can't control themselves. I think the risks are much greater for young people. And drugs are illegal. I don't want you to break the law. That's my point of view."

I would save the issues of addiction, peer pressure, and lack of life experience for later, once the flow of the discussion is going.

I personally believe that as a society we should send a no-drug-use message to children. Even if many children experiment without harm, too many of them are harmed. I see no reason that children should be using drugs, and I think we should not accept the notion that drug experimentation by children is inevitable. It's inevitable only if we fail to set a high standard.

You may have different ideas about the unequivocal "say no" attitude I just described. A convincing argument could be made that certain older teenagers have the ability to control their use of alcohol or other drugs and could use these substances without substantial harm, even though it would be illegal. Literally millions of adults smoke pot without significant harm and that, too, is illegal. Many of these adults have not developed a dependence and are willing to take the risk of breaking the law. It is possible, therefore, that some older, more mature teenagers could do the same and that some parents would approve. These are personal decisions involving risks that you and your children may be willing to take.

I trust you're aware of the dangers of drugs. I'm not going to try to scare you away from your position. This doesn't mean, as I'm afraid some readers might misunderstand, that I approve of drug use, only that I can't tell people what to do with their own children. However, I do *not* recommend allowing drug use, and I urge you, if you permit it, to closely and carefully monitor what happens to make certain that no self-deception takes place about possible harm.

Because most parents share my point of view about children—even

149

older ones—not using drugs, this chapter and the next are written from this perspective. If you accept drug use by older teenagers, you can still use the same principles of communication and negotiation, but you will have to extrapolate the specific applications.

STOP TO LISTEN

Now that you've started the discussion, it's time for your children to talk. Ask them what they think. For a dialogue to occur, the atmosphere has to remain loving and supportive. You want your children to feel safe. Like anyone else, they won't talk openly about personal matters if they feel threatened.

If I had only three words to say about good dialogue, they would be: *Listen to understand*, that is, listen without defensiveness or distortion. When emotions are aroused, this is sometimes easier said than done. However, try to avoid interruptions and the temptation to pick apart, rather than to understand, what your children say.

Concentrate on listening. Try to avoid distortions. In an extreme example, a teenage girl asks to have her curfew extended past midnight because of a very special party. Her father says: "You're telling me that you want me to say it's okay for you to use drugs and have sex. Well, I won't say that." This father is listening to his own assumptions and not to the words of his daughter.

One helpful listening technique is simple—to pause and take a moment to think about what you heard before responding. This prevents interruptions and reduces defensiveness.

Another excellent technique for good listening is to paraphrase what someone said: "Let me see if I understand you. It sounds like you feel . . ."

When paraphrasing, you don't agree, disagree, or interpret. You just validate your understanding.

WHAT YOUR CHILDREN THINK ABOUT DRUGS

Younger adolescents and more protected ones might be confused by the question: "What do you think about drugs?" They might answer with a question of their own: "What do you mean by that?"

A parent could answer: "I mean what's your opinion? Do you know about them? Are they available in your school? Do you know people who use them? Have you thought about using them? Do they scare you? Do they interest you? These are the sorts of things I mean."

Even the most frightening statistics about drugs show that a large percentage of teenagers do not use them. Don't be surprised if your teenager says: "I think drugs are stupid. I wouldn't touch 'em with a ten-foot pole."

Even if your children say this, *it's still important to talk.* Remember that the discussion isn't simply for your reassurance. The idea is to help expand the thinking of your children. Calling drugs stupid is an interesting remark, but reveals very little about underlying thoughts. You can ask your children why they think that drugs are stupid. Perhaps point out the positive uses of some drugs—aspirin and penicillin, for example. Ask them if they know that some people take drugs to "feel good." You can mention the responsible way that some adults drink alcohol.

It might appear that this is encouraging drug use. On the contrary, these are facts that do not have to be hidden. Children will eventually see the positive side of drugs. Full disclosure gives you credibility. Children can deal with the truth, especially at this point, when they're not even inclined toward drug use. Now is a good time to catch their attention. Your candor puts you in good standing for future discussions. Later, when they may be more interested in experimenting, they will think: "I can trust my parents to be honest and open-minded."

At this point, your children might ask: "So, why shouldn't I take drugs?" This would be an opportunity to help them see that the dangers and risks outweigh the benefits. Remember the idea is to get them thinking. If this thinking doesn't occur, a child who calls drugs "stupid" at one stage, without thinking, might call them "super" a short time later, also without thinking.

Here are some additional questions you could ask:

- Do you know kids who use drugs in your school?
- How has it affected them? How do you think it will affect them later?
- Have you ever been offered drugs?
- (If so) What did you say? Were you tempted?
- (If not) What would you say if you were offered drugs?
- (This can be taken further) What if friends really pushed you

151

to try them? What if they said, "Don't be so chicken. They're a lot of fun and *we're all doing it*"?

The intent of these questions is to help expand your children's consciousness. Fo you, it's an opportunity to assess their knowledge of the topic and their ability to respond to pressure. If it appears your children might have difficulty resisting peer pressure, you can review Chapter 4 and help them learn the skill of assertiveness.

If your children are not interested in using drugs, it will be easy to reach a no-drug-use agreement.

Much of the rest of this chapter is about discussions with children who have used or are considering the use of drugs. Even if your children do not fit this description, you'll probably find the communication techniques of value for discussions of other topics and possibly for future discussions about drugs.

THE BIG LIE

With the exchange of information process, you can be direct and ask your children whether they've ever used drugs.

Of course, any former drug abuser worth his salt would surely tell you that he frequently lied to his parents.

"My parents were so stupid," an addicted teenager once told me. "They used to drive me to parties where we did a ton of drugs. They had no idea what was going on. If they'd asked, I would have lied."

"So," you might wonder, "how can I know whether to trust a child, and what's the use of asking if I'll never get an honest answer anyway?"

Many former addicts and parents of addicts, drawing on their own experience, say that people who use drugs can't be trusted. They recommend an inquisition of teenage children, extending to room searches and urinalyses.

People who have endured serious drug problems may not be aware of something very important: Many people have *excellent* family relationships and *will* be honest about drugs. Many children who think about using drugs or have experimented with them are not pathological liars. They may even be frightening themselves with their drug use or with their temptation to use drugs and therefore welcome an opportunity to talk.

Certainly you don't want to be a patsy to drug use by your kids. However, if they are past the stage of honesty and are harmfully involved with drugs, there are signs that give it away. Keep your ears up and eyes wide open. These are the best safeguards against naive unawareness. Stay alert to the signs and symptoms discussed in Chapter 2, keeping in mind, though, that these indicators can also be caused by other problems.

You should be concerned, for example, if a child's performance begins to decline at school, if he is suddenly found to be in possession of large sums of money, if he shows less motivation to succeed, if he has less interest in extrcurricular activities, and if he is increasingly absent or tardy at school. If several of these events occur, you would be unwise to accept a simple "I'm not using drugs" assertion. These are signs that something is wrong. Whether it's drug related or not, it demands your attention.

On the other hand, you don't have to accuse a child of anything. If signs of some sort of a problem are clear, you don't look away from it. The question shifts: "If you're not using drugs, then how do you explain what's happening? What is the problem? What are *your* solutions? When can we expect changes? How can I be helpful?"

The other effective deterrent against overlooking a drug problem is a good sense of intuition. Parents with keen intuition detect cues that may indicate dishonesty. It would be going too far to say that they should assume they are right, that their child is definitely lying. The best way of handling intuition is *not to assume you are right, but also not to assume you are wrong.* In other words, if something doesn't seem right, you ask about it. For example, one father said: "It seems like a long time since I saw your last report card. When did you bring one home last? It also seems as if you don't do as much homework anymore. What's happening at school?"

"Why are you so suspicious?" was the reply.

"I just have a feeling that something is wrong."

"Well, you should trust me."

"I want to be able to trust you. Let's talk some more so I can be reassured."

Note that the parent doesn't back down. He says he wants to trust and is open to trusting. He simply says he needs to talk further in order to be reassured. The feed-it-back approach, discussed later in this chapter, is excellent for exposing problems, such as when a child says drugs haven't affected his school performance yet his grades have fallen dramatically.

When there are compelling reasons to believe that problems do exist, parents should persist in seeking an explanation of what is happening. They should not stop until the problem is identified or they are convinced that everything is okay.

But you can't forget another possibility. Your child might be telling you the truth. For every parent who naively accepts a drug-using teenager's denial of drug use, there is another parent who unfairly accuses a child and drags him in for a urinalysis or places him in some sort of unnecessary hospital program.

REACTING TO WHAT YOU HEAR

As you and your child engage in dialogue, you'll certainly have reactions, probably strong ones, especially if you hear hints or a confession of drug use, or serious consideration of that option.

Let's say the alarm goes off. You have heard information that makes you squirm, perhaps that your child has smoked pot.

At this moment you might question your solemn pledge to remain calm and supportive. Isn't it time to get tough? You might think that your child needs a lecture about the good old days, punishment to teach him a lesson, and a threat to keep him in line. The lure of "Rambo parenting" will be strong. With one overpowering attack, everything could be fixed; at least so goes the fantasy. Here's the scene, straight from the movie:

"After all we've done for you," the Rambo parent says, "how could you do this to us? How can you look at yourself in the mirror? Your behavior is disgusting.

"You're grounded for a month and you can't hang out with your friends anymore. They're a bad influence. If I ever hear of anything like this again, I'll tan your hide."

"Thank you," the child responds. "You have saved me from the blight of drug addiction."

The fantasy is a quick fix. But the real outcome, as you know, would be bitter feelings, the end of the discussion, and possibly increased rebelliousness. When the dialogue ends, so does the educational influence of parents.

In real life, you know that you need patience. You certainly will be concerned, perhaps frightened. But if you push the panic button, it's not likely you'll be able to help your child get a grip on things.

If you feel like a failure because your child is using drugs, my warning is to be careful not to turn that feeling into a self-fulfilling prophecy. Don't allow yourself to fail by panicking. Remember, this is your first attempt to talk openly. You can still have a dialogue, become a strong influence, and solve any problems that may exist.

Using "I" Messages

Begin first by expressing your feelings and concerns about what you heard. An important part of the exchange of information process is being able to honestly express emotions in a disciplined way. This is accomplished through the use of "I" and "my" messages, as discussed in Chapter 3 in the section on fill-in-the-blank sentences. These are statements of personal feelings and concerns. They are not judgments about your children, especially not "you" statements, as in "You are an irresponsible kid." Clearly, "you" statements would end the dialogue.

"I" and "my" statements start with clauses such as these:

- "My concerns are . . ."
- "My fears are . . ."
- "I get alarmed when I hear that . . ."

An example of an "I" statement is the following: "When I hear you have smoked pot, I get scared that you could get busted."

The immediate reaction of your child may be, "Don't worry, I know what I'm doing."

Rather than getting into a power struggle, consider your statements at this early stage of the dialogue as planting seeds. You are simply expressing your feelings. There will be plenty of opportunities to express them again later. Don't try to bulldoze your way through. You could say:

"We clearly see things differently. But I am concerned and I wanted you to know it."

One of the skills that teenagers often need to learn is to identify and express their feelings. If you can handle your own feelings well in these discussions, you will help your children by providing important feedback, showing that you care, and modeling positive ways to communicate feelings.

Gathering More Information

If alcohol or other drugs have been used, you need more information in order to make a good assessment.

As you gather information, you also will be helping your children look at important issues about their own drug use. You are helping them make a self-assessment.

(1) What, When, How, Where?

If your children have used drugs, it is important to discuss the experience. You will want to know: Which drugs have been used? How often were they used? How much was used on each occasion? How did it feel? What happened when drugs were used? In what setting were they used, that is, where and when? (Was it at home? School? Parties? Friends' houses? Was it on schooldays? Weekends? Before school? During school? In the evening?)

(2) The Reasons for Drug Use

You will want to know why drugs were used. What was the motivation? What needs were met by the drugs? For example, was the purpose to have fun? To alleviate boredom? To escape pain? To conform in a social situation?

There may be multiple reasons for drug use and different explanations on different occasions.

(3) Drug Effects

You will be interested in the impact of drug use. How have drugs affected your child? Has harm occurred?

What happened at the time drugs were used? Potential problems include fights, driving under the influence, and unplanned sexual activity.

You will also want to consider long-term effects. Potential problems include damaged friendships, strained family relationships, problems in school, and legal problems.

It's also possible that the child used alcohol or drugs the way some mature adults can, without any significant damage. Though reassuring, this doesn't preclude the possibility of problems in the future. What is the potential for harm?

(4) Your Child's Attitude

Another important assessment is your child's attitude about drugs. Is it rebellious? Is it "I do it and I'm proud"? Is it "I do it and I'm frightened about what I'm doing"? Is it "I do it because everyone else does it"? Find out whether your child wants to continue using drugs or to stop.

(5) Your Child's Knowledge and Self-Awareness

Another important part of the assessment is understanding your child's awareness and knowledge about his drug use. You will want to know what your child knows and doesn't know about drugs, what he has thought about with regard to dangers and consequences, and what he hasn't thought about.

Before the current discussion, has he considered the immediate or long-term dangers and risks of drug use? Has he looked at the effects of his own drug use? Is he aware of why he is using drugs? Is he self-critical?

In other words, you not only want to know why your child uses drugs, but you want to know if *he* is aware of why. You want to know the effects of his drug use, but you also want to know if *he* is aware of them.

(6) The Current Status of Drug Use

You'll be interested in the current status of drug use. Has the use stopped? Is it increasing? Decreasing? Stable? When was the last time? If use is continuing, at what level and under what circumstances?

A crucial question in evaluating the current status of drug use is harm. Are drugs being used dangerously? Is harm already occurring? Is it imminent?

In evaluating the status of drug use, figure out where your child

157

stands on the drug use continuum, described in Chapter 2. Is it experimental use? Regular use? Harmful use? Or addiction?

Too Much, Too Soon

Once the dialogue commences, children vary in their readiness to openly disclose personal details. With so much information needed for a good assessment, you will be eager to get the facts. In your eagerness, you can get too pushy or overbearing. Sometimes the result is an onslaught of questions, one after the other, called "pumping for information":

- When was the first time?
- Who were you with?
- Who got the drugs?
- What was it like?
- When else did you use drugs?
- Where are you getting the drugs?
- Which of your friends use drugs?

All these questions will be of interest, but asking them one after another will probably create resistance. Remember, the discussion is just beginning. If you try to find out everything right away, you may find yourself locked in a power struggle. You'll be trying to extract information and your child will be trying to withhold it. Think of this initial discussion as the beginning of a long-term process requiring patience.

Defense Mechanisms

If your teenagers do have a problem with drugs, several forces work against their recognizing it: feelings of invincibility, the defense mechanism of denial, the defense mechanism of externalization, and erroneous information. In a dialogue, in order to reach an understanding, you may have to reckon with any or all of these forces.

Teenage children typically have false *feelings of invincibility* that extends to many types of behavior: "Nothing can happen to me. I won't get pregnant from unprotected sex. I won't get AIDS. I won't get hooked on drugs. I know what I'm doing."

With the defense mechanism of *denial*, drug users say: "Drugs aren't a problem. They don't affect me. I can stop whenever I want to." (Sometimes this is true. Sometimes it's a denial of reality.)

Still another characteristic defense of teenagers is *externalization*. They blame everyone and everything except themselves for their drug use, and they take no personal responsibility for their own behavior: "I only use drugs because school is so bad and this city is so boring." It's as if drugs have been imposed on them by outside forces. If the world would change for the better, their drug use would cease of its own accord.

Erroneous information about drugs and their effects is another factor preventing teenagers from accurately assessing their drug use. Teenagers may, for example, assert that there are no dangers in smoking marijuana. They may also have mistaken notions of what a drug problem looks like. In their mind, the only real alcoholics are the guys lying in the street drunk. They don't recognize subtler forms of addiction.

Another misconception is about the "norm." Many teenagers enormously overestimate the number of their peers using drugs, and therefore see their own use as "normal."

Because of all these factors, you may find that your child is unaware of the extent of his drug use, his motivation for drug use, and the consequences and risks of his actions. You may find that he is contradicting himself. He may be misleading you, himself, or both of you.

Rebuttal Cycle

With all these many obstacles to an objective assessment of the problem, many parents feel the urge to make an aggressive challenge, either by asking accusatory questions or by rebutting what their children say. Unfortunately, this causes the discussion to degenerate into a no-win argument, with your children getting defensive. It goes something like this:

"You said there weren't any drugs at the party, but now you're telling me that Joan was there. You've told me that Joan uses drugs. You're contradicting yourself. You're lying."

The message here is: "I don't trust you. We're in a competition. I'm gonna try to prove you wrong."

The rebuttal cycle is a serious pitfall. Parents get hooked into it when they are too eager to disprove their children's point of view. They tear down what their children say instead of helping to broaden and expand their thinking.

Children will answer a rebuttal with a counter-rebuttal of their own. When engaged in the rebuttal cycle, no one listens seriously to anyone else:

Child: "There's nothing wrong with pot."

Parent: "But it's illegal."

Child: "Driving over the speed limit is illegal and you do that."

Parent: "I'm a grown-up and you're a child. I have some prerogatives that you don't have. I don't want you breaking any laws."

Child: "Oh, a double standard. Anyway, all the kids in school use drugs."

Parent: "I doubt if Jane and her friends use drugs."

Child: "Yeah, but they're nerds."

In this "discussion" (really an argument), the parent has some serious concerns about his child's seeming disregard for the law and what appears to be an inaccurate assessment of the extent of drug use among peers. But by falling into the rebuttal cycle, the parent fails to get any serious attention. As you will see later in this chapter, there are better ways to communicate without trying to "win" in a contest for dominance.

POSITIVE WAYS TO GET MORE INFORMATION

In making an assessment, you want more information but don't want your child to feel that he's on trial or under investigation. You're not trying to catch wrongdoing.

Open-Ended Questions

One underused strategy for gathering information without cross-examining is to invite openness and self-disclosure by asking open-ended questions. These are the questions that allow people to answer on their own terms, in contrast with closed questions that allow only limited possible responses.

To illustrate, consider the difference between these approaches in gathering information from a child who has smoked marijuana.

Closed questions: "Did you enjoy it?" (yes or no) "Who gave you the drugs?'' (name the person) "Will you ever do it again?'' (yes or no).

The open-ended approach goes like this: "How did it feel? What was it like? What are your thoughts about smoking in the future?''

These open-ended questions encourage the child to think and to talk. With the open-ended approach, you could even say:

"You know that I'm very curious about what's happening with you and drugs, but I don't want to start bombarding you with questions. Could you tell me what's going on?''

Don't give up if you get an "Oh, nothing'' response. Encourage further discussion:

"What do you mean by 'Oh, nothing'? I'd like to know more.''

Or you can ask a few closed questions—such as "Where were you? Who were you with"—before switching to open-ended ones.

Lighten Up

During this early part of the dialogue, as you are gathering information, you should be developing sensitivity about the amount of questioning that is appropriate with your own child and when you need to lighten up or back off. Remember, nobody likes to be put through the Spanish Inquisition, especially teenagers, who are forming their independent identities.

If at any point your child indicates he can't talk or feels too pressured, show that you're not going to be pushy. Sometimes it helps to say something encouraging, such as: "I know it's hard for you to talk. But I think it's important. Please hang in there with me.''

As it becomes clear to your child that you're not going to send in the cavalry, as he feels more comfortable about opening up, he'll gradually disclose information. Later you can ask more detailed and specific questions. Your child will answer if he feels safe.

Some teenagers will protest: "You're asking a lot of questions. I thought we were going to have a discussion. I wish you wouldn't pry.''

You can remind them of the purpose of the discussion:

"Let me explain why I'm asking these questions. I want to help you think through what's happening with drugs. It's my responsibility as a parent to help you learn to make wise choices. That's why I'm asking. But if it feels like a lot of questions too soon, I'm willing to back off. We can talk again later.''

"But,'' your child protests, "why are you so uptight?''

It's an important question. If you are uptight, you won't be helping matters. In that case, your child has given you important criticism. If you're not uptight, only concerned, make that clear to your child.

If your child still feels stuck about talking further, ask about the guarantees he needs to feel safe. (Refer back to the previous chapter for how to do this.)

If for some reason your consistent and patient effort to maintain a dialogue hasn't been successful, you can suggest alternatives. Again, it's important to insist on discussion:

"These are tough times for kids. Everyone is entitled to support, to someone to talk with. If you can't talk with me, I'm willing to set up an appointment with a professional [or a clergyman]. But I can't look away from this. I'm disappointed we're stuck, but maybe a psychologist can help us get going together. Or maybe you would want to talk with him or her alone. One way or the other, I want you to have the support you deserve."

Columbo Style

When drug abusers are asked about their drug use, some of them lie by omission—not by giving false information but by withholding important details. To a lesser extent, even people who dabble in drugs sometimes distort the truth.

"Okay, I confess," Michael tells his father. "I'm gonna come clean with you. I drank alcohol."

He also has smoked pot and tried cocaine, but doesn't offer this information.

Because of distortions like these, to get an accurate assessment of the situation, you need to ask specific questions about which drugs have been used, how much of them, and how often. This is a delicate process. You don't want to start cross-examining. Yet you want to be informed. The tone of these questions should be supportive, not confrontational. I think of the television character Columbo. You sort of scratch your head and ask some questions to get a few more details. Instead of saying to your child, "I don't believe that you've told me everything," or "Stop lying," you communicate interest and support.

Ask direct questions, but be intuitive about how rapidly to proceed. Start with, "Have you tried any other drugs?"

"I told you once before I smoked pot."

162

"Anything else?"

"Just because I smoked pot doesn't mean I've used any other drugs."

"I know that, but I'd like to know if you've used anything else. What about cocaine? Have you tried it?

"Well, yeah, I tried it once."

"Is that all?"

"No, actually a few times."

"How many times?"

"Three."

"Is that all?"

"Yes."

"You sure?"

"Yes."

"How about crack?"

And the questioning would continue with other drugs.

In therapy with seriously addicted clients you quickly learn about the importance of this type of questioning. I remember a college student telling me he had had only one vodka.

A tumbler?

No way. It was a bottle.

Thought-Provoking Questions

As information unfolds you will begin to have thoughts you want to share with your children. You may want to challenge misinformation or provide a different perspective about something that was said.

Before you offer your perspective, consider taking the approach of asking thought-provoking questions. This means asking a child if he has ever considered the flip side, the opposite, of what he is saying.

I was talking with a sixteen-year-old girl who was smoking pot and drinking alcohol on a regular basis. Her drug use was clearly creating problems for her in school and at home, yet she was boldly proclaiming the merits of drugs. She focused on how great she felt when she was high.

I sort of rained on her parade by changing the focus with a couple of thought-provoking questions: "Is there another side to this? Do you ever worry about your drug use?"

Taken aback, she admitted she had worried, then added: "But I don't dwell on it."

"It's unpleasant to think about, isn't it?" I asked.

"Yeah," she said.

"But not thinking about it doesn't make it go away, does it?"

"No, I guess I need to deal with it," she said.

And I agreed.

Because thought-provoking questions are so effective, I've listed a few that I frequently use in talking with teenagers:

- Is there another side to this?
- Do you worry about your drug use?
- Do you feel your drug use may be out of control?
- Have you thought about the potential dangers?
- Do you see any risks?
- Do you have any concerns?

Thought-provoking questions are also a good opening for you to express your own thoughts and feelings. For example, I asked Jane, age sixteen, if she was worried about her drinking. She said no. Then I said: "I guess you're not worried about how much alcohol you're drinking, but when you tell me you have been drunk several times in the last couple of months, it concerns me."

This is a way to keep the discussion personal rather than abstract, to state your concerns rather than to get argumentative.

Directed Questioning and Labeling

You want to understand your child's drug use and to help him understand it. Certain questions not only help you gather information, but also broaden his thinking about drug use. These are directed questions, so named because they increase awareness by pursuing a direct line of reasoning. As your child answers directed questions, certain information and patterns of behavior become apparent. You can ask your child if he notices the patterns, or you can point them out yourself.

Many times children do not know why they are using drugs. They may not have thought about it. Their own reasons may be hidden from themselves. Directed questioning is particularly helpful in uncovering motivation.

"Okay," I said in a counseling session, "you don't know why you use drugs. Let's take a look at *when* you use them and see if together we can figure out why."

"I just do drugs when I feel like it. No special reason."

"Well then, let's look at when you've been feeling like it. When was the last time?"

"Saturday night."

"Where were you? What were you doing?"

"I was at Ken's house. We were bored."

"So, at least one time when you used drugs, you were feeling bored."

"Yeah, so what?"

"Well, I don't know, let's keep looking at this. Maybe we'll find a pattern."

"And maybe not."

"That's possible. Let's see."

"Okay."

"When was the next to last time you used drugs?"

"It was the weekend before. I had nothing to do."

"Kind of bored then, too?"

"I guess so."

"What do you think? Maybe one reason you use drugs is because you get bored and want something fun to do."

This dialogue shows a pattern of drug use for fun or to avoid boredom.

Similar questioning of the same child uncovered other reasons for drug use at other times.

With directed questioning about motivation, it's important to search for root causes and not to stop with vague generalizations.

Betty told her parents that she used drugs "to feel good." At first they thought she meant she was using them for a "trip," to alter her consciousness. But as they asked more questions, it became clear that she was smoking pot to self-medicate against depression. She was having problems in school and didn't know how to cope with them, so she used drugs to escape the pain. That's what she meant by "to feel good."

As children explain the context of their drug use, you can identify the underlying motivation:

- "I wanted to see what cocaine was like. I wanted to try it." (experimentation)

165

- "At parties, everyone does drugs." (peer pressure, conformity)
- "When you guys [Mom and Dad] fight, I get high." (to cope, to kill pain)
  - "I drink on dates." (for fun and possibly to deal with stress)
  - "I take downers before exams." (to deal with stress)

Sometimes the motivation is subtle. A boy who says he smokes pot because he "likes it" may appear to be enjoying the sensation of being high. But another question revealed a different motivation:

"What is it you like best about it?"

"I can brag to my friends. I'm the only kid in my class who has smoked pot."

Besides revealing important information about patterns of drug use, directed questions are also useful in uncovering contradictions in thinking. This is a special type of directed questioning, called the feed-it-back approach.

The Feed-It-Back Approach

As information begins to unfold, you will probably see gaps in your child's knowledge base and contradictions in his reasoning that you want to discuss. For example, your child might say he has not been harmed by drugs when it appears that there is evidence to the contrary.

The feed-it-back approach is a way to gradually help children see the contradictions in their own thinking. It helps them overcome denial mechanisms and other obstacles that could interfere with objectivity. Through careful questioning about feelings and experiences, hard facts are brought into the open. Parents "feed back" what they hear through simple comments about the hard facts.

Swiss psychologist Jean Piaget once said that every time you teach a child something, you deprive him the opportunity of figuring it out for himself. This maxim has special relevance when the child is a young teenager who is determined to take charge of his own life, determined to reach his own conclusions.

The feed-it-back approach is an excellent teaching method to help children see all the facts clearly and arrive at their own conclusions. With skillful and tactful questioning, you can help them gain valuable knowledge about themselves with a minimal amount of explaining.

Even with this nonthreatening approach, most children will not immediately acknowledge contradictions in their thinking. The feed-it-back approach is not a quick solution. It is an educational method for the long haul, a way to plant some seeds of wisdom, to begin to gradually crack the defenses. Often you have to discuss the same material several times until the child can clearly see the facts.

The feed-it-back approach is best illustrated by actual transcripts. Below are examples of using the method to explore the assertion that "drug use hasn't affected me;" to explore the assertion that "I could stop at any time;" and to determine whether a person is dependent on drugs. As you read the dialogue, remember that the tone of voice of the parent is always warm and supportive, not confrontational.

The feed-it-back approach is here applied to the question: "How have drugs affected you?"

PARENT: "How has smoking pot affected you?"

CHILD: "It makes me feel good."

PARENT: "I know it does, but I want to know more. How has it affected your life in other ways?"

CHILD: "I feel good more often."

PARENT: "Have there been any negative effects?"

CHILD: "No."

PARENT: "Well, let's look at this together. When did you start smoking marijuana?"

CHILD: "About a year ago."

PARENT: "What were your grades back then?"

CHILD: "A's and B's."

PARENT: "What are they now?"

CHILD: "C's and D's."

PARENT: "It sounds like the drugs may be having an effect in school. What do you think?"

CHILD: "Yeah, they make me feel better when I go to school."

PARENT: "I know that. But it sounds like maybe your schoolwork has suffered and the drugs are part of the problem. Maybe I'm wrong. Do you have any other ideas about why your grades have fallen?"

CHILD: "No, not really. I hate school."

PARENT: "I'm sorry school feels so bad to you. I'd like to talk with you about that, to see if we could figure out some solutions. But maybe drugs are part of it. It sounds as if they could be. Anyway, why don't we drop it for now."

CHILD: "Okay. Fine with me."

The facts speak for themselves. The child has revealed a potential problem. The parent isn't avoiding the problem, but maneuvering to reduce defensiveness. If the parent tries to hammer it home, he will only meet resistance. It is a wise move to back off. Soon another discussion of the same issue can bring these thoughts back to the attention of the child.

The feed-it-back approach is here applied to the question: "Could you stop using drugs if you wanted to?"

MOTHER: "Sounds like you use drugs whenever you feel bad. I wonder if you're becoming dependent on them."
CHILD: "I can stop whenever I want to."
MOTHER: "Have you ever tried?"
CHILD: "Yeah."
MOTHER: "Tell me, what happened?"
CHILD: "I didn't smoke for a couple of weeks."
MOTHER: "How was it?"
CHILD: "Fine, no problem."
MOTHER: "Good. Then what happened?"
CHILD: "My teachers started hassling me at school."
MOTHER: "Then what? Did you smoke again?"
CHILD: "Yeah, because my teachers were hassling me."
MOTHER: "Well, I'm pleased you could stop for a couple of weeks. But I'm concerned that you started again when you were feeling bad. I guess it helps kill the pain."
CHILD: "Well, my teachers were hassling me."
MOTHER: "I believe you. But, you know, I'm not sure the solution is to get high. And I'm concerned that you smoke pot when the going gets rough. Are there any other times you stopped using drugs?"
CHILD: "Yeah, there was another time."
MOTHER: "When was that?"
CHILD: "Uh, about six months ago."
MOTHER: "How long did you stop?"
CHILD: "About a month."
MOTHER: "What happened?"
CHILD: "Well I started again when you and Dad were fighting about the divorce stuff. It was really depressing."
MOTHER: "I know, those were tough times for all of us. I'm sorry it

was so hard for you. But you know, I seem to be hearing two things here. One is that you must be concerned about your drug use, because you've attempted to stop it, at least twice. The other thing is that you can stay off drugs as long as nothing is really bothering you. But when the going gets rough, you start using them again. Drugs kill the pain. You know, there's an alternative.''

CHILD: "What's that?''

MOTHER: "To figure things out, to deal with problems without getting high, and even to learn to prevent problems.''

CHILD: "I know. You've told me that before.''

MOTHER: "I guess it's a thought to keep in mind.''

CHILD: "Maybe you're right.''

MOTHER: "Will you think about it?''

CHILD: "Yes, I will.''

The parent has planted some seeds of wisdom. Again, in this example it's wise to back off and allow the child to think about what was said.

The feed-it-back approach can also be applied to the issue of whether a person is dependent on drugs. As you will see, this issue is related to the one discussed above—a person's ability to discontinue drug use.

CHILD: "It's not a problem. I'm not dependent.''

PARENT: "But you say you smoke pot when things bother you at home or in school.''

CHILD: "Yeah.''

PARENT: "Does this solve your problems?''

CHILD: "Well I feel a whole lot better.''

PARENT: "I know that drugs help you feel better, but I'm concerned that they just help you escape from difficult situations. Do you know what I mean?''

CHILD: "I need to escape. I *have* to live at home. I'm still a kid. I *have* to go to school. I'm too young to drop out.''

PARENT: "But there is an alternative.''

CHILD: "What's that?''

PARENT: "We could talk things out at home. If you're upset, I'd like us to deal with the problem so you don't feel bad. I don't want home to feel so bad that you need drugs to escape from feeling rotten.''

CHILD: "What about school?''

169

PARENT: "Look, I'll be honest. I didn't exactly love school either. No one does. But there are ways to make it feel better. I'm concerned that you're getting into a habit of running away from things."

CHILD: "But I like drugs. They don't harm me."

PARENT: "I don't deny you like them. I don't deny they lessen the pain. But I don't think they're a long-term solution. We all face lots of things in life that are unpleasant. If we take drugs to deal with them, we'll have some serious problems."

CHILD: "Well, I don't take drugs *every* time I feel bad."

PARENT: "I'm glad to hear that. But I still think the number of times you *do* take drugs is worth thinking about, isn't it?"

CHILD: "Yeah, I guess so."

In this dialogue the parent almost lapsed into lecture by discussing the long-term risks, but the comments were relatively brief, so this still can qualify as the feed-it-back approach.

ANSWERING THE TOUGH ONES

No matter how skilled you are in helping children make their own discoveries, you will certainly have issues to raise with them—eye-openers that they may not have considered. As always in the exchange of information, you want to state your point of view not as the ultimate truth but as the way you see things. The tone is respectful and supportive. Often you will find yourself going back and forth between expressing concerns, asking questions, making observations, and stating opinions.

Below I have listed some of the major areas of disagreement that arise in discussions with teenagers, along with suggestions on how to respond.

Everyone's Doing It

Many teenagers defend their own drug use by saying: "All kids are using drugs." Research has indicated that children tend to overestimate the number of their peers who use drugs.[1]

You could say: "I think you know it's not true that *all* kids use drugs. I suspect fewer of them use drugs than you think. What do you base your conclusion on? Do you want to check some statistics together?"

If your child says he's not interested in statistics, you can still say: "I guess that's one fact we have a different opinion about."

Then there's the matter of conformity: "Just because many of your peers are drinking and taking drugs doesn't mean that you must do it, and it doesn't mean that it's no big deal."

You can discuss the merits of having an independent opinion, making one's own choices, and being willing to be different from a crowd. This is of special value to teenagers, who are at a stage in life when they are trying to determine, for themselves, exactly who they are.

It's Not My Responsibility (Externalization)

In discussions about drugs, many teenagers externalize their motivation for drug use, denying any and all responsibility for their own behavior:

"I smoke pot because there's nothing fun to do in town." (Not because I'm bored and don't know how to find fun or make my own excitement.)

"I drink because my mom is always hassling me." (Not because I try to escape. I can't deal with her and work out problems at home.)

I smoke pot because school is so boring." (Not because I can't cope with school. I can't concentrate or get the sorts of grades I want.)

"I drink beer because everyone does." (Not because I am choosing to conform.)

When statements such as these are made, you can introduce the concept of "externalization," or blaming the world, and explain to your children that they aren't taking responsibility for their own behavior. You can show that they blame other people and other life experiences for their own choices. This can be done without invalidating their explanations. It's possible to accept their underlying feelings, without agreeing that this entirely accounts for, or explains, their drug use.

A mother said the following to her thirteen-year-old daughter:

"You say you smoke pot because there's nothing fun to do. I don't doubt that you feel bored, but I don't agree with you that there's nothing else to do that would be fun. I think you could find fun things to do or even invent them. That's my opinion. I'd be happy to help you plan activities. I think it's important to learn to be able to entertain, amuse, and excite yourself in life. I'd like to see you do that."

A father said this to his fourteen-year-old son:

"I notice you say you use drugs because of us [Mom and Dad] and school. It's as if you imply we *make* you take drugs. I know you're having problems with us. But it's been *your* choice to deal with these tensions by using drugs. I think there are better solutions. Let's talk about some of them."

Another rationale given for the use of drugs is "Why not? We're all gonna be nuked someday anyway." It would be entirely unreal to discount the ever-present danger of nuclear destruction, the cloud of doom that we all live under. On the other hand, the threat of nuclear destruction doesn't necessitate drug use. Parents can be reassuring. Humans are learning that war with nuclear weapons is no longer possible. It would mean total destruction. People are getting smarter. We will prevent it from happening. In a different vein, the nuclear threat could even be turned around and used to motivate productive activity: "Why don't you work to help make the world a safer place?"

Drugs Are Harmless

"Pot is safe. Alcohol is harmless. —— is harmless."

You should disagree. All drugs have their risks:

"I disagree with you on that. I'll be happy to gather some scientific studies and we can look at the research together. I'm not saying everyone has problems with these drugs, but I know there are dangers and risks with all of them."

Many teenagers who are harmfully involved with drugs do not realize the damage that has been done. They say, "Drugs haven't hurt me."

One good way to settle the difference of opinion is to refer to the discussion of the drug use continuum in Chapter 2. Ask your children to determine where they would place themselves on the continuum and why. Explain where you would place them and why.

I'll Never Get Hooked

Many children are unaware of the realistic dangers of drug dependence. Or if they are aware, many feel *they* could never fall victim to it. Teenage invincibility is most evident in terms of sexual behavior. Teens who intellectually understand how a woman becomes pregnant somehow believe they are immune to that possibility, that they can engage in risk-free sexual activity. That same tendency can be seen

172

with drugs. They believe, quite simply: "It can't happen to me. I can control my drug use."

The best response is the straightforward truth: "Yes, it's true that many people can control their drug use. Only a certain percentage have problems with drugs. But there is no special reason to believe that you're immune to the risks. And the risks are greater for young people, who have only had limited life experiences, than they are for adults."

Another important point to make is that nobody ever starts using drugs expecting that they will become addicted. If people thought they would get addicted and suffer the tragic consequences, they wouldn't start in the first place. Everyone thinks they can handle the substances, including that percentage of people who end up with serious problems.

Mistaken Notions of Addiction

As I mentioned before, many teens visualize skid row bums and heroin shooting galleries when they think of drug addiction. They are unaware of the subtler forms.

You can talk about drug problems in which people seemingly carry on a normal routine but spend much of their time in a daze or compulsively focusing on getting their next fix. You can refer to adult friends who are miserable from drugs. Cite examples of students who certainly aren't shooting heroin, yet are suffering the academic or social consequences of problem drinking or drug use.

Drugs as Crutches

Many adolescents don't grasp the full significance of their drug use. Their limited viewpoint is reflected in statements that begin, "I only use drugs for . . ." or "I just use drugs for . . ."

- "I just do drugs for fun. Everything feels better when I'm high. It's no problem."
- "I only do drugs when my teachers hassle me or you guys [parents] yell at me. Drugs relax me. It's easier to deal with school and you guys when I'm high."
- "I only do drugs when I'm depressed. They cheer me up. They make me feel good."

It would be a mistake to discount these motivations. Drugs can make a person feel good. They can help with coping. They can relieve tension and stress. You can validate this point of view but also help them see the risks, and especially help expand their thinking about the future.

"So," you say, "drugs cheer you up when you feel down. How long does it last? When the drugs wear off, how do you feel? Don't you want more drugs because you still feel bad? It seems to me it doesn't ever really solve the problem.

"I understand that you enjoy everything more when you are high, but I see some serious risks. If you always seek this sort of a high, you'll be disappointed much of the time when you're not high. You might end up being high all the time, and then you'll miss some of the other satisfactions of life, such as school success and eventually work achievement. Not to mention, great relationships with a boyfriend or girlfriend. You can't succeed in school and be high. You can't work out a relationship if you're always high.

"If you start using drugs to accomplish these goals, they can become a crutch. You'll depend on them to create the feelings and won't learn other ways to do it. You might think, So what? But there's a catch here. Our bodies grow accustomed to the substances and we need more and more of them for the same feelings. In fact, we can get so accustomed to drugs, develop such tolerance, that we need a huge amount just to feel normal. Drugs may seem fine at the moment, but over the long haul they can create serious problems. This isn't to say that everyone who uses drugs has problems. But when you say you use drugs *only* for fun, it worries me that you're not seeing the bigger picture."

One parent made this statement to a teenage son who used drugs to calm down before going on dates:

"I don't think it's a good idea to get high to relax yourself for dates. There's nothing wrong with being nervous. We all have to go through that. It's part of growing up."

MAKING YOUR ASSESSMENT

After engaging in a thorough dialogue about drugs, you and your children will know all the facts and potential dangers. You each will have shared your values and opinions and the reasons behind them. It's time to make an assessment.

In the most general terms, the important questions are: (1) Are drugs being used? and, if so, (2) Has harm occurred or is it likely to occur? Answers to these questions influence the types of agreements and rules that you will want to establish and your strategy for negotiating.

If drug use is already causing harm or puts your children at high risk for harm, you'll probably want to take quick and decisive action. If use is at a lower level, you have the option of being more gradual in your intervention. You can pay more attention to your educational role, that is, helping your children learn to make good decisions. In some cases, it pays to be patient.

It is also possible, although some people consider it unspeakable, that some older teenagers can use certain drugs *without* significant harm. As much as it might seem desirable to oversimplify and say to older teenagers, "Never, never use drugs, they always cause harm," and as much as this would be more comforting and acceptable to those who are panicked by the drug problem in this country, we must be intellectually honest. Although drug use certainly is not ideal for developing minds and bodies, some teenagers can use drugs, even regularly, without advancing to dependence and without harming themselves.

This doesn't mean that drug use should be accepted. There's no good reason to take unnecessary health risks. But the truth is that some teenagers can use drugs without injury. Unfortunately, many drug *abusers*, children and adults alike, *mistakenly* assume that they are indulging without harm.

Risk Factors

If drugs are being used and harm hasn't occurred, there are some important risk factors to consider.

Children who are deficient in basic life skills and using drugs to compensate for the deficiency are at higher risk for dependence than others. For example, if they have difficulty coping with stress, say in

175

school or social encounters, and use drugs to deal with their anxiety, they might start to depend on drugs on a regular basis.

Other risks occur without dependence or even regular use. Some involve recklessness, such as drinking and driving, or drinking (or drugging) and unplanned sexual activity. Some involve the choice of drugs. For example, it is risky to experiment with highly addictive substances, such as crack.

Another risk factor is a family history of alcoholism or drug abuse. From a statistical point of view, families with this history need to be more alert to potentially harmful use of substances by their children.

YOUR CHILDREN'S OWN ASSESSMENT

If your children are using drugs, part of your assessment is seeing how *they* assess the situation.

Are they aware of the risks and dangers? What stage of drug use do *they* think they are in? It is likely that you and your children will have some differences of opinion. Thought-provoking questions and the feed-it-back approach are helpful in reconciling differences. But drug users—young and old—are often defensive in looking at their behavior. They say: "No big deal."

This hooks many parents into an aggressive war of words, an attempt to talk their children into believing that they have a problem. Lots of luck. The teenagers smile and say: "Why are you so uptight? Go take some Valium and call me in the morning."

LOVING CONFRONTATION: ADDRESSING THE ISSUE OF HARM

Loving confrontation is a way to address the issue of harm and potential harm from drug use, without locking horns with your children. With information gained from discussions and observations, you begin by stating your opinion about the seriousness of the problem, with love and concern, as this mother did:

"I believe that you're hurting yourself. I love you and I'm very worried about this. I've noticed that you're not doing your homework and your grades are falling and that you're not coming home on time for curfew.

"You seem very moody. You often seem tired. I've also noticed that you have a persistent cough. I'm concerned about you."

After making the observations, you ask some questions: Have you been aware of this? What do you think? How do you explain it? How do you feel? Are you concerned?

Your child might give the classic answer: "I don't care."

"What about school?" you ask.

"I don't care. School is boring."

It's usually a case of denial. I try to cut through this defense mechanism with a statement like this:

"I don't believe you don't care. I know that deep inside you must. It's hard to feel good about yourself when you're failing, even if you think the teachers are unfair and school is boring. I suspect you probably don't *want* to care, and sometimes you feel so frustrated that you don't care, but I believe it does matter to you."

Drug users in the denial stage will insist that everything is okay. But you can challenge this assertion with more loving confrontation:

"Regardless of what you say, I see a problem and I believe it's related to drugs. If you can explain it otherwise, that's fine. I would like to know how you explain it. But I love you too much to look away from this, to allow this type of self-destructive behavior to continue. We need to keep talking."

If harm has not yet occurred, but your child appears to be at high risk, you can use loving confrontation to explain the risks you see. Here are a few examples:

- "I love you very much and I'm concerned about what's happening with you and drugs. I know you are shy in social situations. You told me you're using drugs to go out on dates and be with your friends. I think this is a very dangerous practice. It's how drug problems develop, when people use substances to deal with stress in life."

- "I'm worried about something I've noticed. I know you've been upset about the divorce, but you haven't been talking with me or anyone. I'm concerned that since the divorce you seem to be using drugs to deal with how you feel. This is a serious matter. I don't want you to become dependent on drugs to deal with problems. I want to help you learn how to cope with stress without relying on chemicals."

- "I'm concerned about your use of drugs. You know we have a history of alcohol problems in this family. For whatever reasons, children of alcoholics seem to be more prone to dependence on sub-

177

stances. I don't want you to suffer with drugs the way I have. You may feel that everything is okay, but given our family history, I'm worried about you."

We've now discussed the skill of loving confrontation that you can use to respectfully challenge the point of view of your children. Don't forget, however, that they might have some challenges of their own, and good ones, too. You need to listen with respect.

The beauty of a good dialogue is that it promotes learning and understanding. With the exchange of information process, new insights bring family members into closer agreement about issues that may have separated them in the past.

Clearly the issue of drugs is not an isolated one. Drug use influences how you feel about use of the family car. It influences your thinking about which parties your child can attend. It influences your decisions about curfews. Therefore, in a broad-ranging discussion about drugs, all of these issues may surface.

Once drugs and related issues have surfaced and everyone has listened to one another, it's time to make agreements. That's the topic of the next chapter.

7

MAKING AGREEMENTS

"Yeah, sure," a parent says to me in a workshop, "make an agreement with my son. I've made hundreds of them and he has never done anything he said he would do. I've tried this agreement stuff. It doesn't work."

Clearly this parent did not have *valid* agreements with his son— not if he had made so many of them without success.

Valid agreements are fully understood by everyone involved. They are made in good faith, that is, with the intention of following through. They are based on mutual respect and careful thought and consideration.

Every day, children make millions of *invalid* agreements with their parents: "Sure I'll do my homework. Sure I'll be home by eleven o'clock. Sure I won't use drugs. Now leave me alone [so I can go and do whatever I want to do]."

Children know that invalid agreements are a handy way to silence their nagging parents.

Sometimes invalid agreements are made unintentionally. Children may quickly say they'll do what their parents want, believing at the moment that they will keep the agreement but never *really* resolving to do so. They attempt to do as promised, but their efforts lack resolve and ultimately fail. It's an unthinking knee-jerk response to pressure rather than deliberate dishonesty.

This chapter is about parents and children making valid agreements with each other: how to make them, how to keep them, and what to do when they are broken.

179

We begin the discussion with some general principles, but then get more specific about drug-related issues.

PERCEPTIONS AND STANDARDS

After a parent-child dialogue, it's time to compare perceptions, to identify areas of agreement and disagreement, to attempt to reconcile differences and then come to terms.

An important parent-child issue is establishing reasonable standards of behaviors, for example, concerning bedtime, curfew, drug use, and household chores. A good discussion always results in greater understanding of the facts and usually narrows the gap between differing points of view. After a discussion, remaining differences can be openly acknowledged, later to be negotiated and resolved.

Here's the way a discussion about housework was summed up in one family:

"Let's compare our opinions. Tell me if I'm wrong. It seems that we both agree that we should all carry a share of household responsibilities. I think you should continue to be responsible for your room, take out the garbage, feed the dog, and empty the dishwasher. You feel that this is too much to ask and that it should be up to you to choose your own standards for your bedroom. You think someone else should handle Quey [the dog]. You've done it for so long that now you think it's someone else's turn. Is that right?"

"Yes, that's a good summary."

Once the differences are clarified, parents will either make compromises and concessions or insist on the final word.

Parents and children sometimes have very different ideas about the current situation, about how well children have been meeting their responsibilities, whatever they may be. A father claims his sixteen-year-old daughter has been missing her curfew, but she insists she has not. In situations such as these, it usually doesn't make sense to argue. A good way to reconcile differences is to "watch together" and keep track.

The father says: "Let's not argue. Let's agree to watch the next few weeks and keep track of when you're late and when you're on time for your curfew. Okay?"

Agreeing to watch not only increases objectivity but also encourages "best behavior."

When negotiating about issues—such as curfew, use of the family car, attendance at certain parties, dating rules, sex, eating habits, homework, grades, housework, choice of friends, and drug use—the more you and your children think alike, the easier it will be to make agreements. The longer you and you children have been having open discussions, the greater the likelihood of agreement. But you can't always agree on everything.

In a negotiation between equals, people try to meet each other halfway. Although parent-child negotiation should be based on mutual respect, it is not between equals. Parents have the ultimate authority. Still, the goal of parenting is to empower children. With the transfer of power, you extend trust by giving children increasing freedom as they get older. You want them to have experiences that they can handle, to help them learn responsibility and control. You want them eventually to be fully independent and capable of making their own decisions without your help. Fewer and fewer rules are needed.

With older teenagers, it doesn't make sense to be unbending, to think that you can set down all the rules and limits on your own terms without making concessions. By the time they are sixteen or seventeen, your children should be making most of their own decisions, and they should have had enough learning experiences to make wise ones. This is the ideal, although not always the reality.

If you have been slow to transfer power, it's time to get moving. Soon your children will be on their own. You don't want to send them into the "cruel" world unprepared for what they will face, having had only limited learning experiences and opportunities to talk it out with Mom and Dad.

When you and your teenagers have differences of opinion, some of your rules or standards of behavior may be non-negotiable:

"We disagree. We see things differently. This is something I feel strongly about. I ask that you do as I tell you."

In other words, you ask for an agreement based on respect for your authority. If necessary, you may have to ask for an agreement based on your power, as in, "Do as I say or the consequences will be . . ."

All through the process of transferring power to your children, you make rules and set limits that serve at least three purposes: (1) establishing a high standard of behavior; (2) protecting your children from danger; (3) helping them develop self-control. That is, you set limits so that they will learn to set their own.

During childhood, and especially during the intensely emotional period of adolescence, it's important that children understand the reasons behind your authority and use of power. Your purpose is not to dominate and certainly not to make their lives miserable. Rather it is to protect them and help them learn to cope successfully.

When asking for compliance with rules, it's important to make it clear that you're on their side. You want them to be able to stay out as late as is healthy. You don't want to limit their social life. You want them to have the car. You just want to make sure that they are prepared to handle these responsibilities. You look forward to backing off and letting them take over for themselves.

It's very important to be clear in these ways because the purpose of authority is often misunderstood, as in the following case:

Mrs. Schneider told her sixteen-year-old daughter, Judy, to be home by 11:30 on Saturday night. She had a great deal of confidence and trust in Judy, but this was her first date with a boy who had a driver's license. Mrs. Schneider wanted to set limits that she thought would help her daughter deal with this older teenager. Later, when Judy had more dating experience and knew what to expect, Mrs. Schneider would extend the curfew. Her logic was sound. Her limits were fair. But she didn't explain her thinking process to Judy, who was terribly disappointed by the curfew and wanted to stay out later. Judy thought the curfew meant that her mother didn't trust her.

Some children, angered by what they consider to be unreasonable limits, become rebellious. Judy happens to be a responsible daughter and didn't do that. But the damage in this case was that she believed her mother was working against her. Mrs. Schneider didn't come across to Judy as supportive, which was unfortunate because really she was highly supportive.

Many children, like Judy, fail to understand the purpose of rules and agreements. These misunderstandings can be prevented with greater clarity of purpose (to protect) and intent (to eventually give more freedom).

REACHING A COMPROMISE

When you and your teenagers disagree, before reaching the non-negotiables, there is a wide range of cooperative possibilities for compromise. Some are listed below, along with examples for each.

(1) You can lay out the conditions and reassurance you need in order to give permission for certain activities:

- "I want to give you the car even though it makes me a little nervous. What I need to feel comfortable with this arrangement is your guarantee that you don't drink or use any drugs."
- "I'll give you the later curfew you wanted, if you'll agree to call me at eleven o'clock and tell me where you are and how things are going. That way I'm reassured that you're safe and can go to sleep without being upset. I don't see phone calls as a long-term solution, maybe just for a few weeks."

(2) You can give permission for certain activities (for example, going on a date, using the family car, or visiting particular friends) with an agreement to talk openly afterward about what happened. Then you have an opportunity to evaluate the experience and to determine which coping skills your children may need to develop:

- "I'll let you go away for this weekend if you'll agree to talk about what happened in some detail so we can see if it was a good idea and what to do about situations like these in the future."
- "I'll allow you to have a later curfew on this special occasion if you agree to honestly discuss what happens when you keep these late hours so we can see if it poses any special problems."

(3) You can explain the type of evidence from the past or the future that would lead to greater freedom:

- "Let's talk about how you've handled peer pressure to try drugs, and I'll consider letting you cruise down Speedway Boulevard and letting you hang out behind McDonald's, even though I know some of the other kids who cruise have used drugs."
- "Do a good job of coming home on time with this curfew and after a couple of months of success we can extend it."

In many situations, if you are willing to be flexible, you can find a workable compromise. If not, you hold the line. And if you have listened to them, explained your logic, and made it clear that you *eventually* want them to have more freedom, then usually your children will agree to your terms.

If your children will not accept your terms, then you must rely on your power as a parent. The effectiveness of this strategy depends on how many "chips" you have. That is, you need to be giving something of value which would make your teenager comply if you threatened to take it away. For example: "If you stay at parties with drugs and don't leave, I won't let you use the car," or "you'll lose your allowance," or "I won't pay for your auto insurance."

If it reaches this point, don't get hooked in a power struggle. Make it clear that you value cooperation: "I wish we could reach an amicable agreement. But under the circumstances, I must insist."

There is an art to maintaining parental authority with grace. When you have to establish a "bottom line" that your children find objectionable, tell them that you are sorry they are disappointed, that you don't like disappointing them, but that you find it necessary. If possible, make it clear how things could change with time.

MAKING VALID AGREEMENTS

After the give and take of discussion, agreements are made. They can be based on a shared understanding ("We see things the same"), respect for parental authority ("I ask that you agree to my terms"), or parental power ("Agree to my terms or the consequences will be . . .").

A good agreement is crystal clear, understood by all, and accepted by all. Your children may not be thrilled with some of the terms you set, but that doesn't keep them from agreeing in good faith to comply. By the same token, you don't want to establish unnecessary limitations.

Agreements that are not fully understood and not truly accepted will probably be broken and should be considered invalid. Intuition is your protection against accepting invalid agreements:

"It doesn't sound to me like you really have decided to stop using drugs. It sounds like maybe you're just saying so, maybe even to get me off your back. Do you really intend to stop? I don't want you to make an agreement unless you plan to keep it."

Even with a "Yeah, I'll keep the agreement" response, you have to listen carefully and perhaps ask your children to be more convincing.

Also you have to be alert to situations in which your children agree to your terms, but without carefully thinking it through. To this you might say:

"I appreciate your willingness to agree to my request that you stop using drugs. But you agreed so quickly, I want to make sure you have thought it through fully. I'm sure opportunities for drug use will

184

present themselves. Are you determined that you will resist these temptations?''

You don't want to be a doubting Thomas, but on the other hand, you have to recognize that you're not negotiating with peers. You're talking with your children, who might be feeling intimidated. This makes it more difficult to establish valid agreements. Also, you yourself may be tempted to believe anything, because it would relieve your own anxiety. Therefore it makes good sense that you fully use your intuition and establish valid agreements, even if it slows down the process.

Once a valid agreement is made, the expectation should be that everyone will uphold their end of it. So if your seventeen-year-old girl says she'll come home by her midnight curfew, if the agreement is valid, you don't have to wait up for her. That would be indicating mistrust. To do so is to invite childish behavior. However, it makes sense to establish evaluation points: "Let's talk about this after a couple of weeks to see how the curfew is working."

Broken Agreements

Another important aspect of making rules and agreements is establishing consequences for broken agreements.

If there is a history of broken rules, then you need to start with clear consequences from the beginning: "If you don't do your household chores, you won't get your allowance."

If there is no history of problems, then you don't have to lay out consequences. The starting assumption is that everyone will do as agreed. There's no need to assume failure.

When agreements *are* broken, a nonpunitive educational approach will usually get things back on track.

Step One: Begin with a reasonable talk: "You were supposed to be home by eleven o'clock and I noticed you were half an hour late. What happened?"

Then you listen to the explanation. If it was a deliberate violation, you determine whether your agreement was valid, that is, if it was understood and accepted in good faith. If not, you need to talk again and establish an agreement with validity:

"Do you think the curfew is reasonable? If not, say so. I'm not saying I'll necessarily change it, but if it's bothering you, we need to have more discussion."

If the agreement was broken due to an error in judgment, or because your child forgot, you ask what will be done differently to avoid repeating the problem in the future. Then you say you are serious about the curfew and want to make certain that your child is. You ask for assurance that this won't happen again and listen to hear if the agreement is valid.

You may uncover problems, such as "I wanted to come home, but my friends were teasing me about my early curfew."

This shows that you have to help your children learn the necessary skills to keep the agreement. In the above example, the child needs to learn how to resist peer pressure.

By the end of Step One, you want assurance that the agreement will be kept.

Step Two: If the agreement is broken again, you discuss it again, reminding your children that this is the second time it was broken: "Once again you were late for curfew. I'm very concerned about this. You have to start keeping our agreements. What happened? We need to get to the bottom of this."

Depending on the importance of the broken agreement and the history of the child, this step may be repeated another time if the agreement is broken again.

Step Three: This is the same as Step Two, except that at the end you discuss consequences: "This needs to stop or the consequences for breaking the agreement will be . . ."

Step Four: This is when you follow through with the consequences. You might say: "You will stay home for a weekend to think about what has been happening with curfew. Then we'll talk and we'll see if we can make workable agreements during the next week. I want you to be able to go out on weekends. I don't like grounding you, but I need to see improvements."

The goal of all these measures is to promote clear thinking and responsible behavior. You should always bring the discussion back to building good judgment by explaining the reasons for a rule or an agreement and the reasons for setting consequences for misbehavior.

If antagonism has reached a very high level, teenagers sometimes go for broke: "I don't care what you do to me. I'm gonna do what I want to do anyway." This is a serious problem, discussed in the following chapter.

What you want to avoid in all these discussions is losing control and starting to rant and rave. I've seen this over and over again.

186

Children misbehave. Parents lose their temper. The children then back off, donning a self-righteous smirk, waiting in silence for the storm of words to blow over. They've gained a certain measure of control by staying calm while their parents got hysterical. To an outsider, it looks like child against child—the parents have lost their status.

Halfhearted Effort

Broken agreements come in many forms, from blatant disregard of a commitment to a sloppy, halfhearted effort at compliance.

Fifteen-year-old Tom did his chores around the house only sporadically. His parents resented the inconsistency, but held back their feelings because they always hoped for improvement.

Halfhearted compliance such as this poses special problems. Parents tend to tolerate it longer than blatant disregard. Eventually, however, they get angry. Then, the day they plan to talk about their feelings, their children do as they are told for a short period of time.

My suggestion is to treat a halfhearted effort as you would any broken agreement, using the several steps outlined above. For example:

"I've noticed that you haven't been meeting your curfew *regularly* [or "doing your chores," or "cleaning your room"]. Our agreement was that you would do it regularly. You agreed to come home in time for curfew and I expect you to be on time, always, without my reminders. What's been happening?"

"Oh, I'm sorry, I forget."

"What do we need to do to make sure you remember. After all, I expect you to keep our agreements consistently."

The discussion then continues, following the same progression it would take with any broken agreement.

PRINCIPLES FOR MAKING AGREEMENTS ABOUT DRUGS

Many books offer oversimplified advice about drug use or potential use, as if all parents and children were the same, as if all families had the same experiences, and as if the same strategies would be appropriate in every situation and with every age child.

187

The gospel of prevention books is no drug use, ever. Set a rule, enforce it, and punish infractions. I wish it were so simple. However, determining the best strategy for preventing or minimizing drug abuse is a complex matter. It depends upon a careful assessment of a number of factors, including age, maturity and your child-rearing history. It also depends on whether drugs are currently being used and, if so, at what level and with what amount of harm or potential harm.

As a parent, you have many ways to prevent drug abuse. First and foremost is to establish agreements based on a shared understanding. Another way is to make agreements based on respect for your authority as a parent. If needed, you can make agreements based on the threat of punishment. If all this fails, you can use a method called "watching closely," discussed later in this chapter or take more drastic measures to intervene, as described in the following chapter.

In assessing a situation and taking action, I suggest a few guiding principles:

(1) Make it clear that drug use is not for children.
(2) Remember, the goal is not only to prevent harm, but also that your children learn to make wise decisions on their own.
(3) Bear in mind that older teenagers are in a transition to adulthood. They will soon be adults who must make their own decisions.
(4) Recognize pragmatics. Most parents have enough power and influence to stop drug use by preteens and young teenagers. However, it is *impossible* to prevent determined teenagers from acquiring drugs. As your children become older, you have less control over what they do and have to rely on other types of influence.
(5) When children are using drugs and harm is occurring or imminent, it's important to draw the line and make a strong stand quickly.
(6) When the risk of harm is less, you can use more subtle, long-range strategies of influence.

A Word about "Responsible" Drug Use by Children

As I have said throughout this book, my strong recommendation to parents is to say: "The use of alcohol and other drugs is not for children."

I put it in these terms, rather than the alternative: "Only adults can use alcohol and other drugs."

The latter statement makes it sound as if taking drugs is the "grown-up" thing to do.

In recent years, many parents and professionals have accepted the inevitability of drug experimentation by children. They say: "It's a rite of passage of adolescence. We must accept it, learn to deal with it, and minimize the damage."

Although the use of alcohol and other drugs is certainly a common occurrence, it should be noted that a large percentage of teenagers do *not* use drugs at all. I believe that even more would abstain if we set a clear "no use" standard and believed in our ability, as adults, to inspire adherence to this standard.

A consequence of accepting drug use by children has been the practice among some parents and professionals of teaching "responsible use." Since children will take drugs anyway, they say, we must teach them to be responsible users who do not abuse the substances.

The problem with this argument is that it seems to legitimize drug use by children. It seems to me that instead of teaching them how to use drugs responsibly, the effort would be better invested in teaching them how to meet their needs without drugs and how to resist peer pressure. If children are already using drugs, efforts should be made to help them stop.

It would be far too hysterical to state that *all* drug use by teenagers automatically causes harm. However, there are significant risks. In view of this, the goal should be *no drug use*. Only in those situations when use by older teenagers cannot effectively be stopped does it make sense to settle for the lesser goal of preventing a harmful level of use.

Adult Decisions

The "no use" rule for children has to be seen in the context of a cultural standard that allows adults to legally use some drugs, such as alcohol, nicotine, and legally prescribed mood-altering substances, including tranquilizers. Millions of adults use legal and sometimes illegal substances, presumably without impairing their health, and with a willingness to bear the legal consequences.

At some point a child will become an adult and can make his or her own choice. Although we arbitrarily assign ages for certain "adult" behaviors, such as driving a motor vehicle, voting, and drinking alcohol, there is no magical moment when a child becomes an adult.

Adolescence is the transition period to adulthood. In terms of drug use, some adolescents are ready to make adult decisions before others. Determining the readiness of an individual for mature decision making is an important issue and often a source of dispute between parent and child.

Depending on age and maturity, there are differences in how to approach making agreements about drugs with your children. For the sake of explanation, I will somewhat arbitrarily divide the discussion about making agreements into two parts: making agreements with children and young teenagers (up to age fifteen) and making agreements with older teenagers and young adults (sixteen and up). This is not to suggest that all sixteen-year-olds are capable of mature decision making. As you know, other factors enter the equation.

We begin with a discussion about making agreements with children and young teenagers.

MAKING AGREEMENTS WITH CHILDREN AND YOUNG TEENAGERS (FIFTEEN AND UNDER) WHO ARE NOT USING DRUGS

If your children are not using drugs, it may be due to lack of interest or lack of access. Regardless, it is important to make it clear that drugs are not for children, and "no use" is a family rule.

If obedience in your family has been based on punishment for misbehavior, then your children should be told about the consequences of using drugs. At the same time, it's wise to begin to phase out "the threat." Encourage your children to think for themselves and to make wise decisions without your supervision, so that as they get older, they will become increasingly more responsible.

The most important agreement to make with children who have not used drugs is that they will talk with you if they begin to consider the possibility. Above all, you want honesty and dialogue:

"I'm pleased you're not using drugs. If you ever get interested in them I would like you to talk with me right away. Will you do that?"

You might add: "Sometimes people impulsively do things without much forethought. Personally I think it's a bad idea to start using alcohol or other drugs that way. But if this does happen, I want you to agree to talk with me afterward. This isn't to say I think it's okay for you to use drugs. I would be disappointed and angry if you did. But I want us to be able to talk, regardless. Okay?"

Most children who are not using drugs will be willing to agree to these terms. If you encounter resistance, the task is to figure out the obstacles: "What makes it hard for you to talk with me?"

From the diagnostic point of view, what this means is that your children agreed to talk now because they knew you would approve of what they were doing, that is, *not* using drugs. However, you don't yet have the sort of home atmosphere that allows for complete honesty and openness. If this is the case, I suggest you backtrack and work on that.

If your children have already tried drugs and stopped, you will have discussed the experience and the motivation that led to the experimentation in the earlier stages of the exchange of information process. Now you will want to set up the same agreement about being honest in the future as you would with children who have never indulged. You will also want to be certain that your children have the ability to resist future temptation.

The key to finding out whether a decision has been made to stop using drugs is to ask the question: "What if alcohol or pot or some other drug were *put in your hand*? Would you use it?"

Sometimes children think they have stopped experimenting because they haven't sought the drug, but really they have not decided that they would reject drugs should the substances become available.

MAKING AGREEMENTS WITH CHILDREN (FIFTEEN AND UNDER) WHO ARE USING DRUGS

If your children are using drugs—so far without harm—and want to continue to do so (or if they plan to use drugs for the first time), you can explain the potential risks and, together with them, consult books with drug information.

Ideally, they will agree to stop using drugs. If not, you summarize the differences between their analysis and yours, and then establish the rules:

"You think smoking pot is harmless and I see it as risky behavior, especially for someone as young as you. You could be right. It is possible that you could use drugs infrequently, as you say, without substantial harm. But I believe it is not likely and I'm unwilling to allow it. I want you to agree not to use drugs."

Another possibility is that your children understand the risks, but are willing to take their chances. To this you say:

"We each agree that drug use is potentially dangerous. We also agree that it involves substantial legal risks. You're willing to take these risks. I don't want to allow it. That's the difference in our thinking. I want you to agree to refrain from taking drugs."

If drug use has already caused harm, you will have uncovered it in the dialogue. You might say:

"You don't think that drugs are part of a problem, but I do. I see that your grades have fallen in school and that you haven't been doing your chores at home as well as you used to. I won't allow you to continue using drugs. I want you to agree to stop."

You can state the proposed agreement in a gentle yet firm way. You want a valid agreement based on respect, and an important goal is to promote good, clear-headed thinking. Even though you have the ultimate job of setting a standard, it's important that the discussion remain respectful.

After a respectful discussion, many young teenagers will agree to comply with your rules, even if they disagree with your point of view.

As a last resort, a hard line is usually effective with the fifteen-and-under age group. If they intend to use drugs, then you will stop their allowance, restrict their social life and after-school activities, and take other necessary actions. As always, the intent is *not* to hurt them but to protect them from engaging in a risky activity. Children should not be using drugs. You inform them of the consequences of continued drug use and then follow through.

Some children will agree to stop, but won't mean it. You need to use your intuition to watch for phony, invalid agreements designed to end discussions. Listen to the tone of voice to detect sincerity. Listen for an angry "giving-in" tone or for a quick "Yeah, yeah, sure" tone, either of which could indicate an invalid agreement. If you doubt the sincerity, say so in a nice way:

"It doesn't sound like you *really* are agreeing to this. I don't want you to say you'll stop until you intend to follow through. Of course I'll be delighted if you assure me that you mean it. But I want honesty in our relationship. If you haven't really decided to stop using drugs, then we need to keep the discussion going."

The dialogue *must* continue until drug use ceases, no matter how long it takes, and regardless of what consequences you need to impose.

MAKING AGREEMENTS WITH OLDER TEENAGERS (SIXTEEN AND UP) WHO ARE NOT USING DRUGS

Most parents want their older teenage children, ages sixteen and up, to remain drug free.

This age group has easy access to drugs. So if they haven't been using them, then they probably are not interested *at this time*. It's still important to establish a clear "no use" expectation and to make an agreement to maintain an ongoing dialogue.

The way to communicate a "no use" expectation is highly individualized. Thinking about your child-rearing practices will help in assessing where you stand in the transfer of power and in determining the types of agreements you want.

If you have given increasing freedom and responsibility over the years and the transfer of power is on schedule, by age sixteen or seventeen mature children should be ready to make their own wise decisions, even about drugs. All they need is guidance. It would be regressive to set rules and make threats when your children are capable of making good decisions without them.

If the transfer of power is lagging behind schedule, children need a rule to guide their behavior. And if they behave properly only because they are scared about punishment, they need to know the consequences of misbehavior. But it is also important to work toward phasing out this method of control. Soon these children will be young adults without parents around to supervise them. They need to learn to be responsible for themselves.

If you've been overly permissive, that is, allowed too much freedom, and your children have been unable to develop self-control, then you need to regain control and establish some limits. Accustomed to their freedom, your children will probably resist your efforts, but one way or another, they need your leadership. Once you succeed in setting limits, they will be relieved that you helped them settle down. Then you can gradually give back freedom as they demonstrate their ability to behave responsibly.

193

Finally, if you've been too much the authoritarian, setting so many rules and restrictions that your children have rebelled, it's advisable to back off, pick only a few rules that *are* enforceable, and make the tone of the communication less threatening. Before establishing new rules, you have to improve the relationship.

MAKING AGREEMENTS WITH OLDER TEENAGERS (SIXTEEN AND UP) WHO ARE USING DRUGS

If older teenagers are using drugs, occasionally or regularly, it's likely that you will have differences of opinion about the risks and effects, and that you'll disagree about future use. The exchange of information should help in assessing the effects and potential dangers, an important consideration in making agreements.

Certain drugs pose inherent dangers, such as crack, which can quickly create addiction, and heroin, which often involves the use of unsterile needles. If these drugs are being used, you will want to read the following chapter about intervening in serious drug problems. But usually the first drugs used, besides nicotine, are alcohol and marijuana, and usually these substances pose dangers that are less *immediate*. These drugs are the focus of our discussion in the remainder of this chapter. The actions taken will be influenced by an assessment of the harm and risks involved in the way these drugs are being used.

First you can use your educational influence to promote a decision to stop taking drugs. Sometimes an initial discussion may be unsuccessful, but by continuing a dialogue, your children eventually agree to stop.

When drug use has been infrequent and harm doesn't seem imminent, the educational approach has advantages. Although it takes longer and causes more discomfort (because you temporarily have to tolerate the use of drugs), family communication remains intact, and the possible outcome is children learning their lessons well and being prepared to make good decisions for life.

If an ongoing dialogue fails, you still have the option of setting a rule about no further drug use, based on either respect for your authority or, if needed, the threat of punishment.

In some families, given the history of child-rearing practices, a quick jolt of punishment effectively persuades teenagers to give up drugs.

One risk with any form of punishment is that it may increase the determination of rebellious teenagers to defy authority. And even if drug use is halted, the gain may be short-lived. Children stop only because of fear. As they begin to feel more powerful or more rebellious, they start again.

Because older teenagers are bigger, stronger, earning their own money, and in possession of a driver's license, they are much less likely to buckle under to the pressure of punishment than younger children. They have more resources of their own and therefore greater independence. With this age group, you sometimes need to use different strategies for making agreements.

WATCHING CLOSELY

If dialogue and rules don't work in getting a "no use" agreement with older teenagers, and punishment either is ruled out or hasn't worked, I recommend an educational process I call "watching closely." The basic idea is to refrain from strong-arm tactics in exchange for an agreement that your children will behave responsibly in all important realms of their life (in school, at home, with friends, with family) and continue to talk with you about the impact of their drug use.

What you do is:

(1) Express your perception of the problems and the risks of drug use.
(2) Set high standards of behavior.
(3) Maintain an ongoing vigil with your teenagers over what is happening in their lives. (That's why I call it "watching closely.")
(4) Hold your teenagers accountable for their behavior.

Watching closely is effective in promoting self-scrutiny. With this approach, older teenagers have an opportunity to really see how drugs are affecting them.

Intense supervision is important. If your children do not meet the standards of behavior you set and cannot keep the agreements that they make, you handle it respectfully, in a disciplined and constructive way, as you would any broken agreement. You walk them through

195

the same process you would use if drugs weren't involved. This gives your children an opportunity to get back on track. If they don't improve, then you make some connections between drugs and their misbehavior:

"You don't seem to be able to handle drugs and these other responsibilities. I think you need to stop using drugs. What do you think?"

At this point, you ask for a drug-free agreement or a more dedicated commitment to the high standards of behavior. If your children still don't meet their responsibilities after trying again, a whole set of natural and logical consequences will come to pass, always with an explanation to promote understanding of the problem. The logic is made clear. The negative consequences are not punishment for using drugs. They result from the fact that responsibilities are not being met.

TOO LIBERAL?

Is the idea of watching closely too liberal? Is it saying that drug use by older teenagers is acceptable?

These are valid concerns, but the answer is no.

You can't physically stop drug use. Teenagers can get substances in school or in other places when you're not looking. The parent-as-police-officer mode doesn't work with this age group. Education and dialogue are your greatest influences.

Watching closely keeps your children thinking and allows them to understand the risks and effects of what they're doing. The goal is to stop drug use, or at least keep it from increasing. The desired outcome is that your children monitor their own behavior. Such awareness helps prevent or minimize problems.

"Isn't this just teaching children responsible use of drugs," you may wonder, "the very thing you said is not a good idea?"

In a sense it is, but only with older teenagers/young adults, not children, and only as a strategic move. It is based on the objective fact that the method of threats and punishment doesn't usually work and isn't always advisable with older teenagers. In many cases it is wiser to keep the dialogue open, to sacrifice possible short-term gains for long-term influence.

In a way this is saying you want responsible drug use. However, it is more like this: If you as a parent can't effectively stop the drug use no matter what you do, then, yes, try to keep the use in the responsible range. Try to prevent or minimize harm. Don't get caught in a power struggle that completely takes away your power.

Most teenagers who use drugs are not significantly harmed. Many of them outgrow it by the late teens or early twenties, when they are freer of peer pressure and have successfully assumed adult roles. However, if the use is clearly harmful or becoming harmful, *they will see it themselves* if they are watching closely. You will then be in the strong position of having open channels of communication. You have time to talk with them before dependence occurs. You can be the calm voice clarifying problems, not the antagonist.

Watching closely is based on two often-forgotten facts: (1) Children and teenagers do not *want* to harm themselves. Like everyone else, they have a survival and growth instinct. (2) Older teenagers have the potential to think with mature logic. Given an opportunity to clearly understand self-destructive behavior, they can take care of themselves.

Sometimes, however, it's too late for watching closely. If drug use has already reached the level of dependence, reasonable discussions are almost impossible. More drastic measures are needed to attempt to break through the denial and jolt the drug user into reality.

WATCHING CLOSELY: NO HARM, LOWER RISK

The process of watching closely varies according to the level of harm or potential harm in different situations. It is especially difficult to persuade older teenagers that drugs are potentially dangerous if they have been using them without evident harm and they have well-developed life skills (which puts them at less risk for developing dependence). These children are getting the pleasures and benefits of drugs without suffering the negative consequences. This is what you could say to them:

"As you know, I'm against your using drugs. I see it as potentially hazardous to your health. I'm also worried about the legal risks. I know I can't stop you, but I do expect you to perform well in school, be responsible at home, maintain good relationships with friends and other people, and stay healthy. I think that using drugs might interfere with this. Let's watch closely and see what happens. I assume if you see drug-related problems, you'll use your good judgment and stop. Right? So, will you agree about doing well at home, in school, and with friends? Will you agree to keep watching what happens and talking about it?"

At this time, you also set rules for your own protection:

"I'm not going to go crazy and get into a big fight and power struggle with you. However, I'll protect my rights. For example, if you have drugs in our home, that puts me in legal jeopardy. I won't allow that. If you drive under the influence of alcohol or other drugs, that too puts me in jeopardy, and other people. You must agree not to use the family car on days you use drugs. If I even suspect you're mixing alcohol or other drugs and driving, I won't let you use the car for a *long* time.

"I hope setting these rules doesn't mean you'll sneak behind my back. I hope my honesty with you now will encourage your honesty and willingness to talk with me. If we lose trust, then we will really have problems."

This appeal to keeping a good relationship usually is enough to convince most children to keep talking.

Then you maintain the dialogue and have regular ongoing discussions: "How are you doing in school? With friends? How's your health? How are you doing at home?"

If harm begins to occur, you use the feed-it-back approach to point it out. For example: "It looks like your grades have been falling. Have you noticed this? What do you think?"

By watching closely, you trade quick intervention for good thinking. With this method, your children will be able to see the harm that drugs cause and stop before trouble escalates. Also, with the passing of time and nothing to rebel against, teenagers sometimes lose interest in chemical substances. Finally—to speak with candor—some of these older teenagers will continue using drugs—without significant harm.

WATCHING CLOSELY: NO HARM, HIGH RISK

If drugs have not yet caused harm, but you see a high-risk potential, you would say something like this:

"I won't stand by idly while I see the dangers of drug use. I love you too much to ignore this. I'm going to keep talking about what's happening. I want you to stop using drugs, but I also know that I can't follow you around and that you don't intend to stop.

"You say that drugs haven't caused any harm yet. I'm nervous that they will. I think I see a problem brewing in that you've been using drugs to deal with stress. I realize your grades are still fine, you are behaving well at home, and you're doing all your schoolwork. But sooner or later, if you don't learn other ways to prevent stress or to deal with it, I'm worried you'll have a very serious problem. I hope you'll take my recommendation to get professional help to deal with stress. I'll help you myself to the extent I can.

"In the meantime, let's see what happens. I'll expect you to keep up your grades in school, come home in time for curfew, maintain good relationships at home and with your friends, and do all your chores."

WATCHING CLOSELY WHEN YOU SEE HARM

The stakes are much higher when harm is already occurring. The critical distinction at this point is whether your child has crossed into dependence. If this has happened or is about to happen, reasoning is lost. The logical faculties are no longer fully functional. Watching closely won't help.

However, before dependence occurs, numerous problems should be evident. Under these circumstances I recommend an accelerated version of "watching closely." You want your child to recognize the harm quickly, before it escalates. If this fails, more drastic measures are needed:

"I see without question that drugs are harming you. Your grades have fallen. You're in trouble in school. You consistently ignore curfew.

"This is very, very serious. I love you too much to look away, to allow this type of destructive behavior to continue. It's urgent that you stop using drugs. The drugs are harming your life and this family. I'm willing to arrange for professional help. You've got to face this problem. Something must be done.

"Do you agree? Will you stop using drugs?"

If he won't agree, you lay out your expectations once again: "I expect that you will not drink and drive or use drugs and drive. That you will get enough sleep and start to take care of your health. That you will bring up your grades and come home on time for curfew. And that your behavior will start to improve *immediately*."

Some children will be relieved by your strong stance and accept the offer of help. Others will say that they can bounce back in school and that they will behave better. You can cut a little slack, giving them an opportunity to improve quickly within a time limit:

"Look, I hear your earnest desire to fix things. I think you need professional help and I'm willing to provide for it. I'm not at the point of trying to drag you into someone's office. Maybe you'll prove me wrong and stop using drugs on your own and get your life back in order. I hope you do. But there's too much evidence of harm for me to wait long. I'm going to check in with you every week this month to see how things are going. We need some big changes. Will you agree to make them?"

If your teenage child won't agree immediately, back off and let him think about it for a couple of days. If he still won't commit to making changes, it's time for more drastic measures, as outlined in the following chapter. If he does commit to making changes, explain the consequences of not following through and then watch closely what happens:

"If you don't come home on time for curfew, I won't let you go out on weekends" (or, if that is unenforceable and your child will go anyway, then) "I won't give you your allowance" (or) "I won't pay your car insurance" (or) "I won't let you use the family car."

As problems escalate, the warnings get more severe:

"If it deteriorates to the point of your being in trouble with the law, I won't hire an attorney. You'll be on your own. I won't bail you out. If you drop out of school, you'll have to get a job and prove you can hold it successfully to stay living here at home. After that I'll charge you rent or ask you to leave, depending on what it's like with your living here."

If parents don't "rescue" their children, drug abuse will create its own problems and bring the matter to a head. You don't have to take your children to the police (although sometimes it's a good strategy) or tell the teachers at school. The problems in school and eventually with the law will surface of their own accord.

In terms of ultimately giving help, there is some advantage to imposing consequences at home but not being the one who turns them in to other authorities, unless absolutely necessary. If you turn them in, then you look like the bad guy. They may say: "I have a problem and it's my parents." If natural consequences occur at school or with law enforcement officials without your intervention, children see for themselves that drugs are causing harm. They're forced to face the real problem: their use of drugs.

Sometimes it seems you need the patience and discipline of a saint to walk your child through a calm reasoning process when you are frightened about the outcome. However, children who are empowered to think can usually see what is happening. Their logical powers click and they recognize potential or existing problems *before* the harm is too serious.

If drug use already borders on dependence or your child has serious underlying problems, it's possible that this vigilance will not succeed. If the drug use escalates, your child has clearly indicated to you by his behavior, and more important, to himself, that something more drastic must be done.

WALKING THE TIGHTROPE

I speak with experience when I talk about the difficulty of watching something very scary, but holding back just a little to see if long-term benefits will outweigh short-term gains.

I was counseling a sweet but very confused seventeen-year-old girl, Laura, and her parents. She was struggling with her use of pot and, mainly, alcohol, and just barely passing in school. Her parents were upper-middle-class and had given her a car of her own. From time to time they would punish her for one transgression or another by not letting her use the car. The punishment was ineffective. It didn't stop Laura from doing everything she wanted to do. She always managed to find a friend's car to drive.

Soon after the initial session, her parents and I learned that Laura was drinking and driving.

"Don't worry," she said, "I'm a safe driver, even when I drink." Her parents took away her use of the car for a week until she said she would stop drinking and driving.

No problem for Laura. When I met with her separately, she told me that she had managed to drink and drive a friend's car that week. Also, she would lie to her parents about drinking, so they would get off her back.

201

Furthermore, Laura was angry that her parents had used the car as punishment.

"Don't you think it's unfair?" she asked.

"What?" I replied.

"That they punish me by taking away the car."

"I wouldn't say unfair," I answered with candor, "so much as ineffective. It didn't really make a difference, did it?"

"No, not really," she answered.

"I want to be very honest with you," I said to Laura. "It scares me when I hear that you're drinking and driving. I think it's very dangerous, and *no one* should do it. You risk your own life and the life of everyone else who's on the road."

Laura assured me that she was a good driver, even after drinking.

I explained that alcohol is tricky. It gives a false sense of security, causing people to think they can drive fine. But research has proven it slows reflexes. That's why all the drunk driving laws have been passed and are being so strongly enforced.

"You know," I said, "you can lose your license if you get caught drinking and driving. And police are out watching you kids cruise. They'll pull you over, even if you haven't violated a law."

This really caught her attention. She valued her driver's license as much as anything.

She asked about the legal level of intoxication. I explained and promised to bring a little cardboard device for calculating the amount of blood alcohol based on consumption, body weight, and the time elapsed since the last drink. She was interested.

As the session ended, I felt a sense of responsibility for her, her parents, and innocent drivers and pedestrians. I thought about my options, including breaking the confidentiality and telling her parents what was happening. What could they do? Not let her use the car again? Keep her at home? She was clever and would get around any punishment they dished out. Taking away the car for good would lead to a mammoth power struggle. I decided to trust that Laura was a reasonably intelligent human being who, given an opportunity to think, would make a good decision.

I admit to some trepidation.

The next week I brought the device for calculating blood alcohol to the office and gave it to her. Together we figured out how it worked. She discovered for herself that she had often been clearly over the

202

legal limit of intoxication. She worried about losing her license. She took the device home.

The following week she told me she had decided she would never drink and drive again. "It's too dangerous," she said.

She stuck to it, too. When she didn't feel threatened by her parents, and cooler heads prevailed, Laura was able to make good decisions on her own. This was a turning point for her. Later that year I proudly attended her high school graduation.

PROFESSIONAL HELP

The family is one place to confront personal problems, but it's not the only resource. Often families find that they cannot solve their problems alone. If problems are not being solved at home, then it's important to seek help elsewhere, the sooner the better. Counselors, psychologists, social workers, and other mental health professionals are an excellent resource. Ideally, they should be consulted before drug dependence develops, to assist with preventive efforts. If dependence has already occurred, the help of professionals is urgent.

Getting to the bottom of a drug problem involves more than abstinence. The underlying causes must be addressed, and mental health professionals are trained to help with this. Often, remediation involves professionals helping children learn basic life skills—the ones we discussed in the context of prevention—so that they can meet their needs without drugs and without hurting themselves.

Attitudes about psychotherapy have come a long way since the old days, when consulting a professional was seen as a major source of embarrassment, a family secret. And services have become much more accessible with the advent of community mental health clinics. Free and sliding-fee-scale services are widely available.

When you discuss problems with your children, one of the offers you can make is to seek professional help. You can call it the help of an impartial third party trained to deal with problems. Keep it positive and be careful not to present it as a threat: "If you don't shape up, I'll take you to a psychiatrist."

Some children will gratefully accept your offer, others will be reluctant. Unless harm is serious, rather than trying to force the issue, professional help can be an ongoing offer as you continue the dialogue. That way, when children finally acknowledge problems, they won't have to feel that they are giving in to pressure.

Seeking professional help is a family matter. Alcohol and other drug problems do not occur in a vacuum. They are affected by the family situation and will have consequences on a family dynamic. As parents, you can benefit from professional help when the family has a drug problem. An ideal offer is:

"Let's all go for some help to deal with this problem. We can go separately or together, whichever makes you more comfortable. I'm sure we [your parents] share some responsibility for what's happening. Let's solve these problems together."

In selecting professional help for substance abuse issues, I have two precautions. One is that you want to make sure that the professional has had experience in working with alcohol and other drug-related problems. Not all of them have had this experience, although training programs are increasingly recognizing this important area of study. Also, be aware that some substance abuse and hospital programs tend to see all drug use as an indication of addiction. Be sure to inquire whether the professionals are equipped to work in preventive ways, to identify and treat less extreme levels of drug use.

One of the biggest obstacles to people seeking professional help is a culture-wide ideology of super-individualism: "It's my problem, and I need to solve it alone." If you or your child is tied to this belief, I suggest you think twice. The argument of the super-individualist is that getting help is a sign of weakness. I think it's just the opposite. It's a sign of strength to be willing to admit to problems and to use all available resources to confront them.

If a child insists that he wants to solve problems alone, you can encourage him to succeed, but keep the option of help in the forefront of his mind. He may say: "Trust me, I'm gonna change things." A good response is: "I do trust you. Suggesting you get professional help doesn't mean that I don't. It means I think you, like anyone else, deserve support in making important changes.

"You say you can solve this alone. I'm on your side. I hope you're right. Let's see what happens."

PROMISES, PROMISES

"I'm gonna cut back."

"I'm gonna stop using drugs."

These are sincere promises repeated over and over again by children who are having serious problems but finding themselves incapable of solving them. Hopeful parents take heart with each new commitment, but at some point they must ask themselves how many times the pledges have been made and then broken.

A good way to keep track of broken promises is by watching closely and using the feed-it-back approach. You can offer help:

"If you want, we can set limits and restrictions that would support you. Like, for example, you can agree to come home right after school and to avoid any party where there might be drugs. You can agree to stay away from your friends who use drugs. If you do this, it'll probably be easier for you. What do you think? Or we can get some professional help. Would you like that?"

Each failed attempt to keep a promise is discussed, and each time it becomes increasingly clear that the child needs assistance.

DRASTIC MEASURES

Drastic measures need to be used when drugs have taken over and reasonable discussion simply is impossible. It also makes sense to take drastic measures before dependence has happened, if it is clear that patient and disciplined watching closely is not working.

But first a word of caution. Many parents make a serious mistake by *prematurely* using drastic measures. They may, for example, humiliate their teenage child with a urinalysis, or try to keep him "imprisoned" at home during all his spare time, or place him in a mental hospital against his will, even when drug use has been only minimal.

When reflecting back on his teenage years, a young man with a serious drug problem told me about his parents going to an extreme after he smoked pot the first time:

"I was almost perfect compared to other kids. I stayed out of trouble and used to talk honestly with my parents. But they went nuts when I told them I'd smoked pot for the first time. They didn't let me out of the house after school or on weekends for a month. They informed my teachers and basketball coach that I had smoked pot. Okay, I decided. If they're going to punish me like that, I won't give them any more information. My parents became my enemy. I stopped telling them anything. I decided they'd have to catch me."

This left the young man at the mercy of the "educational influence" of friends. A more moderate response might well have prevented his ultimate problems.

In recent years, I've noticed a disturbing tendency to place children who have used drugs in mental hospitals as the first alternative, when it really should be one of the last. Seductive advertising by these institutions catches the attention of distracted and busy parents looking for help. Sometimes part of the problem in the first place is that the parents don't have enough time for their children. Hospitals exploit this with advertisements that essentially say: "Turn the responsibility over to us."

Drastic measures should be taken only when all other options have been ruled out. Taking drastic measures to prevent or minimize drug abuse is not the type of prevention we've been talking about in this book. As you will see, however, even though parents sacrifice dialogue for forceful intervention when they take drastic measures, the desired outcome is ultimately the same: to get the young person to think about what he's doing. We'll talk about this in the next chapter.

PART III

INTERVENTION

8

DRASTIC MEASURES

It shouldn't have been such a shock to Mr. and Mrs. Cooper considering all the warning signs. Jeremy's grades in school had fallen dramatically, to the point where this former honor student was failing three classes. The Coopers noticed but figured it was a passing phase. They kept believing the promises of miraculous improvement, even when time and again these promises were empty. Meanwhile, they wrote notes excusing absences whenever Jeremy "ditched" school.

Jeremy's cheerful disposition had long ago given way to nasty moodiness. Ugly remarks were excused as typical teenage rebellion. Missed curfews were brushed aside as a sign of the times: "Kids aren't behaving as well as they used to."

When Jeremy was fired from a job at a fast food restaurant, the Coopers believed his unlikely excuse—that he was being hassled unfairly by the boss.

All along the Coopers gave Jeremy substantial amounts of money so he could buy necessities, such as lunches and gas for the car. But his needs kept growing.

Although the signs of a problem were abundant, Mr. and Mrs. Cooper missed them. Instead, they rescued Jeremy, thus enabling him to consume increasing amounts of pot, alcohol, and cocaine.

When he was finally picked up by the juvenile authorities, the whole story came out into the open.

"How could you do this to your family," his father said, "after all we've done for you?"

Jeremy just laughed at him contemptuously.

At this point, Jeremy's parents read an article about getting tough with misbehaving teenagers and decided to lay down the law at home. No alcohol and no other drugs. Pass all subjects in school. Be home in time for curfew. Accept a share of household responsibilites. No more hanging out with druggies. Go back to his old, nice friends. No more supplements to his lunch-money allowance (because he might use them to buy drugs). No more use of the family car.

In getting tough with their son, the Coopers had no self-criticism about their own role in his problems and their own enabling behavior. They also had no sense of how to go from where the problem stood to where they wanted the changes to lead.

Jeremy who had been the "good boy" protected by loving parents, suddenly became the "bad boy" whose misbehavior could not be tolerated. He had never learned personal responsibility, but now was being asked to be a model child. Failure was inevitable. Jeremy could not, and would not, meet the new expectations.

He retaliated against the tough regime by blasting his stereo in the middle of the night, sneaking out of windows to be with his friends, and getting into even more trouble with the law.

His condition worsened. His mood changed moment by moment. He became increasingly hostile. His life revolved around getting and then using drugs. He didn't seem to care about himself or anyone else.

Now Jeremy is in a drug treatment center, with an uncertain future. This is a sad story of addiction.

The main thrust of this book is *preventing* drug abuse by empowering children to think clearly and to make wise decisions. One of the effects of addiction is to damage relationships and diminish logical reasoning, making reasonable discussions and wise decision making almost impossible. When addiction occurs, it's too late for prevention. It's time for *intervention*.

Ultimately, however, the cure for addiction involves the same outcome as prevention—a person learns to think clearly and make good decisions. But the conditions for this must be established. First, you need more drastic measures to cut through the defenses, confusion, and distortions.

This chapter is about meeting the challenge of drug dependence when it has already developed, as with Jeremy, or when it seems likely to develop because drug usage has been increasing and preventive measures have been ineffective.

210

Drug addiction is easier to prevent than to cure. There is no sure-shot remedy, so parents must be prepared for a struggle. To help your children, you first need to take care of yourself. It's like on airplanes when the flight attendants advise passengers to put on their own oxygen masks before putting them on their children.

TAKING CARE OF YOURSELF

Drug problems of a single individual drain the emotional energy of an entire family, arousing anger, depression, fear, and frustration. The experience is also one of confusion: "What went wrong? I don't really understand."

Typically, parents react to addiction with extreme blame. Some parents hold themselves personally responsible, saying: "I've failed." Anxious and depressed, they start second-guessing themselves: "If only I had . . ."

Other parents explode with anger and put all the blame on their children, whom they now see as misfits and failures.

Either way, this blaming behavior is, at best, not constructive.

If your children are addicted or are using drugs dangerously, I'm sure you realize that they need help. Regardless of what they do, I recommend that you get professional help for *yourself*, or enroll in a self-help group such as Alanon, Families Anonymous, or Toughlove, or do both. You *need* support, for your own sake and for your children's.

In many respects the approach of some of the self-help groups is consistent with the philosophy of empowering children on which this book is based. The idea of these self-help groups is that, when addiction occurs, you don't stop *loving* your children, but you do stop *rescuing* them. You no longer engage in any enabling behavior. You no longer provide the financial resources, phony excuses, legal help, or bail money. Neither do you provide the emotional support that has allowed the drug habit to flourish. Most self-help groups teach you to draw the line, that is, to clarify the limits of acceptable behavior. Before you start offering help again, your children must take important steps toward helping themselves. They must take responsibility for their own behavior. You cannot, and should not, try to save them.

One problem, however, is that sometimes parents in these groups

211

put *all* the blame on their children and don't acknowledge or fully acknowledge their own mistakes. At most they will say: "We should have been more strict sooner." But drug problems *always* develop within a family context. Therefore it is important, when drawing the line, to share the responsibility:

"I'm sure we [your parents] played a part in your problems. I don't think we were as available as we should have been when you were younger. I'm really sorry about that. We also shouldn't have been covering up for you at school. Then we made matters worse by picking on you. But that's in the past. We're trying to understand what we've done wrong, so we can do better in the future. But you've got to do your share of changing, too. Our efforts will be wasted unless you make an equal effort."

LEARNING FROM PAIN

When your children are on the way to becoming drug dependent and attempts to reason with them have failed, they can learn from the pain they experience. Pain teaches, and you can be the supportive ally in an effort to promote self-responsibility:

"I see all the problems you're having with friends, in school, and here at home. I hate to see you hurting so much. I don't think it'll get any better without professional help, and it'll probably get a lot worse. How about talking with someone? I'll be glad to arrange an appointment for you and go along if you want."

Some children will say they've tried to stop or cut back on drugs, but haven't been successful. This, you explain, is all the more reason to get help.

If they won't go for help, make your expectations very clear. At a time when they are not under the influence of alcohol or any other drug, make a gentle yet firm statement:

"I see serious problems. You won't acknowledge the problems or stick with the agreements you've made. I've offered counseling, but you won't accept my offer.

"We have rules at home. We insist that you follow the rules or take the consequences. The rules include keeping your personal living space clean, sharing in household chores, succeeding in school, and showing respect for others who live here. Because of your drug habit, I don't think you can do this. I don't think you're capable of making valid agreements, but I'll give you a final chance to prove me wrong."

You and the rest of the family will get angry as your children break rules and behave irresponsibly. It's important to express your resentments, which are the natural consequences of drug use. (For more information on disciplined ways to express resentments, refer back to Chapter 3.)

As Fred, a fifteen-year-old, got out of the car at his friend's house, he was swearing at his dad. It was the type of hostile nastiness that often goes with drug dependence. The father didn't get into a verbal power struggle. He simply said: "I'm very angry about what you called me. You'll have to arrange another ride home or take the bus."

When children consistently fail to fulfill their responsibilities because of drug problems, parents should begin to withdraw the benefits and privileges of family membership. Children lose the financial and emotional support that was being misused to perpetuate bad habits. The explanation is not punitive:

"It doesn't feel right to launder your clothing, prepare your meals, or transport you around town while you're being so rude to us. You blast the stereo, lie to us, and don't do your share of the work around the house. Your friends call at all hours. We want to do nice things for you, but not under these circumstances. Being thoughtful and cooperative is a two-way street."

A drug problem will create natural consequences not only at home, but also in school and possibly with the law. If children are expelled or flunk out of school, you'll ask them to get a job and pay rent. Drugs are the problem, and you'll be the reasonable adult expecting adult behavior:

"As you know, we expect you to succeed in school. If you're expelled, we'll expect you to get a job and pay rent."

If children threaten physical violence, as sometimes they do, they should know that you will call the police. Sometimes a single serious encounter with a law-enforcement official is enough to scare children straight.

As awful as it seems, you can't rescue your children from drug dependence. What you can do is: (1) Stop contributing to the problem by rescuing or persecuting, and (2) Encourage your children in every possible way to take responsibility for themselves.

As you do your best and suffer with them, remind yourself that you cannot control their behavior.

TAKING ACTION

It is wise to intervene in a drug problem before dependence occurs, if it is evident that your children won't make agreements to give up drugs and they are using drugs dangerously without thinking about the effects.

By this point you have urged that they go for individual or family counseling. They may have promised or vowed that they would either stop or reduce their drug use. They may have pledged that they would do better at home or school. But instead of improvement, the situation has worsened.

Your children still deny a problem.

It's about time for more drastic measures, including the possibility of forcing them to go for drug treatment or petitioning the juvenile court to declare them "incorrigible," meaning essentially out of control and refusing to accept limits. (Bear in mind, however, that most juvenile court systems are not highly responsive, because they are already overburdened with children who have committed offenses.)

If the children are of legal age, they can be evicted from the home: "You can't live here and behave this way."

These actions will make your children angry and possibly more rebellious. Using this type of power is, at best, a trade-off. You may gain a measure of control. The price you pay is diminished communication and trust. But at this point, you have little alternative. Let your children know that you are considering these drastic measures.

THE WHOLE TRUTH

Drug-dependent teenagers usually get in trouble with many people in their lives—school officials, employers, neighbors, brothers, sisters, friends, and romantic partners. Often these people will come to you, the parents, with complaints about your children. When they come, it's a good idea to ask them to be candid with your children and not to spare them from the truth and also the consequences of their behavior.

In a last-ditch effort to promote voluntary treatment, your strong warning about drastic measures can be complemented by eliciting the candor of other people who are important to your children. You can approach these people and ask them to come forward with their thoughts and feelings, to confront your children, in a caring and supportive way, with their perspective on what's happening. The idea is that no one saves the drug abuser from hearing the truth about the impact of his behavior. This chorus of voices makes it difficult for him to deny a problem.

The drug-abusing person might counterattack. He may offer a string of lies about what's really been happening or about having already stopped his drug use . . . last week. But he knows he will no longer be fooling anyone: Regardless of what *he* thinks about the situation, a whole group of people close to him see things differently. Ideally, the confrontation will break through the denial and he will agree to accept help.

Sometimes families or counselors hold a special meeting to bring significant people together to confront drug-abusing individuals. This encounter is called an intervention. Such a meeting is an ideal not always realizable. However, most people who are concerned about a child will agree to come. Surprisingly, some teenagers endure the encounter, probably because behind their defensive wall, they know something is wrong and are crying for help. They are more likely to attend, and stick it out, if an intervention is held right after a drug-related crisis, such as an arrest or the breakup of a relationship. At this meeting, participants are asked to share their observations and feelings, with care and concern, and without using put-downs or making accusations. The drug-using person can answer, but participants are told not to get into arguments.

It used to be said that alcoholics and drug abusers couldn't be helped until they hit rock bottom. This aroused a vision of skid row bums, sleeping on sidewalks with a bottle of Muscatel in their hands. The idea behind having an intervention (or asking concerned individuals to confront a drug-abusing person on a one-to-one basis) is that the bottom can be elevated. In other words, *existing* harmful consequences can be vividly presented in the hope of promoting an earlier recognition of problems and a willingness to get help.

The Cooper family arranged an intervention for their son, Jeremy, in their home, with the help of a local drug treatment program. Some of what was said at the meeting and over a period of a week after the meeting is condensed and presented below.

A former girlfriend confronted Jeremy:

"You stopped being fun. All you ever wanted to do was get high. You kept breaking dates. You seemed more concerned with drugs than me. I was very hurt."

A former friend:

"You borrowed money from me and never returned it. You called me names because I didn't want to use cocaine. We used to have good times together. We used to be close. Now you've left me."

A teacher:

"You don't hand in your assignments. You don't study. You're failing in my class. This doesn't fit at all with what your previous academic record indicates about your capabilities."

Mrs. Cooper:

"You've stopped doing your share at home. You don't keep agreements. Money keeps disappearing. I suspect you're stealing it. You're rude and insulting to me, like this morning when you yelled, 'Get lost, bitch.' "

The manager at the fast food restaurant where he had worked:

"I fired you because you came late and didn't show up for shifts. I gave you fair warning."

Mr. Cooper:

"You seem high, either stoned or drunk, almost every day. You don't even look me straight in the eye when we talk."

Jeremy Cooper angrily left the intervention session, threatening to run away. A couple of weeks later, he agreed to enter treatment of his own accord.

TREATMENT UNDER PRESSURE

With some children, a hostile, go-for-broke attitude accompanies drug problems. Children essentially say: "I don't care what you do, you can't stop me."

In school they say: "Go ahead—send a note home, suspend me, expel me. I don't care."

At home they say: "Go ahead—take away the car. Ground me. Take away financial support. I'll climb out the window and steal a car if I need to."

If your children won't talk and won't voluntarily go for help, you face a very tough decision about whether to coerce them into treatment. You see the problem getting worse. You've stopped enabling. You're not persecuting. What's left?

The idea of people being forced into treatment is an objectionable one. Most of the time, it fails. But if I look at my own experience as a psychologist, I realize that I've worked with teenagers who were initially coerced into my office by their parents. I tell the parents up front that I won't work with children who do not agree there is a problem and want help. Then I make my position clear to the children:

"It doesn't seem that you really want to be here. It looks like you were kind of dragged into the office. Is that right?"

"Yes."

"Well, I don't want to be your punishment. It doesn't feel good to me, and I can't be of any value to you if you're here under duress. But it does seem like you have at least one problem: your relationship with your parents. I'd be happy to talk about that with you, and I'd be happy to talk about your life and your drug use if you want, so you and I can reach our own conclusions."

Almost invariably, if the pressure is lifted, these children welcome an opportunity to talk. After all, they usually do have serious problems and many things on their mind, and usually no one with whom to talk.

I also know of situations in which children did well after being coerced into residential treatment and forced to "detox" from drugs. They get greater clarity of thought once the chemicals are out of their system, and sometimes they are able to recognize and admit to problems they had been denying. Usually, however, they are angrier and more determined to defy authority. In part, the outlook of individuals who are pressured into treatment depends upon the way they are received. If mental health workers start dishing out punishment or acting as if they are dealing with a voluntary client, the outcome will probably be negative.

Treatment under pressure has no guarantees. But sometimes you run out of choices and have to take your chances.

DRUG TREATMENT

The major treatment options for substance abuse are outpatient therapy, inpatient hospitalization, and residential treatment (nonhospital settings, such as therapeutic communities). These options describe settings for treatment. The specific type of counseling varies according to the orientation of the provider.

Another option for confronting alcohol and drug abuse is self-help groups such as Alcoholics Anonymous and Narcotics Anonymous. These peer groups help support individuals in a drug-free lifestyle. Countless numbers of people have benefitted from affiliating with these organizations. For some, the strength gained through shared vulnerability at a self-help group is a good complement to their professional counseling, which is aimed at uncovering the underlying causes of drug abuse. Sometimes, however, individuals discover contradictions between the orientation of professionals and that of the self-help organizations.

The evaluation of treatment for drug dependence is neither conclusive about what works best nor highly encouraging about outcome. Each variety of treatment claims success, but persuasive scientific evidence to back up the claims is lacking.[1] A variety of factors have confounded the validity of results in terms of evaluating programs.[2] For example, what a reasonable person would consider success is often not what is measured in evaluations. Sometimes the criterion for success is merely a client's completing the program, or remaining abstinent while in the program, or maintaining short-term abstinence after discharge. From the family's point of view, this hardly measures up to what is desired.

The research on effectiveness of treatment is filled with contradictions, some reports favoring residential treatment, others saying it is costlier but no more effective than outpatient treatment. Some stress longer duration of treatment, others say this is not more beneficial.[3]

The confusion in the research literature is matched by anecdotal observations of inconsistency. Children sometimes go through very expensive inpatient treatment at private substance abuse centers and use drugs the day they are released. Sometimes drugs are smuggled into treatment centers. Sometimes teenagers who are getting help for a marijuana or alcohol problem learn about heavier drugs, such as heroin, while in a treatment center.

Some residential treatment centers are run by former addicts who have become intoxicated with their newfound power and cultlike in their practices.

Some counselors offering outpatient or inpatient care have never been trained in dealing with substance abuse problems. Some try to deal with underlying causes, without even insisting that the drugging and drinking cease—a naive but still widely practiced endeavor.

SUCCESSFUL TREATMENT

Clearly there is no simple formula for overcoming drug addiction. But there still is hope.

Some teenagers find the power from within to get off drugs.

Some programs work for some people. And sometimes it takes two or three visits to programs before success is achieved.

Some teenagers seek help and find relief by joining Alcoholics Anonymous.

In selecting a counselor or a program, I suggest looking for certain characteristics:

Family involvement: Ideally the whole family system is involved, so that as an individual changes the system changes as well.

Geared for teenagers: Many programs accept adolescents but were designed for adults with completely different life experiences. An ideal program should be specifically geared to the experiences and needs of teenagers. Counselors should be experienced in working with youth.

Positive peer influence: Because peer influence is so strong, an ideal program should use this force for positive peer pressure.

Focus on positive attitudes and life skills: Some counselors and some programs focus only on drugs and addiction. They should also promote the development of healthy attitudes and life skills—helping children learn social skills, problem-solving skills, and positive ways to deal with stress. They should promote self-esteem and self-respect and *not* tear a person apart. These goals are best accomplished in a homey, noninstitutional environment. Residential programs should include an array of recreational and educational activities, not merely encounter sessions aimed at confronting drug use.

Focus on drugs: Some counselors only focus on the underlying psychological causes of drug abuse and fail to empower children to overcome the existing dependence. It is important that a counselor dealing with addictions insist that children stop using drugs, help them break ties to their drug-using past, and prepare them to resist future pressures and temptations.

Transition and after-care: After the program ends, attention needs to be paid to what comes next. Good programs help clients avoid relapse, yet give them the strength to cope with all eventualities. They provide after-care services or a plan for ongoing support. Hospital and residential programs should help arrange a good transition back to home and school.

Philosophy of empowerment: Good counselors in good programs are cautious not to take away the power of people who come for help. Counselors do *not* tell children what is wrong. Rather, they help children see it themselves. Good counselors encourage and require children to use their personal power and resources to take responsibility for themselves and don't foster dependence.

Professional training in substance abuse issues: An ideal program is under the direction of a person with extensive professional experience in the field and recognized credentials.

In making your choices, I suggest that you talk personally with people who offer the services. I'd be wary of programs making grandiose promises and claims of 90 percent cure rates. The treatment of substance abuse has become big business. Like other businesses, profits are sometimes put ahead of concern for the individual.

Still, you have to choose the person and place to go for help. You have to try something. If the first choice doesn't work, you keep looking, because ultimately your child and your family need help. You simply can't give up. It's sad that we have such troubles in our society. We need to work for social changes that reduce the occurrence of drug abuse. That's the topic of the next chapter. But until those changes occur, we have to use all our power to protect the people we love and to find the help they need.

9

FAMILIES WORKING TOGETHER: COMMUNITY STRATEGIES FOR REDUCING DRUG ABUSE

About twenty years ago I was in a hotel room in Chicago with my college roommate and twelve to fifteen other people, mainly his relatives. We were packed together like sardines. My roommate was recovering from a knee operation. His normally cheerful face was all scrunched up, and his moans sent shivers up my spine. One of his uncles, a physician, suggested Valium and was about to write a prescription.

"No need, I have some," someone said.

"So do I," someone else added.

"Me, too," was offered by a third person.

Then I witnessed that funny scene you sometimes see when you ask to borrow a pen. Everyone starts fumbling through their pockets and handbags to see who can find one first.

I didn't count, but about half the people in the room were carrying a supply of psychoactive drugs.

Back in those days, the mass media were talking about drug problems and a drug culture, referring mainly to pot and LSD. When I observed this group in action, I recognized for the first time the full extent to which drugs permeate our entire society.

We live in a drug-filled and drug-oriented world. If you have a headache, you take an aspirin. If your back hurts, you take pain pills. If you feel depressed, you take antidepressants. We also live in a

221

consumer-oriented society in which people buy and consume products to make themselves feel good.

Under these circumstances, it's impossible to isolate children from exposure to drugs and from the consumer mentality. But as you've seen in the previous chapters, with dedicated and sustained effort, parents can prepare their children for coping with the pressures to use drugs.

To solidify your efforts at home, you can begin to look beyond your own family—to other parents, to schools, and to your community. These are important influences on your children. You want them to be teaching, encouraging, and reinforcing the same healthy behaviors and attitudes that you promote at home.

This chapter is about parents expanding their influence and working together with other parents to bring about social changes that reduce the availability and acceptability of drugs in our communities. As an organized force, parents can achieve goals that they could not reach as individuals.

Every community has a message about children using drugs. The message is what parents, schools, policy makers, and law enforcement people *really do* about drugs, not necessarily what they *say* they will do. Until recently, most communities in this country had a message of indifference that went something like this:

"We will tolerate children drinking alcohol and using other drugs as long as there's no serious harm, even though we *say* children shouldn't do it."

This laissez-faire attitude allowed children to start taking drugs at an early age. It allowed recreational use of most substances, including illegal ones. It even allowed certain high-risk behaviors, such as driving while intoxicated.

As drug problems escalated, there was an uproar. An enormous movement of activist parents, alarmed by the extent of drug use by children and the indifference of adults, began to change the message in their own communities and around the country. Parents set higher standards of behavior and insisted that their schools and communities do likewise. In response to this grassroots movement, social institutions and government responded with corresponding changes.

The new message about drugs is still evolving, but its leading edge is quite clear: Alcohol and other drugs are *not* for children. We cannot overlook the risks and dangers of children using drugs.

222

PARENTS HELPING PARENTS

The starting point for cooperating with other parents is getting to know each other. The simplest way to do this is to introduce yourself to the parents of your children's friends. As you get acquainted, you share experiences and perspectives. At some point you can make the discussion more formal by suggesting that you start talking about the drug issue and other pertinent topics, and that you work toward establishing clear community standards and mutual support in maintaining the standards.

Some of the best results of parents talking with each other have been in making guidelines for parties. Parents have agreed to policies such as these: to have invitation-only parties, to make sure the parties are chaperoned (at least casually), to make it clear that alcohol and other drugs will not be tolerated, and to set an agreed-upon reasonable hour for parties to end.

In some communities, parents make a commitment to call each other if a child is found to be in possession of alcohol or any other drug. That way the parents are not the last to find out, as is too often the case.

PARENTS AND SCHOOLS

One of the most important ways for parents to take positive action in a community is to make sure that local schools have a comprehensive substance abuse prevention and intervention plan. This should include clear school policy and procedures about drugs, a kindergarten through twelfth-grade substance abuse prevention curriculum, an array of alternative activities, and a system for the identification and referral of drug problems.

Ideally, every school district should establish a community drug advisory committee on which parents are represented. In communities where there were no such committees, parents have been successful in lobbying for them.

Policy and Procedures

One way to create a healthy and safe school climate is by establishing clear school policy prohibiting drug use and by firmly and fairly enforcing it. Procedures are needed for handling drug possession, drug use, and the suspicion that someone is under the influence of drugs. The roles and responsibilities of schools and local law enforcement agencies should be clarified.

Curriculum

Ideally, the school prevention curriculum would be much like your own curriculum at home that we've discussed in this book, emphasizing the attitudes and life skills that build resistance to substance abuse and providing accurate information about alcohol and other drugs. Some of the curriculum can be included in existing classes. But this type of learning also takes a place of its own. It is *social and psychological knowledge,* and it's as important to an individual's intellectual development as is physical and logical knowledge. Historically, it has been neglected in our schools.

Aternative Activities

Alternative activities, so named because they serve as a positive alternative to drug use, are part of a comprehensive prevention program. These activities show that life can be enjoyable and fulfilling without drugs. They provide positive growth experiences, reinforcing the attitudes and life skills in the prevention curriculum. By participating in these activities, students learn leadership skills and are influenced by positive peer role models. Examples of alternative activities are: Project Prom and Project Graduation (programs in which students plan drug-free celebrations); student retreats; tutorial programs (older students tutoring younger ones); teen leadership training; "Just Say No" Clubs (for students who want to support each other in remaining drug free); and SADD groups (Students Against Drunk Driving).

Another type of student activity that has been used in preventing drug abuse and other problems is peer counseling. Often fellow students will discuss problems with peers that they would not reveal to adults. Peer counselors offer help or make referrals.

Identification and Referral of Problems

School personnel and peer counselors need to stay alert to the early warning signs of problems and to know how and where to make referrals. Also, students themselves need to know where they can turn for help if they feel the need.

Ideally, a school would offer support groups or special individualized services for students at high risk for drug abuse and for those who have been referred for help. Schools should also designate a staff member to stay abreast of available community resources.

School Climate

The attitudes and life skills that protect against substance abuse do not lend themselves well to brief and simplistic instruction. For example, self-esteem cannot be increased simply on the basis of a few hour-long modules in the classroom. To promote self-esteem and other positive attitudes and to teach basic life skills, the *entire* school climate must support wellness, self-respect, and respect for others. It must provide opportunities and incentives for success. The whole system must be geared to healthy development. Parents can be a strong force in working for this type of school climate.

COMMUNITY INVOLVEMENT

Parents uniting with each other is the beginning of building a sense of community. Working with schools expands the impact of parents. But to really change the messages about drugs and to fully empower children to resist drug abuse, the *entire* community should be mobilized. This includes media, local business leaders, law enforcement, health professionals, elected officials, civic groups, youth leaders, and churches and synagogues.

In recent years, action-oriented groups have been formed in communities around the country. Some have taken a hit-or-miss approach to creating change, although recently these groups have become much more systematic, in part because local and statewide professionals have offered "team training."

Systematic approaches to community change pull together all segments of a community. Members inform themselves about drugs. They assess community needs and resources. They examine prevailing attitudes and practices. Then they decide what changes they want, and make an action plan.

Organized communities can influence and change everything—attitudes, practices, laws, norms, and behavior. Community groups have used the media to deliver positive prevention messages. They have worked with policy makers to initiate enlightened legislation about drugs and to increase financial support for substance abuse prevention programs. They have raised private funds from businesses to cover the expenses of prevention programs. They have pressured convenience stores and other businesses to stop selling alcohol and tobacco products to minors. They have created alternative activities for young people, such as teen institutes, and recreational and leadership programs. They have opened lines of communication between schools and health professionals and helped coordinate services.

As communities organize, they establish standards for behavior. Children need clear and consistent boundaries. They need to know what type of behavior is accepted in their community and what is not. In the past, boundaries about drugs have been weak, vague, and inconsistent.

By joining an existing community group or by forming a new one, you demonstrate your own serious, personal commitment to preventing drug abuse. You serve as a role model of taking control over your environment, of social concern and social responsibility. You show your children the importance of being involved in social causes, in something bigger than oneself.

THE BIG PICTURE

Drug abuse is not just a personal or family problem. It's a social problem as well. When substantial numbers of children abuse drugs in a society, you have to wonder why. You have to pull back and look at the larger picture.

What you see is that drug abuse is not an isolated problem. It is only one of many problems plaguing children and teenagers. Crime, school failure, teen pregnancy, eating disorders, depression, and suicide are others. It is evident that *many* children are having *many* problems growing up.

When I think of drug abuse I think of people running away from problems. I think of people who can't make a good life for themselves. Sometimes it's because of lack of opportunity, no jobs, no education, no future. Poor people living in the most impoverished and troubled neighborhoods are increasingly using drugs to seek relief from their struggles. Some of them sell drugs because that's the only way to have a standard of living above the poverty level. The drugs they are using are the most dangerous ones. More and more they are using crack. And they are injecting heroin into their veins. The sad picture is made worse as alarming numbers of addicts are infected by the AIDS virus from sharing needles.

In these settings it is almost impossible to have positive attitudes. Life skills don't necessarily help. The root cause of drug abuse in this population is the conditions of poverty.

Even in these extreme situations something can be done right now. We have proven programs that can break the vicious circle of poverty and despair that has been passed on generation to generation. A national commitment to services aimed at the seriously disadvantaged—high-risk youths—could break the circle. Such a program would include prenatal care, child health services, child care, and efforts to strengthen families through outside support. Expanded preschool programs and the prevention of school failure would be a high priority. This would be cheaper by far than the price society now pays for neglected health needs, unemployment, crime, and, of course drug abuse.[1]

In this book we focused on preventing drug problems among people who live above the poverty line. The economic opportunity is there, but still there is a form of impoverishment. We have children who don't know how to enjoy life and can't cope with pressures. They are deficient in life skills. They are lacking in meaning and fulfillment in life. The don't feel good about themselves.

In many of these families, economic pressures have forced both parents to work outside the home, even the parents of infants and preschoolers. Because of geographical mobility, the support of an extended family and a close neighborhood have been lost. Tired and exhausted parents run out of energy, causing them to neglect important child-rearing, educational, and nurturing roles. The demands of juggling pressure from work and family sometimes create what psychologist Urie Bronfenbrenner has described as "havoc in the home."[2] Children feel the stress and become insecure, which causes problems in school. Meanwhile, television and the mass media increasingly fill the void left by the disorganized family, taking over its role as the transmitter of culture and values.

Economic pressure and "havoc in the home" probably contribute to problems leading to divorce. Divorce, in turn, creates additional emotional and economic problems. Some single parents are forced to fulfill the double duties of full-time breadwinner and full-time parent.

The situation is critical. Not only are children being forced to make decisions about drugs at an early age, but they do it at a time when the family, the chief source of emotional and economic support, is disorganized, fractured, and under severe stress. All of this creates alienation, a lack of connectedness. Alienated children seek acceptance from their peers and affiliate with other troubled youth.

As has been suggested through this book, children need more links to their parents. They need more time and attention. They need more from their families.

But parents need something, too. They need support.

For example, the situation in middle-class homes would be greatly improved if affordable and adequate child care were available and if employers would offer flexible work schedules. Much can be done on the social level to improve situations in families.

In a sense, parents need to unite for their own benefit, to fight for the type of social support they need from health providers, government officials, employers, and educational institutions.

THE VISION

The drug problems we face as a society will be solved only through social change. The process involves building the kind of world in which people don't need to escape. They are happy. They have hope, opportunities, pleasure, and meaningful work. They have a sense of community, belonging, and purpose. They support each other and create positive social institutions. This is *ultimate drug prevention*. By working for these ideals we teach children a great lesson about responsibility and good citizenship. It is the very opposite of the escapism and defeatism that motivate drug abuse.

Meanwhile, empowering your own children and working in your own families, schools and communities is a good first step toward making the type of world that we can now only imagine. Raising brilliant, loving, self-confident children who can make wise decisions about drugs is an accomplishment worthy of praise.

REFERENCES

CHAPTER ONE
1. Lloyd D. Johnston, Patrick M. O'Malley, and Jerald G. Bachman, *Drug Use by High School Seniors: The Class of 1986* (Rockville, Md.: U.S. Department of Health and Human Services (DHHS) Publication No. ADM 87–1535, 1987).
2. J. Michael Polich, Phyllis L. Ellickson, Peter Reuter, and James P. Kahan, *Strategies for Controlling Adolescent Drug Use* (Santa Monica, Ca.: The Rand Corporation, 1984).
3. National Institute on Drug Abuse, *Adolescent Peer Pressure: Theory, Correlates, and Program Implications for Drug Abuse Prevention* (Rockville, Md.: DHHS Publication No. ADM 84–1152, 1984).
4. Daniel Goleman, "Parents' Oh-So-Subtle Influences," *San Francisco Chronicle,* August 8, 1986, p. 28.

CHAPTER TWO
1. Andrew Weil and Winifred Rosen, *Chocolate to Morphine* (Boston: Houghton Mifflin, 1983).
2. Ibid.
3. Ibid.
4. Barbara Critchlow, "The Powers of John Barleycorn: Beliefs about the Effects of Alcohol on Social Behavior," *American Psychologist* 41, 751–762 (1986).
5. National Institute on Drug Abuse, *Let's Talk about Drug Abuse: Some Questions and Answers* (Rockville, Md.: DHHS Publication No. ADM 81–706, 1981).
6. D. B. Kandel, "Drug Use by Youth: An Overview." In D. J. Lettieri and J. P. Ludford, eds., *Drug Abuse and the American Adolescent* (Rockville, Md.:

National Institute on Drug Abuse. Research Monograph No. 38, 1981).

7. Weil and Rosen, op. cit.

8. National Institute on Drug Abuse, *Cocaine* (Rockville, Md.: DHHS Publication No. ADM 83–1304); *Inhalants* (Rockville, Md.: DHHS Publication No. ADM 83–1305); *Hallucinogens and PCP* (Rockville, Md.: DHHS Publication No. ADM 83–1306); *Marijuana* (Rockville, Md.: DHHS Publication No. ADM 83–1307); *Opiates* (Rockville, Md.: DHHS Publication No. ADM 83–1308); *Sedative-Hypnotics* (Rockville, Md.: DHHS Publication No. ADM 83–1309).

9. Clay Roberts and Don Fitzmahan, *Yellow Pages Resource Supplement for Here's Looking at You, 2000* (Seattle: Comprehensive Health Education Foundation, 1986).

10. Weil and Rosen, op. cit.

11. Kenneth S. Schonberg, ed., *Substance Abuse: A Guide for Professionals* (Elk Grove Village, Il.: American Academy of Pediatrics, 1988).

12. Terry Todd, cited in Louis Lasagna, "Breakfast of Champions," *The Sciences*, vol. 24, no. 2, 61–62 (1984).

CHAPTER SIX

1. Anderson C. Johnson, "Project Smart: A Social, Psychological, and Behavioral Based Experimental Approach to Drug Abuse Prevention" (paper presented at the Annual Convention of the American Psychological Association, Anaheim, Ca., 1983).

CHAPTER EIGHT

1. Polich, op. cit.

2. Chad D. Emrick and Joel Hansen, "Assertions Regarding Effectiveness of Treatment for Alcoholism," *American Psychologist* 38, 1078–1088 (1983).

3. William R. Miller and Reid K. Hester, "Inpatient Alcoholism Treatment: Who Benefits?" *American Psychologist* 41, 794–805 (1986).

CHAPTER NINE

1. Carnegie Corporation of New York, "Bringing Children Out of the Shadows," *Carnegie Quarterly* 33, 2, 1–8 (1988).

2. Urie Bronfenbrenner, "Alienation and the Four Worlds of Childhood," *Phi Delta Kappan* 67, 430–436 (1986).

INDEX

abuse of drugs
  definition of, 32
  evaluation of, 24–32
  explaining to children, 92
activities
  decision making, 105–6
  fun and good feelings
    compliments, giving and receiving, 97
    fun things to do, discussion of, 98
    goal formulation, 99–100
    liking oneself, 98–99
    role models and pride, 97–98
    truth in communication, 100
  problem solving, 104–5
  risk taking, 106–7
  social influence, awareness of
    age and maturity, concepts of, 110–11
    assertiveness skills, 112–14
    bullying and power plays, 111–12
    media manipulation, 109–10
    peer pressure and individuality, 111
  stress management
    "Barbara the Beaver" story, 103–4
    decision making, 105–6
    defining and recognizing stress, 101–2
    in home life, 108

    positive options for coping, 102–3
    problem solving, 104–5
    relaxation process, 107–8
    risk taking, 106–7
addiction. *See* dependence
agreements with children
  broken agreements and consequences 185–87, 205
  children and young teens, making agreements with, 190–93
  compromises, 182–84
  drastic measures. *See* drastic measures
  feed-it-back approach to broken promises, 205
  halfhearted compliance, 187
  invalid agreements, 179
  no drug use as goal, 188–90
  older teens, making agreements with, 193–95
  perceptions and opinions, comparison of, 180–82
  principles of drug-use agreements, 187–90
  professional help, regarding, 203–4
  "responsible" drug use, idea of, 188–90
  standards, comparison of, 180–82
  valid agreements, 184–85
  walking tightrope, 201–3

233

agreements with children (*cont.*)
"watching closely" approach, 195–96,
195–201
"Albert the Ant" (Horne), 103
alcohol, 7, 22, 23, 24, 46–48, 94,
95
drunk driving, discussion of, 96
excessive use, effects of, 47–48
media manipulation and, 109–
10
tolerance to, 47–48
use, evaluation of, 24–25, 27
Alcoholics Anonymous, 218, 219
amphetamines, 44–45
anabolic steroids, 40, 51–52, 93
angel dust, 49
athletes, 51–52
authoritarianism, 14–16

barbiturates, 45–46
benzodiazepines, 46
boredom, 76

caffeine, 22, 42–43, 93
chocolate, 22, 43
CIA, 49
clear thinking
about consequences, 69–71
about goals, 67–68
about rules, 68–69
home discussions, 66–67
problem solving, 72–75
Coca-Cola, 41, 43
cocaine, 22, 26–27, 41–42, 53, 96,
145
codeine, 48
coffee, 22, 23, 24
combinations of drugs, 28
communication skills, 77–81
community involvement, 225–26
constructive criticism, 63–64, 79–
80
crack, 42

decision-making activities, 105–6
Demerol, 48
denial, 9–10, 12–13, 159

dependence
on amphetamines, 45
on cocaine, 41, 42
definition of, 33–34
drastic measures to confront. *See* drastic measures
explaining to children, 92, 94–95
on marijuana, 50
on nicotine, 43, 44
depressants, 45–48, 96. *See also* alcohol
Dianabol, 51
discussion of drugs and drug use
abuse, dependence, and tolerance, explanation of, 92–93, 94–95
agreements. *See* agreements with
children
assessment of problem
children's own assessments, 176
important questions, 175
loving confrontation, 176–78
risk factors to consider, 175–76
basic information, 91
contradictions in children's thinking,
pointing out, 166–70
crutches, drugs as, 173–74
dangers, explanation of, 94–97
directed questioning and labeling,
164–66
disagreement, major areas of
crutches, drugs as, 173–74
denial of responsibility, 171–72
dependence, mistaken ideas about,
172–73
harmlessness of drugs, 172
invincibility, attitude of, 158–59,
172–73
peer use of drugs, overestimation of,
170–71
distortions of truth, 162–63
drunk driving, 96
exchange of information process
beginning, 147–48
benefits of, 123–26
children's thoughts about drugs,
150–52
clarification of point of view, 131–
32

discomforting responses from children, 134–36
lies, 152–54
listening to children, 150
objections to talking, 138–41
parental authority, effects on, 126–29
passionate opinions, discipline of, 130–31
personal basis for point of view, expression of, 133–34
position on drug use, 148–50
preparation for discussions, 131–36
proposing a discussion, 137–38
reasons for discussions, 123–24
rolling papers in child's dresser, finding, 142–44
shyness of children, overcoming, 136
taking time to establish, 141
thoughts and feelings of parent, 147–48
trust vs. control, 129–30
externalization of responsibility by children, 159, 171–72
feed-it-back approach, 166–70
illegal drugs, 96
immediate negative effects of drugs, 95
keeping cool, 89–90
lies, 146, 152–54, 162–63
loving confrontation and issue of harm, 176–78
missed opportunities, 145–46
more information, gathering of
Columbo-style questioning, 162–63
defense mechanisms of children, 158–59
kinds of information needed, 156–58
lightening up, 161–62
open-ended questions, 160–61
too many questions, 158
motivations for drug use, uncovering, 164–69
normal behavior, clarifying, 96–97
objections to talking, 138–41
opportunities for, 86–87, 88
overdose, risk of, 96
position on drug use, 148–50

preparation for, 131–36
proposing a discussion, 137–38
reacting to knowledge of drug use
attitude of child, 157
conditions of drug use, 156
current status of drug use, 157–58
defense mechanisms of children, 158–59
effects of drug use, 156–57
"I" messages, use of, 155–56
knowledge and self-awareness of child, assessing, 157
more information, gathering of, 156–58
"Rambo parenting," 154
reasons for drug use, 156
rebuttal cycle, falling into, 159–60
too many questions, 158
reasons for discussions, 123–24
specific drugs, descriptions of, 93–94
starting discussions, 85–89
substance of, 90–97
thought-provoking questions, 163–64
when to start, 88–89
drastic measures
actions to take, 214
dangers of, 205–6, 209–11, 214
guidelines for treatment programs or counseling, 219–20
options in drug treatment, 217–19
pain, learning from, 212–13
sharing responsibility, 211–12
support groups, 211
treatment under pressure, 216–17
truth-telling confrontations with others, 214–16
drugs
addiction. *See* dependence
age of user, 30–31
combinations of, 28
dependence, 33–34, 36
discussions about. *See* discussion of drugs and drug use
effects of use, 31–32
experimental use, 35
food and drugs, 22
harmful use, 35–36

drugs (*cont.*)
  health of user, 31
  legality, 28–29
  methods of use, 30
  mood swing, seeking, 35
  patterns of use, changes in, 29–30
  personality of user, 30–31
  pervasiveness of, 221–22
  pharmacology of, 28
  physical evidence of drug use, 38
  prevention. *See* prevention of drug
    problems
  purity of, 29
  quantity, frequency, and length of use,
    29
  reasons for use, 31
  scare approach to deter use of,
    52
  setting for drug use, 30
  signs of drug use, 36–38, 153
  stages of use, 34–36
  tolerance to, 33
  types of drugs
    anabolic steroids, 40, 51–52
    depressants, 39, 45–48
    hallucinogens, 39–40, 48–49
    inhalants, 40, 49
    marijuana, 40, 50–51
    narcotics, 39, 48
    stimulants, 39, 40–45
  use, misuse, and abuse, evaluation of,
    24–32

economic factors, 227–28
empowerment of children, 11, 17–18
  activities to promote. *See* activities
  agreements. *See* agreements with
    children
  clear thinking, 57, 66–71, 72–75
  definition of, 4–5
  healthy lifestyle, checklist for, 115–
    17
  limits, setting of, 71–72
  prevention of drug problems, steps for,
    55–58
  problem-solving abilities, 58, 72–
    75

relationship values and skills, 58, 76–
    81
  report-card problems, 81–84
  self-esteem, 56–57, 58–65
  as transfer of power, 18–20
  unconditional love, 61–65
enabling behavior, 13–14
exchange of information process. *See* dis-
    cussion of drugs and drug use
experimental drug use, 35

Families Anonymous, 211
first use of drugs, 3–4
flashbacks, 48
food and drugs, 22
Freud, Sigmund, 41

goals
  activities to promote, 99–100
  clear thinking about, 67–68
A Guide to a Happier Family (J. P. Tarcher,
    1989), 81

hallucinogens, 48–49
hashish, 50
health effects, 31, 32
heroin, 48
Hicks, Tom, 51
Hofmann, Albert, 49
Horne, Jessica, 103

identity, sense of
  authoritarianism of parents, effect of,
    15–16
  damage caused by drugs, 9, 10
inhalants, 49, 94
intervention. *See* drastic measures
invincibility, feelings of, 158–59, 172–
    73

legality, 28–29
Librium, 46
lies, 146, 152–54, 162–63
love and affection
  and constructive criticism, 63–64
  giving and asking for, 58–61
  mixed messages, 60

self-acceptance and confidence, 61–63
unconditional love, 61–65
LSD, 49

marijuana, 24, 94, 96, 145, 146
amotivational syndrome and, 51
effects of, 50–51
rolling papers in child's dresser, finding, 142–44
use, misuse, or abuse of, 25–26, 27
media manipulation, 109–10
mescaline, 48
methaqualone, 46
misuse of drugs
definition of, 32
evaluation of, 24–32
morphine, 48

narcotics, 48
Narcotics Anonymous, 218
negative feelings, expression of, 77–78
negotiation of differences, 80–81. *See also*
agreements with children
Nembutal, 45
nicotine. *See* tobacco

overdoses, 96
overprotection by parents, 17, 19

parents
agreement between, 27
authoritarian approach, 14–16
denial or ignoring of problem, 12–13
empowering family life. *See* empowerment of children
enabling drug use, 13–14
limits, setting of, 71–72
organization and involvement of, 222–26
overprotection by, 17, 19
permissiveness of, 19–20
as role models, 20–21
schools, involvement with, 223–25
wait-and-see approach, 12
PCP, 49, 96
peer pressure, 111, 112–15
Percodan, 48

permissiveness, 19–20
pharmacology of drugs, 28
Piaget, Jean, 166
pot. *See* marijuana
poverty, 227–28
prevention of drug problems, 11
activities to promote. *See* activities
empowerment of children, components of, 55–58. *See also* empowerment of children
healthy-lifestyle checklist, 115–17
message to give, 90–97
normal behavior, clarification of, 96–97
starting discussions, 85–89
problem solving, 104–5
after-school behavior, regarding, 75–76
boredom, regarding, 76
importance of abilities, 72–73
process of, 74
teaching of, 73–75
professional help
agreements with children regarding, 203–4
forced treatment, 216–17
guidelines, 219–20
options in drug treatment, 217–19
psilocybin, 48

Quaaludes, 46

reacting to drug use. *See* discussion of drugs and drug use
Reagan, Nancy, 11
reasons for drug use, 31, 54–55
relationship values and skills
constructive criticism, expression of, 79–80
negative feelings, expression of, 77–78
negotiation of differences, 80–81
resentments, expression of, 77–78
suspicion, communication of, 78–79
report cards, 81–84
resentment, expression of, 77–78
risk taking, 106–7

role models, 20–21
rules, clear thinking about, 68–69

Sandoz company, 49
scare approach, 52
school drug prevention, 223–25
Seconal, 45
self-esteem, 56–57
  activities promoting, 97–99
  affection and praise, giving of, 58–61
  discussions promoting, 126
  strokes, giving and requesting, 58–61
  success and mastery as part of, 65
  unconditional love in building of, 61–65
self-help groups, 211
signs of drug use, 36–38, 153
social change, 227–29
social influences, awareness of
  age and maturity factors, 110–11
  assertiveness, teaching of, 112–14
  bullying and power plays, 111–12
  media drug dealers, 109–10
  peer pressure, 111, 112–15
"speed," 44–45
statistics on drug use, 7–8
Steiner, Claude, 6
steroids, 40, 51–52
stimulant drugs, 39, 40–45
stress-management activities
  "Barbara the Beaver" story, 103–4
  decision-making process, 105–6
  defining and recognizing stress, 101–2

home-life problem solving, 108
positive options for coping, 102–3
problem-solving skill enhancement, 104–5
relaxation techniques, 107–8
risk taking, role of, 106–7
sugar, 22
support groups, 211
suspicion, communication of, 78–79

THC, 50
thinking clearly. *See* clear thinking
tobacco, 7, 24, 27, 43–44, 93, 95
  media manipulation of, 109–10
tolerance
  to alcohol, 47
  to amphetamines, 45
  to barbiturates, 46
  to caffeine, 43
  explaining to children, 92–93
Toughlove, 211
treatment programs
  forced, 216–17
  guidelines, 219–20
  options, 217–19

ultimate drug prevention, 228–29

Valium, 26, 45, 46

Xanax, 45

Ziegler, John, 51

ABOUT THE AUTHOR

Since receiving a doctorate in clinical psychology from the University of California at Berkeley, ROBERT SCHWEBEL has had more than twenty years' experience treating substance abuse, including developing prevention programs for schools and public agencies, working in private practice with youth and families, and presenting lectures and workshops to professional and community audiences. For three years he served as director of Matrix Community Services in Tucson, the largest drug prevention program in Arizona. He currently serves as Vice Chairperson of the School Chemical Abuse Prevention Interagency Committee for Arizona. For seven years he has written a weekly column on families and relationships for the *Arizona Daily Star*. Dr. Schwebel has hosted a local NBC-TV talk show about relationships, "Good Loving," and he is a coauthor with his mother, father, brother, and sister-in-law—all health professionals—of the book *A Guide to a Happier Family*. This is his second book.